CHINA
LOOKS
FORWARD

中國的前途

孫科

CHINA
LOOKS
FORWARD

by

SUN FO

London

GEORGE ALLEN & UNWIN LTD

FIRST PUBLISHED IN 1944

To the memory
of my father
SUN YAT–SEN
Father of the
Chinese
Republic

BOOK
PRODUCTION
WAR ECONOMY
STANDARD

PRINTED IN GREAT BRITAIN AT
THE UNIVERSITY PRESS
ABERDEEN

Preface

A FEW words of explanation may be in order to acquaint the reader with the origin of this book.

Since the winter of 1939-40, after my return to Free China from my second mission to Moscow at the end of 1939, I have had numerous occasions to speak on the world situation with particular reference to its effects on China. These speeches and lectures were delivered extempore without written texts or even notes. My secretary, accompanying me on these speaking engagements, acted as my stenographer, and took down the speeches verbatim. After transcription, and with my own revisions, these speeches were then released to the Chinese Press for publication.

With the lapse of time a mass of material was accumulated. A young literary friend and playwright undertook the task of collecting and editing them for publication in book form. This was done in the autumn of 1942, when the collected speeches, together with some of the articles I had published in the Press, appeared in a volume in Chinese as *Chung-kuo di Ch'ien-tu*, or The Future of China. It aroused a good deal of attention and elicited favourable comment on the part of my Chinese readers.

Early in 1943 friends, both foreign and Chinese, had suggested the publication of an English version, but I was undecided. I had reasons for this hesitation. These speeches and most of my published writings were delivered to and intended for my own people, especially the younger generation, who are being reared in war and are now preparing themselves for the tremendous task of national reconstruction in post-war China. Would Western readers be interested in what I have to say to my own people?

But my friends were insistent that an English version be brought out. Two of them, my colleague Mr. Yeh Ch'iu-yuan of the Legislative Yuan and Professor Sun Ta-yu of the Central Political Institute, volunteered to make a draft translation during the hot summer months of 1943. I had practically put the matter out of my mind when my son, Tse-ping, wrote me from New York that my American publishers were anxious to have a translation made and published by them. I then decided to take a personal interest in its preparation. It has occupied most of my spare moments for two months this autumn to whip it into shape, revising and re-writing the manuscript.

5

In its final form, the bulk of this volume is taken from its Chinese original, with some new material added. In order to round out the contents I have written two new articles, "China Marching Toward Democracy" and "Writing China's Constitution," especially for this purpose.

I have to thank my other friends who have had a hand in the work. Mr. Percy Chen, editor of the *National Herald* in Chungking, has contributed much time and labour in reading over the translations. Dr. Mei Ju-ao of the Legislative Yuan has assisted me in preparing my article on the Constitution. Mr. Wen Yuan-ning, member of the Legislative Yuan and now with the Goodwill Mission to England, also read over some of the material and gave his advice on the English version. Finally, there is my good friend and collaborator, Dr. John C. H. Wu, who was so kind as to come especially from his home in Kweilin to participate in the final editing.

I must not forget to mention my wife, my constant comfort and unfailing source of inspiration, especially during these many trying war-years, without whose encouragement and selfless devotion even the ephemeral task of preparing this book for publication would not have been done at all.

SUN FO.

Yuan-lu,
  Chialing Village,
    Chungking,
      November 29, 1943.

Contents

8

CHINA LOOKS FORWARD

PART FIVE

TO PEACE

PART ONE

To Freedom and Equality

Dr. Sun Yat-sen and Soviet Russia *

I

IT is fifteen years since the death of Dr. Sun Yat-sen, the guiding spirit of the Chinese Revolution, prophet and champion of human freedom. In commemorating the anniversary of his death to-day, in the midst of our patriotic war of resistance against the invasion of a ruthless enemy, we should take greater courage, and derive renewed inspiration, to execute the political testament left to us by the Father of the Republic. Even in this dark day of disaster and suffering we may look forward to the dawn of a brighter future, with the promise of a better world after the present war is terminated in victory.

Dr. Sun's goal, during the whole of his life, lay not only in the salvation of China, but also in the emancipation of the rest of the oppressed world. His primary aim was, of course, the emancipation of his own people, but his ultimate purpose was that of humanity.

The most cherished wishes of his life are best expressed in a letter to Soviet friends which was written during his last days. He wrote : " You are the leader and vanguard of that grand union of free republics which look to the future. That great federation of nations is truly the priceless heritage bequeathed to all the oppressed peoples by your immortal Lenin. Turning their eyes to you, the enslaved millions under the yoke of imperialism will nourish their faith and courage to win their own freedom, thereby working to liberate themselves from the shackles of the existing international order which is based on age-old wars of enslavement. What I shall leave behind me is the Kuomintang. It is my hope, while accomplishing its historical mission of ridding China of the bondage of imperialism and helping other fettered nations to free themselves, the Kuomintang will co-operate with you in the days to come as fully as possible. I have already directed the Kuomintang to establish lasting co-operation with you, earnestly believing meanwhile that your Government will gladly continue to lend its assistance

* Commemoration article published in *Free China*, March 12, 1940.

unstintingly. Dear Comrades, while taking my final leave of you, I wish to express my ardent hope that before long the dawn will break. This will be the time when the Soviet Union, as a good friend and an ally, will greet a strong and independent China. Both countries will emerge victorious, I am sure, from their gigantic struggle for the freedom of the oppressed peoples of the world."

No letter of more world-historical moment has ever been written ; it exists to point out to mankind the road towards the realisation of a happier world.

The emancipation of China and that of the world are fundamentally inseparable. There can be no real freedom and equality in the world so long as a fifth of humanity, the four hundred and fifty millions living in China, are not free. If we ask for these things for ourselves, we must demand the like for others. The disease of imperialism which infects the whole society of nations is a cankerous malady of the old world. If we can cure this plague we shall have made a great contribution to humanity.

That is the reason why the leader of our Revolution, throughout the long, single-handed struggle against the feudal Manchu Monarch in China, hourly awaited the rise of new revolutionary forces to help in the overthrow of oppression. Not until the outbreak of the Russian Revolution was this hope of his realised.

Seeing clearly the portent of this historical event, the Father of the Revolution was not blinded by the flood of propaganda let loose in all countries against the Russian Bolsheviks. It was apparent to him that the success of the Russian Revolution would not only deal a death-blow to imperialism in Czarist Russia, but would undermine its strength elsewhere and, at the same time, strike at the root of its existence, world capitalism.

The Father of the Republic, veteran leader of our Revolution for some two-score years, was not deceived by the deluge of scandalous propaganda. Therefore, he showered sympathy upon, and pinned unwavering hopes in, this vindication of universal human rights.

He said : " Every one is aware that the Russian Revolution is a replica of its Chinese forerunner. But it has been carried to a success far in advance of our own ; its great achievements are unprecedented in the history of revolutions." Later, commemorating the death of Lenin, in an address to the first Kuomintang Congress in Canton early in 1924, he said : " The reason why the Powers of the world are blackening the name of Lenin is because he dared to say undauntedly that the twelve hundred and fifty million inhabitants of the majority nations are being oppressed and exploited by the hundred and fifty millions of the minority nations. Besides, Lenin was the champion for self-determination of oppressed peoples." Therefore, to the founder of the People's Party, the "Russian Revolution has kindled the hopes of mankind." If we add Russia's hundred and ninety millions to China's four hundred and fifty millions, the task of regenerating the world does not seem such a fantastic dream.

Dr. Sun Yat-sen's great revolutionary aim was not accomplished in his lifetime. Even now, fifteen years after his death, we have made but slight progress. Still, we have succeeded in achieving internal unity in the midst of a war of national salvation—a stage of organised armed struggle against imperialism.

Soviet Russia, on the other hand, has wellnigh finished the third of her five-year plans, a stage of the construction of Socialism.

Thus it may be said that the two countries are forging ahead for world regeneration. What is our main task henceforth? In the midst of our war against aggression and through our efforts in State-building, we must realise the cardinal aims of our Revolution : first, we must practise San-Min-Chu-I within our borders ; second, with the power of a strong, independent nation and in co-operation with Soviet Russia and other friendly Powers, we must achieve final victory for the freedom of the oppressed and enslaved peoples of the world. This responsibility rests on the shoulders of every one of our comrades and our countrymen.

2

The Russian Revolution took place in 1917, just eight years before the death of Dr. Sun Yat-sen. In these eight years internal strife and intervention by the great capitalistic Powers, France, Japan, Great Britain and the United States, led to one of the most bloody of revolutions. The young Soviet Government had to conquer internal counter-revolutionary forces, repel the Japanese and other interventionists in Siberia and Karelia, and cope with a hostile blockade.

The social structure of the new State was undermined, economy was disrupted, and famine swept the land. The sufferings of the people were unbelievable when the bare necessities of life were unobtainable. Russia was in chaos.

In the midst of these catastrophes, the leaders of the Soviet Government tackled the three great questions which faced them : on the score of nationalism, more than one hundred different ethnic groups, each with its own language and culture, had to be welded into a coherent whole to live in harmonious accord and unity ; on the score of democracy, the masses of the people had to be lifted up from the serfdom of Czarist autocracy to a state of popular self-government ; on the score of livelihood, the capitalist economy monopolized by nobles and big land-owners had to be replaced by a Socialist economy where all the means of production were to be possessed by the State for the welfare of the people.

Here was an advance in economic and political theory which had never been attempted before by any other nation. There were no precedents to follow. But, taking their destiny with both hands, the Soviet Government, in the space of twenty-one years, found a solution to each and every one of these problems.

Dr. Sun Yat-sen died too early. Nor could he have imagined that San-Min-Chu-I, which was propounded by him, would be first brought to fruition by our great neighbour. Even now there are some among our leading intellectuals who do not understand that the building up of a Socialist state in Soviet Russia will mean the realization of our own San-Min-Chu-I, albeit, according to her own lights, and on the basis of her own economic and political background.

How, one may ask, did Soviet Russia tackle these three questions : why do we say that their successful solution is equivalent to the realisation of the San-Min-Chu-I ?

In the case of nationalism, Soviet Russia is a state comprising a host of ethnic groups. During the days of the Czarist regime the ruling caste cared for naught but autocratic government and bar-baric aggression for loot and expansion. The question of nationalism was completely ignored. The Romanoff Empire consisted of the " Herrenvolk," the Great Russians, and the subject-peoples, like the Ukrainians, Tajhiks, Turcomen, Kalmuks and a hundred others. One of the first tasks undertaken after the Revolution of 1917 was to find a solution to this problem of nationalism which lies at the base of the existence of nations. Lenin appointed Stalin Commissar of Nationalities. Soon a policy was formed upon the basis of which the unification and internal construction of Russia was founded. Thereafter, in the early days of the building of the new State, the Russian Bolsheviks pushed forward with the policy of giving equality to all ethnic groups within their borders. They were welded together politically and economically into one fraternal whole, each retaining in full measure its cultural and racial equality and liberty.

Thus, all inter-racial suspicions and discrimination were swept away at one stroke, and union of free and equal republics was formed. At the same time the Soviet Government formulated and initiated a foreign policy of helping the weak and rendering moral and material support to the oppressed nations of the world. Russia's guiding principle in solving her problem of nationalities is none other than that which the Father of the Republic had advanced for forty years.

To unite many ethnic groups in forming one composite modern nation, it is necessary that each and every one should enjoy full equality with the others, political, economic and cultural. None must be the master ; none must be the slave. None the exploiters ; none the exploited. Otherwise, if calamity comes, dissension is bound to be rife, and destruction a certainty. The disintegration of the Austro-Hungarian Empire in the first World War and the annihilation of Poland, though the causes were many and varied, were due mainly to the absence of political, economic and social equality among the various component ethnic groups.

As regards democracy, Soviet Russia, with the proclamation of the Stalin Constitution, has aspired to become, in its political make-up, the most democratic country in the world. It is to be a land where political rights are equal for every man and woman. There is intended to be universal suffrage for the adult population.

In this advance toward full democracy lies the basis for the claim by the Russians that they possess the most democratic Constitution in the world. In this lies the charge against the Western democracies that their democracy is fictitious and limited, and, therefore, not true democracy. Capitalist economy divides the people into the propertied few—the possessing class, and the destitute many— the toiler, the hewers of wood and the drawers of water. There are, therefore, class distinctions, and suffrage is limited to those who can fulfil property or income qualifications.

In Soviet Russia, on the other hand, private property in land and the means of production has been abolished ; class distinctions have been removed, so that everyone enjoys economic equality with his fellow-men.

Political rights are enjoyed by all Soviet citizens in common. They exercise their political power through direct participation in their local Soviets or popular assemblies. In addition, they enjoy economic, cultural and social rights of work, education and racial equality. This is exactly in accordance with the spirit of the San-Min-Chu-I.

2

Built upon the foundation of popular sovereignty, the strength and functional power of the Central Government are well founded and highly effective. This has been proved by the growth of the authority of the Soviet Union in the councils of the leading Powers of the world.

In the case of the people's livelihood, the leaders of Soviet Russia from the very first followed the policies of improving the agricultural production of the country, introducing and developing industry along Socialist lines, strengthening the defensive power of the country, and solving once for all the question of the livelihood of her people.

Since 1928 the energy of the whole nation was concentrated in pushing through two of the five-year economic plans. Now the third one is being completed. Thus, while it has taken capitalist countries a century to achieve industrialisation, Soviet Russia will have reached their level of production in the main branches of industry, agriculture and transport in about a sixth of their time.

The first two five-year plans were devoted to basic heavy industry ; the creation of the means of production, large-scale electrical power plants, and many other branches vitally connected with national defence. Now, in her third five-year plan, emphasis is being laid on the production of more consumer goods.

Progress during these years was not limited to production. The problem of distribution, which is the thorny one in capitalist countries, is being solved.

Since all means of production are owned or controlled by the State, the profits of all Socialist economy are directed toward improving and expanding the productive power of the nation, and not, as in capitalist countries, for building up enormous private fortunes for a few. The distribution of individual income has been equalised mainly by removing the discrepancies in remuneration between mental and manual labour, urban and rural labour, and male and female labour. This is fully consonant with the tenet, " From each according to his ability, to each according to his work," which agrees perfectly with the principle of the People's Livelihood so long advocated by the leader of our Revolution.

3

On this day of homage to the memory of the Father of the Republic we must frankly examine ourselves on what we have achieved. When we do this we have cause, not for being pleased —but rather for being ashamed of ourselves.

When comparing our achievements with those of the Soviet Union we find that in the fifteen years which have elapsed since Dr. Sun Yat-sen's death we have little to show. The Soviet Union, in the short space of little more than ten years, has already realized to a great measure the aims of our San-Min-Chu-I. In China we have not only failed to secure our legacy and the objective we set out to achieve, but by our sins of omission we have brought untold hardships and suffering on ourselves.

The reasons for this failure lie in the fact that we do not fully understand the fundamental principles of San-Min-Chu-I, nor have we acquainted ourselves fully with the actual conditions and the political theories of foreign countries as well as those of our own land. We have failed to regain our national self-confidence which had been shattered by repeated humiliations at the hands of the imperialists for more than a century.

Some of us often imagine that there are newer and better doctrines which could guide us in the regeneration of China and the world. Some even belittle the precepts bequeathed by the Father of the Republic, not realizing that they are the fairest and the most practical doctrines formulated by man. Proof of this lies in the achievements of Soviet Russia which have put these doctrines into practice.

Thinkers on world problems, and statesmen responsible for the welfare and happiness of mankind, will have to put into practice the essential tenets embodied in the San-Min-Chu-I, if the difficult problems which upset the peace and disrupt the ordered progress of human society are to be resolved. The implied objectives of our San-Min-Chu-I, which demand that national, political and economic freedom be recognized as inherent rights for all peoples, must be conceded and guaranteed by world statesmanship before any hope for a better world order can become a fact.

Let us ask ourselves honestly why we, as a nation, have failed to put in force the principles of the Father of the Republic. The causes I think are twofold : on the one hand, we have in China believers in Socialism and Communism. Those gentlemen are woefully ignorant of the meaning of Marxism and the actual conditions in Soviet Russia. They obstruct in word and deed the carrying out of the San-Min-Chu-I. On the other hand, we have the so-called believers in the three principles. These bigots are rather hazy in their notions of Capitalism, Socialism and Communism. They close their eyes to, or even refuse to know, what is taking place in Soviet Russia. As a result, they have no clear conception of the substance of the principle of People's Livelihood. Socialism to them is a terrifying nightmare.

As a matter of fact, what is Communism? It is nothing less than one of the highest ideals of mankind, equivalent substantially to the state of *Tatung* visualized thousands of years ago by our sages. By a state of *Tatung* our forefathers presupposed a society in which its members were so highly developed spiritually and morally that there would be no need even for government. In this "Communist" society, where production of everything needed for sustaining life at an unimaginably high standard of living is attained, there would be real freedom from want. In such society everyone would give to the State the very best of which he is capable and receive from the State all that he needed. Judging from the low standard of morality and intelligence current in the world of to-day, this Utopian condition may not come before the lapse of several historical periods, lasting hundreds of years, or even thousands.

At present the country which approaches nearest to this state of *Tatung* is undoubtedly Soviet Russia. Her progress along the road of San-Min-Chu-I enables her to distribute the national income according to the principle, "A man shall receive from the State according to the amount of work he contributes to the State." This is Socialism. From this it may be seen that the principle of the People's Livelihood is not in conflict with Russian Socialism, and is not opposed to the theory of Communism.

Now, why do these gentlemen reject the principle of People's Livelihood and embrace the Socialism of Soviet Russia? Their error may be traced to their confusion of thought, the confusion of the means with the end. They refuse to acknowledge that every society has its own historical and social background. Civilization, and culture, like economy, did not develop evenly throughout the world. Hence, no two societies are alike, nor can similar maladies in the bodies politic be treated with the same prescription.

The differences of the historical and social backgrounds between China and Russia are manifold. Among those differences the main are the following : first, throughout the past century Russia has been a country of unimpaired sovereignty ; before the downfall of Czar Nicholas II she was even an imperialistic aggressor nation. China, on the other hand, as a sequel of the Opium War with England in 1840-42, has been for a whole century deprived of her full sovereign rights. Foreign penetration, backed by the presence of warships in her coastal and inland waters, foreign garrisons holding strategic points in her territory, and manipulation of finance by the capitalists of the encroaching Powers reduced her to a semi-colonial status. Thus, after the close of the civil wars and foreign intervention, Soviet Russia did not have to continue the struggle for her national emancipation. China's most urgent need was the recovering of full national independence by destroying the political and economic bonds which were throttling her. This patriotic War of Resistance is the climax of that struggle ; for Japan saw in the growing strength of the National Government the end to that bondage. Japan sought to change China's subjection from a semi-colonial status to that of a full colony.

Secondly, during the days of the Czarist Empire class distinction in Russia was fully developed. In China we have a society in which class distinctions are less sharp. This is on account of the primitive state of Chinese economy, and the extremely low standard of production and living which prevailed in the country on account of the maladministration and corruption of the Manchu Dynasty.

Landlordism in China is by no means to be compared with that which existed in Russia. There were also very few industrial capitalists. What monied men there were derived their wealth from trade and usury. In Soviet Russia the Government expropriated the nobles and large landowners in order to carry out their land decrees giving the land to the peasants. This big and influential class of landowners concentrated around them all the counter-revolutionary forces, and the violence and bloodshed of the civil wars resulted. In China, at the present, there is no need for such drastic measures to achieve the end of bringing the land into the ownership of the State, for the benefit of the tillers of the soil, in accordance with the doctrines of Dr. Sun Yat-sen.

Thirdly, China's economic development is far behind that of Soviet Russia, or even Czarist Russia. But even the Bolsheviks tolerated the private capitalist during the period of the New Economic Policy from 1923 to 1926. Lenin pushed this policy through in the face of violent opposition of the so-called Left Opposition because, as he said at that time, " . . . the Government has not the men nor the money to socialize all industry and agriculture." The disbelieving gentlemen must read their Lenin again more carefully and try to understand this teaching. They will be able better to appreciate the meaning of San-Min-Chu-I.

It is clear that if we seek an analogy in Russia our economy is like that during the time of the New Economic Policy. In China we need not abolish private capital. We need its initiative, and its competitive efficiency. But we can restrain it and deprive it of the power to do harm to our social and political structure which we are building up. At the same time, by adopting the system of planned economy, which is an adjunct of the principle of People's Livelihood, we shall be able to quicken industrialization by diverting the greater part of the surplus accumulated national income from private enterprise in the form of income and profit taxes to State industry. Dr. Sun Yat-sen has described State industries which are beyond the scope of private individual enterprise. The Russians socialized their agriculture upon the basis of socialized industry, and not the other way about. And China must have industry before it can be socialized. A few old factories here and there do not constitute industrialization. Industrialization means the ability to equip and expand industry on the basis of our own production instead of imports from abroad.

These differences pointed out above touching the principles of Nationalism, Democracy, and Livelihood merely serve to show the need for different methods of accomplishment and not a difference in the aims. Both ways lead to the same goal.

The more one admires Soviet Russia, the more should one believe in the San-Min-Chu-I. Conversely, the more one believes in the doctrines of Dr. Sun Yat-sen, the more should one study the actual conditions in Soviet Russia and try to understand them.

All of us who are actively engaged in this war of national salvation for the freeing of our country, and have faith in the successful reconstruction after the war, must to-day put aside all doubts and prejudices and dedicate themselves wholly to the San-Min-Chu-I.

As a result of this struggle we are going to make our country independent and free ; a rich and powerful, a happy and peaceful country, a worthy member in the family of nations. The crushing of Japanese aggression will be a fatal blow to predatory imperialism, and the emancipation of Korea and other Asiatic nations enslaved by imperialist Japan will be achieved.

We shall then be contributing a great share to the creation of a new and better world, and at the same time, accomplishing the will of the Father of the Republic to deliver China and ultimately the rest of the oppressed world.

The San-Min-Chu-I, Capitalism and Socialism *

THIS lecture is meant to explain briefly the contents of the San-Min-Chu-I, and then to compare this creed of ours with other current systems of politico-economic doctrine. Sun Tzu, in his *Art of War*, wrote, " To know oneself as well as to know one's enemy is to ensure victory in a hundred battles." We of this generation are devoting ourselves to the great task of State-building in accordance with the San-Min-Chu-I. It is therefore incumbent on us thoroughly to acquaint ourselves with its theory and practice. For this purpose, a comparative examination of this and other systems would be useful toward a better understanding of the subject.

I

The first principle of our trilogy is Min-Chuh-Chu-I, popularly rendered as Nationalism. It aims at propagating and developing all the good and virtuous elements inherent in our national character, which constitute a racial heritage handed down to us from times immemorial. In external relations, this nationalism of ours strives for the attainment of complete independence, freedom and equality for China in the society of nations. Under its inspiration we are to-day fighting a patriotic war against the Japanese aggressor in order to safeguard our national existence, and to liberate our people from a foreign yoke.

In domestic relations, our nationalism calls for equality of status for all racial or ethnic groups inhabiting our vast land. Chinese, Manchus, Mongols, Tibetans, Moslem peoples in the great North-West, as well as other minorities scattered in various parts of the country, must be able to enjoy full equality in their legal, political, economic and cultural positions. There must be no discrimination based on race or religion. Chinese, being more advanced than some of the other groups, may serve as elder brothers and teachers in helping the less advanced to go on to a higher state of culture. All racial groups within the nation must be brought up to the same level in political, economic and cultural development. Only by so doing will China truly attain the position of a modern State.

* A lecture given at the Central Political Training Institute, Chungking, April 8, 1940.

Such, in brief, is the meaning of the Principle of Nationalism. We do not seek aggrandizement at the expense of our neighbours ; nor do we lay claim to any superiority of race over others, such as the misguided Nazis do in their absurd racial doctrines, or like the ridiculous assertion of the Japanese enemy, who traced his ancestry to the mythical " Sun-Goddess." Nationalism to us means just this : National equality and freedom for ourselves, both at home and abroad. Practice of this principle will never involve us in mortal conflict with other nations who would treat us on a basis of equality and mutual respect. Only those who would despoil our land and enslave our people are our enemies.

2

Min-Ch'uan-Chu-I, or the People's Rights, is the second principle. It was Dr. Sun Yat-sen who first evolved and propounded the new concept in political theory, which he called the Five-Power Constitution. He distinguished two sets of powers exercised separately by the people and the Government. The first set, known as Political Powers, is the inalienable possession of the people, and can be exercised by the people alone. The second set, known as Governing Powers, is lodged with the Government, which derives its authority to govern and administer the country from the people. The Political Powers of the people comprise the four democratic rights of Election, Recall, Initiative and Referendum. The Governing Powers of the Government include the following five functional powers : the Executive, the Legislative, the Judiciary, Examination and Control.

The General Principles for National Reconstruction, written in his own hand by Dr. Sun Yat-sen, defines the *hsien* (county) as the unit of local self-government. All officials discharging public duties in various localities, such as the *hsien* magistrate or civil administrator, the village elder or township mayor, the *pao* and *chia* headman, are to be elected by the populace in the respective localities to take charge of the public functions delegated to them. If those elected to office should prove incompetent or be guilty of malpractice and abuse of office, the electorate would have the right to dismiss them and elect others.

Since the people also have the right of Initiative, they could in the *hsien*, village, township, *pao* and *chia*, assemblies, councils, or meetings directly move for the adoption of ways and means in dealing with local affairs. These resolutions, when passed, become by-laws in the respective local districts, and are binding upon all within that area.

Again, as the people have the right of Referendum, they could amend or abolish by-laws and orders of the *hsien* and other local bodies if these are later found to run counter to or conflict with local public interests.

In countries where the populations are small, these four rights, called more specifically direct rights, could be exercised by a large section of the electorate so as to delegate their authority to, and limit the power of, the Central Government through the elected cabinet. But we have an overwhelming population of four hundred and fifty millions ; how are we going to exercise our four rights in matters of national scope and importance ? The General Principles for National Reconstruction answers the question by saying that *vis-à-vis* the Central Government, the people could not exercise their direct rights : they have to elect representatives to the National Assembly for expressing their will.

The main office of the National Assembly consists, according to the Draft Constitution published on May 5, 1936, by the National Government, of the exercise of the four rights of the people, namely, electing the President and Vice-President of the Republic and the presidents and members of the Legislative and Control Yuan ; dismissing the President and Vice-President of the Republic, the presidents of the Yuan, as well as Legislative and Control Yuan members ; exercising the rights of Initiative for the people by making laws to meet the demands of the nation ; and finally, amending or abrogating laws which are found not to the good of the people, by exercising the right of Referendum.

Our system of the People's Rights is quite different from that of contemporary Western politics, in which there is no definite cleavage between Popular Rights and Governing Powers. Again, before the Five-Power Constitution was evolved by Dr. Sun Yat-sen, most Occidental democratic constitutional systems were based on the division of sovereignty of the people into two or three powers, all exercised by delegated authority.

In the case of Great Britain, theoretically there are three Governing Powers or functions of the Government, but in practice two of them—executive and legislative—are exercised by the same organ. Important members of the Cabinet, the Prime Minister and his chief colleagues, must concurrently be members of the House of Commons. They are the representatives of the majority party which is in control of the direction of State affairs. When the House is in session, members of the Cabinet must attend the meetings and make verbal reports and answer questions concerning matters of policies and the administration of their several departments. Parliament enacts laws and decides on policies which affect the interests of the nation and the Empire. So it has been said that the British Parliament is an omnipotent organ capable of doing anything except to change men into women or vice versa. The statement, though humorous, is yet true, because while a legislative body, the House also directs administration, handles political matters, and controls all governmental organs. Cabinet ministers, responsible to Parliament, cannot act independently. Thus legislative and executive functions are interwoven. Only the judicial function is separately exercised by other organs juxtaposed to the main mechanism of the British Constitution.

The Father of the Republic carefully studied the theories of Montesquieu, who divided indirect political rights of the people into three categories, each to be entrusted to a separate governmental organ. This theory was adopted by the founders of the American Republic, and formed the basis of the constitution of the U.S.A., which assigns the functions of legislature to the Congress, of administration to the President, and of judicature to the Supreme Court. The President, under this Constitution, is elected directly by the people. He and his Executive Cabinet are of equal status with Congress. But though he may be censured by that body, he may not be removed by it. Often it has occurred, when there is a conflict in policy, that the Legislature and the Executive hamper each other's activities to a great degree and obstruct the exercise of their respective functions.

3

Dr. Sun Yat-sen realized the drawbacks of tri-powered government. He originated his Five-Power Constitution so, in addition to the three powers of the Executive, the Legislature and the Judiciary, he introduced the powers of Examination and Control. These are set forth as independent functions of government to be performed by separate organs, without interference from each other, yet all responsible to the National Assembly, the elected representatives of the nation.

The power of Control, when transmitted to the relevant machinery and carried out, is an astringent power, and includes inspection, censuring, and impeachment. The system of censure is an old one in Chinese history. The imperial censors, from the T'ang to the late Ching Dynasty, were court officials whose duty it was to investigate, criticize and impeach official corruption and incompetence. Even the actions of the Emperor himself were not immune from criticism of the censors.

The system of Examination was a feature of our social and political organization introduced since the T'ang Dynasty some thirteen hundred years ago, as a means of recruiting the best talents for service as State officials. This institution is especially characteristic of traditional Chinese politics. The point of departure is that, in the days of monarchy, all powers of the executive, the legislature and the judiciary, as well as the two indigenous ones, were centralized in the person of the Emperor. According to the pre-revolutionary system of government, there was only one right and one power, which was the imperial prerogative.

The present system under which the Republic is now being governed is not yet what it should be, although there are five Yuan exercising the powers of government.

We are now governing the country and constructing the State through the instrument of the Kuomintang, the People's Party. This is because the Revolution has not been brought to a successful conclusion, and hence we are still in a transitional period in our political evolution.

In this period of Party Tutelage our permanent Constitution has not been adopted and put into force. It is a period when the people are being taught to exercise their four rights. Under these circumstances, the five Yuan are not in a position to discharge their offices independently upon a direct mandate from the people. They have to subject themselves to the direction of the Central Political Council of the Kuomintang. For example, an administration measure passed by the Executive Yuan could not be enforced without the sanction of the Council. Since the outbreak of the war the functions of the Central Political Council have been assumed by the Supreme National Defence Council, into which it was reorganized, in order that all matters can be handled with dispatch. Acts and statutes enacted by the Legislative Yuan must receive the approval of the Council before promulgation. After the adoption of the Constitution each of the five Yuan will be able to act independently in the exercise of its powers derived from the National Assembly, the elected representatives of the people. Then all acts and measures passed by the Legislative Yuan will become laws upon promulgation. There will be no need for first submitting such acts to a higher political body for review and final approval. In this way the Five-Power Constitution will function through the Five

Yuan, in accordance with the plan laid down by the Founder of our Republic.

4

At different times in the lives of nations certain problems and tasks take the leading place. In the present stage of the National Revolution which is continuing in China, the primary task, as I have stated above, is the recovery of the sovereign rights which were lost by the Manchus during the last century. Until national freedom has been recovered by arms, as it is being done to-day, the whole energy of the nation must be concentrated on this great task. This does not mean that preparations for the carrying out of other tasks should not proceed. But the attention of the nation must not be divided so that the current main task is lost sight of.

When national freedom has been recovered, when all Chinese territory is liberated from enemy occupation and has once again come under Chinese administration, when there are no foreign troops upon our soil under any pretext whatsoever, and when sovereignty has been fully and unequivocally restored throughout our land, then the National Revolution can proceed to the fulfilment of the other tasks which have been placed so clearly before it by the Father of the Republic.

It is probable that immediately after the regaining of our sovereign rights the Period of Political Tutelage will come to an end, and the adoption of the Constitution will become the order of the day. Then, side by side with the development of democratic government on the basis of the Five-Power Constitution, we shall turn to carrying out Min-Seng-Chu-I, the third principle of San-Min-Chu-I, that of the livelihood of the people.

In this sense the third principle is the final aim of the San-Min-Chu-I. It is the principle of the economic freedom towards a better and higher standard of living for the masses of the people. Only on such a basis of economic freedom can the nation fully develop to a higher and broader level of culture than ever before in the vast extent of our long and fruitful history. China had for centuries past served as the guiding light of civilization and culture for the billion inhabitants of the Asiatic world. It is the final aim of the National Revolution that we should regain that moral and intellectual leadership and show the way to a better and happier world, and achieve an even higher civilization.

As two fundamental steps toward the realization of the principle of the People's Livelihood, Dr. Sun Yat-sen taught the Party and the people that : first, the land must be evenly distributed among the tillers of the soil ; second, the abuses of capital must be restrained, and the economic life of the country directed along socialized lines.

The country's lands are the heritage left to us by our ancestors through thousands of years, they are the gift of nature, not the creation of any group of individuals ; therefore they should be possessed by the nation and enjoyed by all. To carry out such a policy the Father of the Republic had it laid down that the " tilled lands must be possessed by the tiller." We have few large land-owners in China, but while the holdings are relatively small when compared to the large landed estates which were the relics of past feudal ages in Europe, still there is the problem of absentee owners who claim the payment of rent in kind. This is a system akin to feudalism, hence some writers on social conditions in China attach more importance to this than is warranted. The hardship of paying rent in kind makes itself felt in years of famine or calamity when the normal course of the primitive agricultural communities is disturbed. In such years, when the farmer is unable to reap a harvest, he has to borrow either cash or grain from the landlords. High, usurious interests, which are a feature of Chinese agricultural economy, may then bind the borrower to the creditor, who is usually the absentee landlord acting through his bailiff, for years and years to come.

Merely passing a decree giving the lands to the tillers of the soil, if unaccompanied with the machinery to take the place of the landlords, would be of little practical effect. Such an example can be taken from the freeing of serfs in Russia by Czar Alexander in 1861. The freed serfs remained at the mercy of the landowners, and in most cases were in a worse economic position than prior to the passing of the laws obliterating serfdom. It was therefore not until 1917 that vestiges of serfdom finally disappeared from Russia as a social institution. It is interesting to note that the Russian peasant was a free owner of land only between 1917, when the Soviet Government decreed the distribution of land to the peasants, and 1927 when the policies of collectivization again took the land away from them.

Wealth in China, the source of capitalism, has for the last three centuries been derived from trade. The owning of land as such did not lend itself to the accumulation of large surplus which could be diverted into other spheres of production. The income of the landowning class was regulated by extremely low prices for agricultural products. These were the only commodities produced, and their values could not be measured in terms of manufactured products of the cities and towns. Imported articles or industrial products of Treaty Ports were scarce in the hinterland of China, so the glut of agricultural products in the interior resulted in an extremely low standard of living, not only for the farmer, but also for the landowner. An all-embracing poverty had spread its shroud over the entire land for more than two centuries. Throughout the vast recesses of the country the poorer were producing for the poor. Where was the wealth?

5

The wealth of the urban monied classes is invested in trade. Hence there are grounds for stating that out of the primitive rural economy there has emerged a higher system which can be called trade capitalism. Contact with the Western traders and merchants during the past century has tended to increase the wealth of these monied classes, and it was natural that out of the trade capitalists there would develop a body of industrial capitalists. Those who have had experience of the difficulties of industrial development in China will readily agree that among the monied classes there is little industrial sense visible. This applies to the financiers and bankers of China, whose main activities still were, up to 1937, concentrated in foreign exchange and financing of trade operations.

It is only now, as a result of the experience of the War of Resistance, when the need for domestic industries is most clearly demonstrated, that the owners of large fortunes gained from successful trading ventures feel the urge towards investment in industries.

This is the reason why the Father of the Republic asserted that it would be possible to restrain the abuses, such as monopolistic prices and control of markets, which form the main features of the development of industrial capitalism in the West. He felt that by examining the development of Western industrial capitalism we would be able to discover checks and remedies for such abuses, and to make use of the substance characteristic of that system of economy. Dr. Sun Yat-sen realized that China would have to pass through the portals of industrial capitalism on the way to the goal of the People's Livelihood or Socialism. But he did not want the development of Chinese economy and the State to be hampered and vitiated by the obstacles, malpractices, and iniquities of that system.

He taught the Party to discourage the growth of large fortunes and monopolistic private industrial undertakings. He laid down that all industries of a monopolistic nature must be socialized from the inception, so as to prevent the growth of a powerful class of industrial capitalists who might gain control of the State apparatus to the detriment of national interest. His policies were framed to check the greed for wealth and power which is a disease with some men. He took into consideration, however, the striving of the small man to better his position ; he envisaged also the industriousness of the masses of the Chinese people and their ingenuity and initiative, hence, while limiting the growth of large monopolistic, private industries on a reasonable scale, leaving the State to play the predominant rôle in the rapid industrialization of the country.

In this way the people of China would be able to possess the national wealth and enjoy the national income for raising their standard of living and freeing themselves economically.

6

Now that capitalism for profit is under fire from many sides, including the leading social thinkers of the United States and Great Britain, it is easier for our Western friends to understand the differences between that system of economy and the third principle of the San-Min-Chu-I.

Dr. Sun Yat-sen, in his writings and teachings, recognized that imperialism, the subjugation and exploitation of economically undeveloped countries and their peoples, for the benefit of the metropolitan ruler-state, was a logical adjunct of capitalism. Profit must come from somewhere, and as the wages of labour in the metropolis grew the surplus values from which profits came would have to be taken, not from the labour of the men and women of the metropolis, but from the labour of the natives of the areas in which the raw materials were grown or produced.

It was natural that San-Min-Chu-I would be opposed first and foremost to imperialism in any shape or form for several reasons. First, the exploitation of subject peoples was not recognized or tolerated by the traditional Chinese political theory and practice. Second, China herself from 1840 was steadily being reduced to a semi-colonial status, which might have deteriorated into that of a full colony if our power of resistance to Japan had not saved us. Third, it was clear to Dr. Sun Yat-sen that the future of China lay in the industrialisation of the country, and transforming it from a purely agricultural country into one with an economy which was well balanced, so as to give full and steady employment and a rising standard of living to the entire population of four hundred and fifty millions. It was natural, then, that imperialism would strive to resist this economic development, and political obstacles would be placed in the way of realization of the San-Min-Chu-I.

The invasion of China by Japan was the last desperate effort made by World Imperialism, acting as system, to check the victory of San-Min-Chu-I in China. When the National Government was administered in Canton from 1923 to 1926, the major foreign Powers, America and Britain included, still following blindly the dictates of unbridled capitalism and its handmaid, imperialism, tried to check the extension of its power over the whole country. Men like Wu Pei-fu, Sun Ch'uan-fang and lesser militarists were supported by the Western Powers, while Chang Tso-lin, the Manchurian war lord, was supported by the Japanese.

Notwithstanding all this, the National Government made its way to Hankow in 1926, and then to Nanking in 1927. But while relations with the European and American groups became easier and more stabilized, the Japanese continued to obstruct by direct intervention, as well as through counter-revolutionary forces in all parts of the country, culminating in the Tsinan outrage in the spring of 1928, when the Japanese Army occupied the railway from Tsingtao to Tsinan, capital of Shantung Province, in a futile effort to block our advance to Peking.

The growth of the National Government in Nanking presaged that soon China would be able to challenge the control which was exercised over her through the unequal treaties, whereby foreign garrisons and foreign warships could be stationed and maintained to dominate and patrol her principal cities and inland waters. This was the policy of the National Government declared in all the main documents of the period. And the Japanese saw that their special position in China would inevitably be placed on a footing of equality with other nations, and brought under the jurisdiction of the Chinese Republic. This would mean the end of imperialism in China. And China would regain her full sovereignty as a modern State.

The Japanese assumed the rôle of the supreme protector and guardian of imperialism in the Far East, and particularly in China. They invaded Manchuria in 1931 under a lame pretext, and finally in 1937 started on their war of total conquest against China.

The Chinese Government placed excessive faith in the League of Nations principally because, to Chinese political thought, here was an organization which had the proper authority to settle such an international dispute and uphold international law and order.

As a result, we were not then ready to mobilize the nation for resistance, and the Japanese war lords were able to occupy the three Eastern Provinces, and set up the puppet State of " Manchukuo."

In doing all this Japan acted as the representative of World Imperialism, and her success was due to some measure of truth in her interpretation of her rôle. Nothing practical was done to help China, and the War of Resistance of 1937 became a necessity. It was the armed clash between the San-Min-Chu-I and World Imperialism.

7

When this war is over and victory finally won, there may still remain the economic victory which San-Min-Chu-I must win over the forces of World Capitalism.

Here, then, we come to the distinction between San-Min-Chu-I and capitalism for profit as two opposing systems of economy.

Production under the capitalist system has brought about an abundant supply of commodities of all kinds. There is no commodity or machine which cannot be produced, be it for manufacture or for consumption. And given the necessary raw materials, there is no limit to the quantity of products which can be placed before the consumers. Capitalism is an economy of enormous potentialities in the sphere of production. In this lies the contribution of the capitalist system to civilization and culture. And this is a great contribution.

Distribution under the capitalist system of economy, however, is chaotic. It is the antithesis of capitalist production. It makes for waste, poverty, suffering, oppression and misery. And to-day, in the span of one generation, two major World Wars are the harvests which it is reaping for the century or so of its development.

Instead of an economy of plenty, for the use and enjoyment of mankind, capitalism produces in such a way that its products may be dumped into the sea or shoved into the furnaces of locomotives in order to prevent them from becoming a glut on the market, thereby cutting down profits ; that its gold may be buried under the ground and heavily guarded that none may use it ; that the wealth of nations may be spent on arms and weapons of destruction instead of life-giving enterprises ; that the enjoyment of the fruits of civilization and culture may be for the few and not for the many ; that there may be no political, economic or social democracy. San-Min-Chu-I is opposed to capitalism of this nature, which is actuated solely by the profit motive.

3

Many Americans are surprised by the fact that Soviet Russia retains the system of industrial accounting which is in vogue in capitalist countries, or the system of wages paid in cash, or even the introduction of the piecework system for increased production in the form of the indigenous " Stakhanovite " movement. These are all forms of capitalist production which have produced results in the United States and Europe. They have also produced results in Russia, and will produce the same results in China. These results are in the form of large quantities of commodities which form a growing part of the national wealth.

San-Min-Chu-I teaches us that we must use these features of capitalism in order first of all to produce in China a sufficiency of commodities. But it also teaches us that we must simultaneously make use of more advanced methods to be taken from the socialized system of production, which has been successfully tried out in Soviet Russia. In this way the good will be taken from the existing leading systems of production, and out of this synthesis China will be able to raise the standard of living for each and every one of her vast population.

One of the greatest problems of modern China is the question of unemployment. In no country is this problem so acute. It resulted in creating a tremendous reserve of labour power, which reacted upon the level of wages, and in general upon the living standard of the entire population. According to the most general statistics, it is said that in pre-war days only one out of every five men in China was engaged in actual production. This includes not only handicrafts and industry, but also agriculture. Surplus labour, which is mostly from the rural districts, seeks a living as transportation coolies, as soldiers, and as boatmen on the navigable rivers.

The present war is modifying the situation, since the loss of man-power through fighting, disease, and famine is counteracting on the annual increase in surplus man-power ; but still the feature of the unproductiveness of labour in the ratio of one to five probably still remains.

When Dr. Sun Yat-sen was formulating the San-Min-Chu-I, he paid the greatest attention to this problem. But in surveying the capitalist system he was not able to find a satisfactory solution. In England, since the first World War unemployment had become a major problem. This resulted in labour disturbances which cul-minated in the great Coal Strike of 1926, and the advance of labour might have been greater had it not been for the ingenious manœuvre employed by the Conservative Government in forcing the Labour Party and the Trade Unions to come out into the open to fight before they were completely prepared.

Still, while political advantage was gained for the owners of capital from those events, they were unable to check the economic consequences which flowed from them. The world depression, which was a forerunner of this present World War, began in 1929, and mass unemployment was concurrently one of the major causes and effects.

Unemployment in any country is a drain on the national wealth. Hence, as it is a feature of capitalism, it was impossible for Dr. Sun Yat-sen to accept that system of economy as a model for his programme for the development of China and the solving of the question of the People's Livelihood.

Taking it for granted that capitalism in Great Britain was less highly developed than in the United States, where industry had risen to great heights of productivity, the survey of the unemployment situation gave no better promise of solution. On the outbreak of war in Europe there were in Britain and America still millions of men and women idle and unproductive, while the aggregate of man-hours of labour wasted through unemployment during the last two decades is wellnigh astronomical.

Min-Seng-Chu-I, the Principle of the People's Livelihood, would solve the question of unemployment by mobilizing the whole mass of the adult population for building up industry and agriculture and supplying the amenities of life for the entire population. By stages the Five-Power Government would take the necessary steps to bring China's economy into the right proportions. That, instead of the misshapen abnormality where agriculture supports upwards of 80 per cent. of the population, there would be an even balance between that branch of economy and industry. The economy of a country must be as proportionate as the figure of a well-built man, in which electrical power takes the place of his heart, and scientific laboratories and institutes guide and co-ordinate and function in all branches of the national economy, just as the head of the man controls the actions of his muscles and limbs. In carrying out this industrialization of China the new economic system of Min-Seng-Chu-I will draw the best from both Capitalism and Socialism, and in the shortest space of time raise China from a backward agricultural economy to one of the foremost industrialized countries of the world.

8

We have already looked at the similarities between the first principle, Min-Chuh-Chu-I, and the Policy of Nationalities of the Socialist system adopted in the Soviet Union. These two systems guarantee to the different ethnic groups within the nation complete cultural autonomy, political freedom and economic equality.

Since China has, for nearly two thousand years, been a homogeneous whole, Dr. Sun Yat-sen had no need to equivocate on the meaning of " nation " and " national independence." As a statesman, Lenin was not placed in so favourable a position. He had to make concessions to the chauvinistic tendencies inherent among the intellectual strata of the populations of the various ethnic groups, like the Ukrainians, the White Russians, the Volga Germans, and the Georgians. As a sop to their chauvinism he quibbled over the meaning of " nation," by proclaiming that each ethnic group had the right of secession. This right, while existing on paper, is really no right at all, for it is unthinkable that any constituent member of the present Union of Soviet Socialist Republics would be able to enforce such right by actually leaving the Union.

The sublime sagacity of our ancestors welded the heterogeneous masses of the inhabitants of the East Asian mainland into one conglomerate mass of the Chinese people ; the inherent tolerance derived from successive schools of philosophy engraved on our body politic the ideas and ideals of internal unity, so that Chinese, Mongol, Manchu, Turkoman, and Tibetan all form the Chung-Hua nation. Hence the absence of the so-called right of secession bespeaks a purer nationalism than the Soviet policy of nationalism.

Again, the principle of nationalism, Min-Chuh-Chu-I, does not visualize the physical adherance of other states or nations to the Chinese Republic. The San-Min-Chu-I of Dr. Sun Yat-sen is a doctrine and a teaching which, by its appeal to reason, will triumph throughout the world. It can never be interpreted as a militant code of intellectual aggression to be used as a weapon in the way the Trotskyists tried to turn the teachings of Marx and Lenin into a dogma for World Revolution and a panacea for all the economic ills of the world.

The defects of such theories pronounced by Marx in the first place, and elaborated by Engels, have been illustrated by the uses to which they could be turned by successive thinkers like Lenin, Trotsky, Kautsky, and the latter day Social Democrats of the European countries. Advocating an economic theory, Socialism, by which the livelihood of the people could be raised to a higher standard, Marx and his disciples grafted upon this a political and social system which tended to ignore the heritage of civilizations and cultures.   In this fundamental defect lie the sufferings of the Russian people from the outbreak of the October Revolution up to the end of the First Five-Year Plan.   It was only at the conclusion of that decisive period that the physical sufferings of the Soviet people came to an end and a new dawn broke for them—the coming of Socialism in their country.

This does not mean to say that the methods employed by Lenin were not necessary for carrying out the basic policies of the Bolsheviks of land nationalisation, and the removal of class distinctions, by introducing democratic principles to a people steeped in the Tartar tradition of absolute government and paternal administration.   The Russians must be taught to know what is suitable for their own country, just as Chinese should be taught to know what is suitable in theirs.   However, when the theory of the proletarian revolution was grafted on to a country like China it required a considerable stretch of the imagination to see in the unemployed coolies anything but a " lumpen proletariat " of social and economic adventurers ; and in the minute number of industrial workers in the Treaty Ports a proletarian mass of skilled and disciplined workers who could assume and control a social revolution.

9

The development of Socialism in Soviet Russia has brought about even closer similarities between San-Min-Chu-I and Leninism. Internal unity has been achieved ; religious toleration has reappeared as a national policy ; unemployment has disappeared ; and the distribution of the national wealth according to the value of work contributed to the State by all strata is tending to be more equalised. This does not mean that in detailed categories of work there is absolute equality ; it merely means that in the major categories, such as between mental and manual labour, between male and female, and between rural and urban labour the discrepancies are lessened.

When we examine the two most important questions of present-day economics which have to be solved—distribution of commodities and unemployment—we find that greater success has been achieved under the Socialism of the Soviet Union than in the capitalism of the Western European and American countries.

In 1932 on all the railway stations of Moscow there were notices giving a list of the factories where labour was urgently needed. Such notices were posted in nearly all parts of the old industrial areas, as well as the new ones being built up in the far-off Urals, Siberia, and even in the former colonial areas of Uzbekistan and Turkmenistan. A year or two later the Soviet Government announced that the problem of unemployment had been solved by having all able-bodied men and women engaged in some productive task. There were housewives, but even they were classed as being in production. Servants were permitted to be members of the Trade Unions which were reserved for productive workers. And by-and-large, the great masses of the annual labour surplus coming from the rural districts were absorbed into the large industrial and agricultural enterprises which were being built under the First Five-Year Plan.

The fact that large productive units were created under planned and socialized economy meant that the question of distribution could be solved more readily. Through factory co-operative distribution, the masses of the industrial workers could be provided with commodities substantially sufficient for their daily wants ; through the village State farm and collective farm co-operatives, the masses of the rural population could be served in the same manner. The workers in the Government and administrative offices also were supplied with the necessities of life in their co-operative restaurants and shops. Over and above these were the commercial co-operatives which stocked commodities, which could be bought by individuals from their surplus wages. Lastly, there were the clinics, rest houses and sports organizations, which assisted in the distribution of amenities of life not supplied by the ordinary co-operatives. By means of the distributor co-operatives the Soviet masses obtain the fruits of national production commensurate with the amount of labour they give to the State.

In these two important questions of national economics, China can study and learn much from the Socialism of Soviet Russia, since in these we find Min-Seng-Chu-I being put into practice. It is as though we have been provided with a laboratory in which the tenets of Dr. Sun Yat-sen have been tried and found to be sound and practical. But among some of the comrades of the Party there still remains much misunderstanding as to the real content of Socialism. They sometimes even think that all property has been nationalized, that no one may own anything, not even his clothes and personal belongings. This comes from ignorance of facts due to refusal to read and study what is being done in Soviet Russia.

In Soviet Russia individuals are permitted to build and own houses, but they may not own the land, which is held on a lease from the Government. They may own motor-cars, which they may purchase with their savings. But they may not own the " means of production " ; that is, machines by the use of which they may exploit the labour of their fellow-men for their own profit. Therein lies the essence of Socialism. However, since China still lags far behind other countries in economic development, the Father of the Republic has recognized this by specifically laying down in his International Development of China that " China has to begin the two stages of industrial evolution at once by adopting the machinery as well as the nationalization of production."

Our broad aim is to develop national capital and increase national production. By national ownership and management of large-scale industries and other enterprises, we shall be able to make great strides in solving the problems of unemployment and distribution among the masses of our people. Then, on this State-owned industrial base, we shall be able to encourage the growth of private manufacturing and agricultural enterprises, so that the general masses of the entire four hundred and fifty million people can be raised to a higher standard of living, and a great step thus taken forward to the realization of the Principle of the People's Livelihood.

10

The doctrinal base of the Soviet Government from its inception in 1917 was in the theory of the dictatorship of the industrial proletariat. The substance of this as applied to Russia by Lenin was that, inasmuch as the Russian aristocracy and bourgeoisie were socially and economically enmeshed in skeins of feudalist tradition and prejudice, and entangled with the big international capitalist and armament magnates, such connections would lead inevitably to policies of expansion, colonial exploitation and the adventures of imperialist wars, the situation called for a radical solution. It called for a major surgical operation on the body politic of the Russian State. It called for the substitution of the aristocracy and bourgeoisie by the workers and peasants as the ruling classes in the Soviet Union.

Trotsky, in his appeal to the Tsarist generals, used the argument that an independent and strong proletarian Russia was better than weak, carved-up, bourgeois Russia, such as would have resulted from the victory of the counter-revolutionary Kolchak, Wrangel, or

Denikin, who were receiving assistance from the main imperialist Powers. This assistance obviously was not being given for nothing. Some *quid pro quo* must have been the case upon which money and arms were being shipped to the White armies in so many parts of Russia.

The measures used by Lenin and his associates were most radical ones. To our minds, they had their historical background in the Tartar tradition of ruling and administration, which was embedded in the mentality of the Russians from their century-long subjection to those alien conquerors from the steppes and the deserts. Hence, it is felt that such methods might have found sympathy among the masses of the Russian peoples and were tolerated by them. But in China such methods would be deplored, and would not receive support from the masses of the people, including the intellectuals, if the Revolution is to succeed.

The doctrine of the Dictatorship of the Proletariat through its " vanguard " the Communist Party in Russia was conceived to give power to the Communist Party for such a period as would be required to establish an economic system whereby the ideal, " From each according to his ability, and to each according to his needs," would eventually prevail. Such a system is based upon a higher development of production than the world has ever seen. From the point of view of practical politics the attainment of that level of production would require upwards of half a century to a full century, even in Russia with its five-year plans. Thus the Dictatorship of the Proletariat through the Russian Communist Party must continue for that period until it is substituted by the withering away of the State and the emerging of a truly Communist society.

In China to-day we have a system of the Dictatorship of the Kuomintang. The Party of Dr. Sun Yat-sen rules the country as the trustees of the people. It rules according to the San-Min-Chu-I, as a dictatorship during a period of political tutelage when the country is being guided toward the consummation of two fundamental tasks : resistance to the invasion of imperialist Japan, and preparing the people for constitutional government.

In contrast to the Russian Communist Party and the doctrines of Marx, Engels and Lenin, the Kuomintang, at the introduction of the democratic Five-Power Constitution, will give up its dictatorial power and become one of the political parties of the body politic of the Chinese Republic. Other parties will be independent and, as associations of free persons, will be free and equal under the laws of the Chinese Republic. The trustees for the welfare and the safety of the Chinese Republic will then be not the Kuomintang alone but the entire Chinese people under a democratic Constitution. This is a very important distinction between our San-Min-Chu-I and the system of the Soviet Government.

In the past the social democracy of the Chinese people and their cultural heritage have been such that we have been able to " calm the savage in man." China was conquered by the Tartars, the descendants of the same Genghis Khan who conquered and ruled Russia for centuries. But in China it was finally the conqueror who adopted the ways of the conquered because there was a higher culture and civilization to dominate, finally, over a lower and less developed one. In Russia the severe, ruthless Tartars implanted their low standards upon a simple forest folk, and left a tradition of intolerance and severity which is only now being erased.

In China through the ages we have experienced the upsurge of movements, " isms," religions, and the expressions of human emotions in different forms. But we have found through our vast history and experience that individual freedom will have its final victory. Therefore the Kuomintang, in accordance with the San-Min-Chu-I, having fulfilled its mission of tutelage must release its power and, through the Five-Power Constitution, establish a full democratic Government within the Republic.

China's War and Peace Aims *

I TAKE this occasion to examine once more the war policy we adopted when, in July, 1937, we first took up arms to oppose the Japanese invader. Let us see what position this War of Resistance occupies in our national Revolution ; its import and significance in the light of our glorious history of the past fifty centuries. Let us inquire into its achievements, and make clear in our minds what is meant by carrying on this struggle to its bitter end, and what is our ultimate war aim. Meantime, in the course of this lecture, we will also analyse the lines of policy to follow in building our new State ; wherein lies the defect of capitalism ; what is the difference between Min-Seng-Chu-I and capitalism. Finally, we must know how a rich, strong and democratic new China may be constructed according to the San-Min-Chu-I.

I

To evaluate the War of Resistance in the light of Chinese history, it is necessary to understand our revolutionary movement. Since 1911, when the Chinese Revolution began, we have overcome many obstacles. The usurper, Yuan Shi-kai, was toppled from his self-elevated throne. The Northern Expedition from Canton against the rapacious war lords was carried to its successful conclusion, and Nanking came to be the nation's capital. Alarmed at our unity and growing strength, Japan struck at Shenyang (Mukden) on September 18, 1931, and rapidly seized all of the three Eastern Provinces. Six years later, on July 7, 1937, she pursued her aggression further by the Lukouchiao attack. Finally, goaded to desperation, we took up the challenge and struck back furiously at the invader at Shanghai on August 13, 1937. This total war, which we are determined to carry on at all costs, is the culminating point in one of the historical epochs in our life as a nation. It is the very opposite of an imperialistic gamble for colonial space and natural resources. It is a war for our freedom to survive and develop as a nation.

The Revolution, since it was first set in motion and then kept in full flood by Dr. Sun Yat-sen, has not yet run its intended course, though it has behind it an eventful history of more than fifty years.

* A lecture delivered at the Section for Party and Political Training, Central Training Institute, Chungking, November 2, 1940.

We are still striving for its full realization according to the instructions of the Father of the Republic.

2

Why do we go through thick and thin and dare death itself to carry on the Revolution? First of all, we want to restore our freedom and independence which has been curtailed since 1842 by the Treaty of Nanking with Britain. Though we still presented the façade of a sovereign State, important elements of our sovereignty were lost after our defeat in the Opium War. Since then, other imperialistic countries followed the precedent thus set and wrested whatever privileges and rights they could from the effete Manchu Government. Unequal treaties have become festering wounds. We were not, it is true, a colony of any particular Power, but became a semi-colonial country under the heels of various Powers. Therefore, over fifty years ago, those patriots who realized the danger we were in, started a widespread movement for national Revolution to halt a decline which was leading to sure ruin.

In a narrow sense, the Revolution was pointed at the corrupt Manchu Government which served as a magnet to foreign aggression. So, our watchword then was, "Expel the Manchus, restore (the sovereignty to) the Chinese." Actually, that was only a small part of the purpose of our nationalist battle-cry. After the downfall of the Manchu Empire in 1911, many thought our work was done. That was not so. After even thirty years, our nationalist movement has not yet reached its goal. From 1911 to 1927 we had not even attained the internal unity upon which to start building a progressive, powerful, modern State. Just when this was about accomplished, foreign invasion struck our land to break up this unity by force and continue the imperialist policy of "divide and rule" a weakened China. To-day, all the unequal treaties, with the Treaty of Nanking at the head of them, are just as binding as ever: we are still far from being a free and independent country.

Therefore, in a broader sense, the Revolution now has to turn its face outwards against the external aggressive forces themselves. For though internal strife due to inequalities among the constituent ethnic groups of a country may be fatal to its independence, foreign aggression in any form, when it is not vigorously resisted, will finish it off even more quickly. Among the imperialistic Powers Japan is the most brutal and rapacious. At Lukouchiao, over three years ago, she embarked on her long-laid plan of military conquest, leaving us no choice but to stand up and fight.

Now, a revolutionary movement can be directed purely against foreign domination, as in the case of the American War of Independence, or have internal political aims to overthrow the ruling autocracy and institute a democracy instead, as in the case of the French Revolution ; or else it may be politico-economic, taking the form of a gigantic class struggle, of which the Russian Revolution is an example. Our Revolution combines the first two qualities with an element of the third. So, although the decadent monarchy was torn down long ago, our mission is but partially fulfilled. The present War of Resistance, when reviewed in its proper background, forms an inseparable part of the Chinese National Revolution.

3

If a nation, unwilling to be the bond-slaves of another one, start a revolutionary war and continue it despite all obstacles, success is a certainty. In the sixteenth century, before the rise of Britain and France as world empires, the dominant power in Europe was Spain. The King of Spain was, at one time, concurrently Emperor of the Holy Roman Empire. At that time, Holland was crushed under Spanish tyranny, her people suffering from a thousand exploitations and indignities from the conqueror, and the Netherlanders, finding it more than they could bear, rose up in rebellion. For seventy odd years they continued their war for national freedom till the Spaniards were driven out of their country and a free, independent State of their own was established. Two centuries and more after the rise of the Dutch Republic, France achieved dominance under the leadership of Napoleon. As she extended her domain to the whole of Central and South-western Europe, Napoleon put his brother on the Spanish throne with a French host of 100,000 to protect him. But the Spaniards had no desire to be French slaves, rebelled, and fought the invaders. After years of heart-breaking struggles, they, too, obtained their emancipation.

I give only two illustrations, though history is full of them. Spain and France, in their heyday, were mighty, imperialistic Powers with matchless armies, while revolutionary Holland and Spain were weak States. But because the fearless revolutionary forces were vital and progressive, they got what they aimed at—freedom.

4

More than three years ago, when our preparations for national defence were yet incomplete, undertaking this War of Resistance was regarded with doubt and apprehension by some of the intellectuals and the general public alike. Without the least semblance of heavy industries, with but the merest cadre of a modern army, navy and air force, they asked, how could we accept the challenge of an antagonist who had had years of peace and preparation since his smashing victory over imperial Russia in 1905 ? It is true that so far as armament was concerned we were pitting sticks against stone. But wars, and particularly wars of liberation, are not fought with arms alone. That sort of armament obsession was found not only in our own ranks, but among the enemy as well. At the first encounter at arms, therefore, the Japanese planned to crush us with five divisions of their well-equipped army within three months. But we are still here, stronger and more determined than ever, after three years, having engaged forty-two of his modern divisions, having inflicted on him over a million and a half casualties, and are bogging him deeper every day in the quagmire.

How could we last so long ? How did we win so many a marvellous success to lay the foundation of ultimate victory ? The answer is this : when we set out in our War of Resistance we had the naked realities of our situation before us ; we saw then the contrast in armaments between ours and those of the enemy. But we were equally aware of historical advantages and natural endowments of our people, to which the enemy was blind, and which happily give us a certain superiority over him.

5

I have already cited two examples from history. If a nation strives heroically for freedom and, when threatened by an aggressor, will launch a nation-wide resistance to fight him to the bitter end, that freedom-loving people is sure to win its liberty sooner or later. This is an immutable law proven by a wealth of historical instances.

Furthermore, we in China are armed with the revolutionary San-Min-Chu-I as a guide to our march, a key to certain success, and a binding force for pitting the whole nation as one against the enemy : such a spiritual fortification can amply make up for our material deficiencies. From the beginning of the war up till now, the enemy has again and again made offers of peace on his own terms, but we have consistently spurned his vile offers. There is no question of our compromising half-way, for ultimate victory is drawing nearer every day.

Our natural endowments are what the Chinese race have accomplished and acquired by patience, endurance, and the

overcoming of myriad dangers through fifty centuries. First, we
have an immense territory of four and a half million square miles,
almost equal to the total area of all the European countries. After
the U.S.S.R. and the U.S.A. we rank first in the size of territory.
Secondly, as our lands extend into the sub-tropical, the temperate
and the sub-arctic climate, we have agricultural products in great
abundance and variety. We have natural resources in store under-
neath the earth in enormous quantities and of many kinds. Although
our industries are still undeveloped, we can make use of our great
reserves of man-power to speed up the work during war-time.
Except Russia and America, again, no other country in the world
is our match. Thirdly, our population of 450 millions are highly
intelligent, if uneducated. Soviet Russia, with her 193 millions,
America with her 135, and India with her 380 are all behind us in
this respect. Before war was waged, we took these facts into our
estimate as potential and ponderous elements which must contribute
to ultimate victory. It has not been, nor will be, proved that we
were wrong.

6

We are used to saying that we will fight on to the bitter end.
Now, what is that bitter end ? Some cynics and sceptics would
explain it as the moment when our armed forces are shattered, our
lands scorched, our material resources exhausted, our morale
broken, and we can carry on no longer. This is sheer defeatism,
nay, it is malicious propaganda from Tokyo. The authentic explanation is that when the enemy is driven clean out of the country
and has to stop fighting, we shall have reached that end. As long
as there is still a single hostile soldier in this land, we have not yet
come to the bitter end. To be more definite, we shall not be satisfied
with the *status quo ante* Lukouchiao, because Japanese aggression
had begun long before the attack at Lukouchiao, Mukden is still
fresh in our memory, and when we have cleared the invading
hordes out of South, Central and North China, we will march
forward in battle array to Manchuria, our north-eastern provinces.
There, 35 millions of our countrymen have been trampled under
the " iron hoofs " of the tyrant for the last ten years ; their groans
are not unheard, their thraldom is not forgotten, by us. If, in the
end, the Great North-East is not restored to our fold, or North
China is to be treated as " a special area," our present campaign of
resistance would be altogether meaningless.

Recently, the blustering Japanese despot began to feel uneasy, so he picks up the trade of peace-mongering, or rather rumour-mongering, spreading rumours of peace through his mouthpiece the *Domei*, or even through foreign news agencies like the *Trans-Ocean* and others. This is only indirectly admitting that he knows the conquest of China is an impossible task. But for the sake of " face," and in order to make good his huge losses (over 1·6 million casualties and about 20,000 million yen military expenses) and escape blame at home, he is loath to go back empty-handed. Thus, he is in a sad fix. Although not long after he launched his aggressive adventure he reiterated his intentions not to have any further dealings with our National Government, yet, since he has come to this awkward pass, he has to eat his own words. Rumour has it that he would withdraw from Central and South China provided that we would be reconciled to the permanent loss of Manchuria, and submit to the conversion of North China as a " specialized area " with the principal seaports along the China coast put under his control. If this is true, then the Japanese are sorry fools. Where is the difference between these conditions and the twenty-one demands of evil memory of 1915 ? If we are stupid enough to stick our neck into such a noose, why have we been fighting these three years and more ?

Our determination to chase the enemy out of our country is no idle dream. It shall be done. Before the war, not a few were incredulous of our power to resist over a long period, but now we have been fighting for some forty months. Formerly, things looked most favourable to the enemy, but to-day there has been a change in our favour. If we continue with tenacity, using all our resources, and turning the international situation to our advantage, the attainment of our war aim will become a certainty.

7

Let us look at the enemy's army. According to our pre-war estimates, his effectives that could be mobilized for service at the front number about three millions. The past three years have cost him over a million and a half in casualties. In the field at present there are about forty-two divisions, each of 20,000 to 30,000 men, totalling over a million ; our north-eastern provinces, Korea, Formosa and Japan must also absorb a considerable number : thus, the enemy's supply of cannon-fodder is already showing signs of exhaustion. If this is kept up for the next few years, even if there are no major battles, we shall wear down his forces merely by guerrilla tactics. Therefore, the enemy's army is nothing to be feared.

His air force, both in quality and in quantity, is the weakest among that of the Great Powers. If we can maintain in the field 1000 war planes, then air dominance over China's skies can be wrested from him. Even as it is, the claim on his air power has been a strain on him. His strength lies, we may safely say, in his navy, upon which he depends to safeguard his empire, but which can never be a mortal threat to us.

8

It is conceded that our enemy is the greatest naval Power in the Far East. Against this element of his strength we can do nothing, since we are not a sea Power. Ever since our last war with Japan in 1894-5, the seas in the Orient have been the preserves of the " dwarf " empire. We cannot produce a navy by magic. But, though powerless, we are not helpless. If this struggle were only a private war between two contestants in isolation, unaffected by international events, we might have reason to despair. As it is, our resistance has become the concern of all countries having interests in the Far East.

On the continent, the country whose interests in the Far East are very great, and closely linked with ours, as she is contiguous to us, is Soviet Russia. On the seas, the United States and Britain stand with us on the same side. As long as we fight on, they are directly and indirectly bound to be affected. All three countries are extending us sympathy and assistance, according to the dictates of a sense of justice as well as to their deep national concern. The material and technical aid as well as moral support which Soviet Russia has been rendering us is daily increasing. Britain is engaged in a mortal struggle in Europe ; we should not expect too much of her ; but her help also could be enlarged when time is opportune. As to America, who is in a position to tip the scale of the world's political balance, and whose naval power has long been the envy and fear of the Japanese, she is accelerating her plan for two-ocean warfare. Her potential aid to us is, of course, incalculable.

Before the triple alliance of the Axis, Britain, hoping Japan would not be an additional foe, made some weighty concessions in an effort to appease the enemy. The silver agreement of Tientsin and the closing of the Burma Road were unfortunate results of such appeasement. But the wolf proved unappeasable : he wanted more. Disappointed, Britain stiffened up. It is obvious that the main objective of the Axis military pact is the United States, for it provides that if any one of the three signatories should be attacked by any country who is not yet involved in the European war or the " China Incident," the other two signatories will at once lend the third partner military, economic and political aid. But America was not frightened by that pact ; on the contrary, her intention of rendering aid to Britain and China has been given an edge. The evacuation of American citizens from the Far East, the extension of the economic boycott against Japan, the rumoured co-defence between America and Canada following a similar arrangement between the U.S.A. and Australia, the parley for utilizing Far Eastern naval bases now going on between Britain and America, the speeding up of the plan for a two-ocean navy, the handing over of fifty destroyers to Britain—all these go to prove that America is not in the least afraid of the Axis threat. America is getting ready to oppose the peace-disturbing bandits both in Europe and in Asia.

Lately (1940) there has been an indication that the American people are in accord with their Government for giving aid to Britain and China. The election of President Roosevelt to a third term seems to indicate that. During the last days of the election campaign, the Republican Party, setting store by the pacifism of the nation, charged Roosevelt's policy with pushing the country over the brink of war ; this move might have been shrewd political tactics, but it failed. The ballot returns show that the people are not afraid of the war threat, and gave a decisive reply to the Axis alliance. At the same time, the election proved that the U.S. Government's past foreign policy had got the full backing of the American nation, and would receive support in future.

The general opinion is that with the re-election of President Roosevelt, America's Far Eastern relations with Japan will be further strained. When the break will happen, it is hard to predict ; but it will come some day, somehow. The enemy's Army and Air Force have been mauled by us these three years, his Navy will henceforth be taken care of by a naval Power of the very first order. If the Japanese, casting all caution to the winds, should drive southward, a war with the United States is inevitable. When his Fleet is sunk, what has he got left with which to blockade us ? By that time, not only would our Manchuria be restored to us, but Formosa too, while Korea will regain her independence. All these are, however, possibilities only, we cannot count upon them. We should not indulge too much in wishful thinking on outside developments ; concentration on our own efforts is of greater importance.

10

If our campaign of resistance is carried to a successful finish, China will then emerge, out of a semi-colonial status, as a Great Power. After having been kept prostrate by aggressive forces for a century, we have not yet (1940) been able to abolish foreign controlled settlements, extra-territorial rights enjoyed by foreign subjects, and alien shipping in inland waters. But the unequal treaties will be annulled, one and all.

To be an independent State, it is necessary to grow rich and strong. There is no question of our being strong after victory is won. Not long ago, both America and Britain promised the revision of their existing treaties with us after the war, thus implying their willingness to abandon these special privileges unfairly obtained from us. As soon as those treaties are invalidated, our freedom and independence will be restored.

What we have lacked are war-planes and guns of large calibre. This will be a matter of no insuperable difficulty. Heavy industries, the basis of national defence, could be established within four or five years after the victory. When the Soviet Revolution was won, the first Five-Year Plan, devoted exclusively to heavy industries, was accomplished in four years. What the Soviet Union has done, there is no reason why we cannot do. After the heavy, the light industries could also be built up by us in due course. Furthermore, when victory is ours, the ocean lanes would be wide open for communications. America is now diverting all industry to armament production ; beginning from 1942, she will be putting out 50,000 aircraft a year. It is a practical proposition that as soon as the European war is wound up, a considerable number of her armament or war plants, which otherwise must be dismantled or fall into disuse, could be bought by us at no considerable cost to be erected here. After 1918, her armament industries were suddenly brought to a standstill. Machinery and ships were laid aside to rust. Had they been acquired by us then, our national defence industries might have had a fair start. Unfortunately, the Peking Government under the war lords paid no heed to that sort of thing. Now, as the opportunity offers itself again, we must not miss it, so that whenever an emergency arises, we shall no longer need to rely solely on foreign help. In one word, the requisites of a strong country are not impossible to attain.

II

To maintain the strength of a State, a liberal supply of powerful armaments is indeed indispensable, but without bountiful resources favoured by nature plus massive economic productivity, that strength may be found standing on feet of clay. Japan, whose national cult is militarism, is definitely not a weak State, but nature is niggardly towards her, and her economy is not really strong. We want China's strength to be well founded.

Economists tell us that national wealth consists in developing the potential productivity of the land and improving agricultural conditions to increase crop production. That is all very well. For thousands of years China's sustenance has come from farming, and yet the peasants are so poverty-stricken that a good, fat year means only they are free from famine, while if a bad, lean one occurs, starvation and death must stalk abroad. Therefore, merely to depend upon agriculture cannot give the people a decent living, let alone make them rich. The conclusion is that we must make industry our major branch of economy and farming our subsidiary occupation, for often the latter had to rely on the former as a motivating force, though in a broad view the two are complementary to each other. But above all, our production should be industrialized and modernised to the utmost degree.

12

The old way for industrializing a country is to develop through capitalism, such as Britain and the United States have done. That may accelerate production, but *laissez-faire* distribution would nullify many of the advantages to be derived from that system.

For example, the achievements of the United States, commonly recognised as " the country of gold," may be cursorily examined. According to certain estimates, the total national productive wealth of the country, if equally distributed among her citizens, would entitle every person to a $5000 share of the division. But actually, as capitalist economics are followed, systematic planning for distribution is absent. Hence, even the people's bare subsistence remains a serious problem in spite of the high efficiency at certain periods in the expansion of industry. A wave of economic depression sweeps over the land about every ten years, resulting in a sharp decrease in production, general unemployment, shrinking of the consumer's purchasing power, and widespread bank failures. The common man not only has no $5000 *per capita* share in the nation's productive wealth, but can hardly obtain his bread and butter.

During the last six or seven decades, such crises have occurred again and again. Thirty years ago, when I was in America, some people blamed the sunspots for causing all these economic troubles, holding that sunspots had some influence on the weather, which adversely affected farm crops, which in turn affected the industrial production. Heaven, therefore, was the cause of American business depressions! The last depression began in 1929. Although it was more than a decade ago, the after-effects still continue. In 1929-32 the unemployed rose to the peak number of some 16 millions; if, on the average, each person had to support two dependants, 48 millions, or about two-thirds of the population of the United States must have been hard hit by the depression. About two-fifths of the people of "the country of gold" were dependent on Government relief. When Mr. Roosevelt first assumed the Presidency in 1933, banks throughout the length and breadth of the country were stopping payments to depositors; Roosevelt then devised and inaugurated his New Deal programme.

The first concern of the New Deal was to raise price levels. It was thought that the falling of commodity prices caused loss to factories, and ultimately forced them to close down, which led to unemployment. This, when general, reduced the nation's buying power. Therefore, to cure the disease, prices should be artificially forced up.

The second remedy was to decrease the output of production. The falling of prices was regarded as due to over-production; hence, productive power should be curtailed For instance, if a farmer had been used to cultivate one hundred acres of land, he was now instructed to reduce his acreage to half; the expected income from the other, untilled half, being subsidised by the Government. What had been planted in excess of the quota was to be ploughed up; reaped crops were to be burned.

Though the New Deal had already been practised for seven or eight years, the army of the unemployed was still millions strong. The Federal Government had to supply them with work. Needless highways were built and unwanted buildings erected. Lately, the armament programme has promised to give employment to a million or two, and the enactment of a new law for nation-wide conscription may absorb another few millions. But the question of unemployment is still not wholly or fundamentally answered. The President of the University of Michigan published, in 1934, his statistics showing that in that year 16 million American youths, male and female, ranging from sixteen to twenty-five, were unable either to continue their education or to get any work. These young people could find no way out ; they were not needed by society or the nation. America, the richest country in the world, on account of her capitalist maladjustments, had thus found her public welfare seriously endangered.

The same thing happened to Britain after the first Great War, for then her unemployed went up to several millions. Even now, there are still over a million without work.

Now, to support a highly industrialized economy, there are other ways. First, Germany, while the main structure of her production is still capitalistic, is subjecting her national economy to Fascist dictation. In 1932, her unemployed numbered 8 millions. After the rise of Hitler, all large-scale enterprises were put under his dictation ; thus the regulation of the quantity and quality of her peace-time production has been turned to her requirements in war-time. State control is absolute. As a consequence, unemployment had practically disappeared.

Next there is Socialist Soviet Russia. Her industries are modernized and rationalized, and her agriculture collectivized and mechanized. Both are either owned or directed by the State. Production as well as distribution is planned throughout by the Government, with the result that of her entire population of 190 odd millions, not a single person is without a job. In the future, when Britain and America attempt, as they must, to solve their problems of unemployment, it is not predictable now whether they will adopt Fascist or Socialist practices.

13

We do not want to traverse the same old way of capitalism which was followed with so much wasted labour and heart-break by Britain and America. We do not wish to let competition or monopoly go unbridled, and increase our social troubles. What we have set our minds to is a State built along the lines of the San-Min-Chu-I. The Min-Chuh-Chu-I aims at internal equality between the different constituent ethnic groups as well as external equality between ourselves and others. The Min-Ch'uen-Chu-I proposes to found a genuine democratic polity, so that the people can participate directly in national and local public affairs alike, and, as the powers of the people and functions of the Government are clearly defined, the latter could be made to perform its tasks efficiently. The Min-Seng-Chu-I is comparatively difficult to understand, for it presupposes a full knowledge both of new economics and of the existing realities of the country.

Here, at this point, we must have a clear understanding of the difference between Min-Seng-Chu-I and capitalism. In the first place, the motive and aim of capitalist production is private gain and profit, while our Min-Seng-Chu-I looks forward solely to affording subsistence for the whole nation. In the system of *laissez faire*, free competition holds indisputable sway ; the volume of production must be swollen to the utmost degree, and the cost of the same lowered as much as possible, in order that the manufacturer may undersell competitors and reap the maximum profit. Thus, the blind expansion of output often leads to excess of supply over demand, which will naturally cause the dropping of prices. On the part of factory owners, therefore, a sharp reduction of workers or outright closing down of workshops is the most rational way to avoid loss. But for the workers, such a dose must be more than they can take.

The Min-Seng-Chu-I proposes, on the other hand, to institute a planned economy. All large-scale enterprises are to be operated and managed by the State for supplying the needs of the whole nation, so that even if there is a loss, no factories will be shut down, provided there is a demand for their products. If it happens that supply does grow excessive, and factories have to be closed down, the labour force thus economized can be diverted to other channels where its use will be equally profitable. This is impossible in the case of the private ownership and operation of industries. For sustaining loss, the State has the capacity denied to individuals or corporations, calling on its revenues and profits, which can be taken and made up from other quarters. Thus, enterprises beneficial to the people will be maintained, while unnecessary ones will not be allowed to exist. Meanwhile, as the quantity produced is planned beforehand, both excess and shortage may be prevented. In this way, the ills of capitalism are anticipated and avoided.

In the second place, the means of production in capitalist countries are private property, while in the economy of the People's Livelihood these would ultimately belong to the whole nation. Through the control of capital during the period of the rapid expansion of our economy, and its transition from agriculture to industry, we shall prevent the growth of large privately owned corporations and companies of a monopolistic nature. Medium-sized capitalist enterprises will be tolerated, but the decisive rôle must be played by State enterprises.

Gradually the private entrepreneur will find that he cannot compete with the large State enterprises, and he will disappear and be absorbed by the national industry.

In our planned economy, all the means of production, including land, will belong to the nation. And so long as the supplies of commodities are insufficient to meet the day-to-day demands of the people the factories will not be closed. By developing an efficient system of distribution the necessities of life will be made available to the masses of the population without allowing surpluses to accumulate in the hands of a few men. For Min-Seng-Chu-I aims at avoiding, or at least reducing, the pains of transforming an agricultural country like China into a well-balanced economy based on industrialization.

14

It is not enough that we as a nation grow prosperous ; we must ensure that our national wealth shall be more evenly distributed. In the words of our ancient admonition : " Do not fret over security but worry about unequable sharing." A state of general poverty is bad enough, but not so bad as inequality in sharing the necessities of life. This is the cause of social disturbance.

During war-time, the war effort and attainment of victory are, of course, given precedence over all other things. While the Government has been thus preoccupied, the price of food has been rising precipitously, causing much social unrest. During these three years of resistance, this province of Szechuan has been reaping good harvests, so there was no real scarcity of supplies. The heart of the trouble is obviously war-profiteering, which could and should be done away with immediately. To remove the cause of unrest, excess stores of food staple in various parts of the land ought to be closely examined and recorded, and then bought up by the Government at an officially fixed price.

To sum up, in constructing a new China, the Min-Seng-Chu-I, not capitalism, nor Communism, is going to be our guiding principle. The Father of the Republic explained this principle, when he formulated the term, by saying that it is none other than Socialism, which means the national ownership of all land and all means of production, such as factories and plants, all communications and transport, with all power plants and mines, and upon the fulfilment of certain conditions which affect farming as well.

At present, we may assert that our Kuomintang is the leading party for waging this War of Resistance. There are others also, such as the Communist Party, which has its own armed force. After the war, however, if a serious effort is not made to build the new State in accordance with San-Min-Chu-I, it is to be feared that there might be again internal strife. In the past, we went through years of civil war; now, in throwing the Japanese aggressor out of our beloved land, we are experiencing an ordeal of fire and death and devastation unknown even in our long history. It is high time, then, that we should accelerate our peaceful State-building as soon as victory comes. We cannot afford to waste time in bickering among ourselves. The enemy will not rest satisfied with his defeat; in six or seven years' time he may come again, taking advantage of our indolence and division. So, to live in glory or to perish ignominiously depends upon whether we are able, in a few years, to build a vigorous and prosperous State, after the pattern mapped out in the San-Min-Chu-I.

When that is accomplished, security can be assured to the Far East, and world peace is possible. Japan's " Co-prosperity " has now proved to be a grotesque lie. In the Far East, and on the eastern shores of the Pacific, we alone are the deciding factor for stability and harmony. Korea was formerly our dependency; Indo-China and Burma once looked up to us as their suzerain State. We cherish no selfish territorial ambitions toward them, but when we grow strong enough to be solicitous of their welfare, they may regard us as their kindly, senior brother. We must have such aspirations and self-confidence as to make China both peaceably strong and equably rich, then to infuse well-being and inspire genuine mutual friendship among all the oriental nations, and finally help to lift humanity of the state of *Tatung* or universal brotherhood.

The San-Min-Chu-I and World Reconstruction *

I

THE Father of the Republic formulated the San-Min-Chu-I with the immediate aim of delivering China, but his ultimate goal was the reconstruction of the world. During the interval between World War I and the present conflict, the attention of our own thinkers was directed more to the application of the Three Principles for the solution of the problems of China than for the purposes of analysing the fundamental ills besetting the world, and of applying the teachings of Dr. Sun Yat-sen as a theoretical basis for a true world democracy, political, social and economic.

To-day the situation is different. Mankind is once more confronted by a catastrophe all the more disastrous because it goes far beneath the physical or immediate causes of the outbreak of hostilities. It goes down into the ethical and moral causes affecting the entire world population, from the highest to the lowest, from the most intelligent to the most ignorant.

Who would have thought that, in the twentieth century, intelligent men of a highly developed people like the Germans would put up with a megalomaniac and intellectual humbug like Hitler as their leader ; or that they would naïvely subscribe to the ridiculous race theories of Rosenberg ? How could men like Petain and Laval sacrifice French freedom by delivering into the hands of the Germans hundreds of thousands of the flower of their youth ? How could Quislings raise their heads and gain the support of even a small part of their countrymen on the pretext of so-called patriotism. And above all, how could the world's leading countries have stood aside with folded arms as disinterested onlookers when, in 1931, the Japanese invaded and seized our three Eastern Provinces, thus initiating and releasing the forces of international lawlessness and robbery culminating in the present holocaust ?

Among the world's leaders in the fateful years of the 'thirties there was no more pathetic figure than that of Haile Selassie, sitting alone in the great conference hall of the League of Nations after the last of the delegates and the spectators had filed out of the chamber. He had been crucified as surely as had the King of the Jews. That was the level to which international morale had sunk.

* Address to Central University students in Chungking, April 20, 1941.

53

And this degeneration of Western civilization has brought it near to disaster, which would have been complete had Hitler, Mussolini and the Japanese militarists succeeded in their plans for world domination.

Amidst this scene of brutish cruelty and moral degeneracy we have come to realize that the principles of San-Min-Chu-I, long regarded as of merely national significance, have suddenly assumed a world-wide importance. By implication they crystallize the aspirations not only of the Chinese people, but also of the peoples of the world that a third catastrophe shall not occur again.

A study of the writings and speeches of the leading men of the world discloses a confused yet ardent groping towards some truth which can be applied to the conditions of the twentieth century. These confused utterances, when sifted to separate the grain from the chaff, show that the higher standard of living so desired in the domestic lives of the nations corresponds with our Min-Seng-Chu-I, and economic freedom with a better and rising standard of living for the masses of the people ; their proposal of the universal application of the democratic principle agrees with our Min-Ch'uan-Chu-I, political freedom within each nation ; their demand for the wholesale liberation of colonies and the granting of independence, freedom, and equality to weaker nations accords with our Min-Chuh-Chu-I, national freedom for the nation-states ; and finally, their design for a world-wide union of the democracies to ensure peace and outlaw war is nothing but the formulation of our ideal of *Tatung* or universal brotherhood. Since these views are all in harmony with our San-Min-Chu-I, formulated scores of years ahead of contemporary thinkers by the Father of the Republic, we become all the more convinced that those principles can be the salvation, not only of China, but of the world as well.

2

One of the first prerequisites for solving the problems of China, as well as of the world, is to analyse frankly and sincerely the causes which underlie the weaknesses and maladies of the nation.

It is common knowledge that though our international status has now been much improved after four years of war against the Japanese invaders, we have since 1842 been treated as a semi-colonial country by virtually all Powers, both great and small.

How did this come about ? It is because China in the past has suffered from chronic internal maladies due to the maladministration of the Manchu rulers. A political and economic system imposed upon us by the alien rulers helped to maintain their domination for three centuries. Politically, the Manchus based their rule upon mass ignorance. In the economic sphere our alien rulers followed policies aiming at a regime of mass poverty, through the exploitation of the peasants and producers for the benefit of the landed gentry and their overlords, the corrupt mandarinate. How did it happen that the entire nation was bogged down in the morass of crass ignorance? The cause could be traced to the people's lack of political power. This had been given some justification by traditional Chinese political theory, which divided the people into two classes : the governing and the governed.

There was an axiom among the governing class : " The people must be made to behave in obedience to orders, but they should not be allowed to know the reason why." The governing class was out for fat and easy jobs, and demanded not only political inequality in its favour, but also the ignorance of the masses. Deprived of the useful knowledge to which they were entitled, the common people had been successfully kept ignorant, and rendered docile, and therefore easily governable.

The second trouble was poverty. How was it that the people were in the grip of gruesome poverty? The answer to this question lay in the complete analysis of economic conditions during the reign of the Manchu Emperors. The process of pauperization which pervaded the entire nation meant a gradual deterioration of the economic life of the Han people, for which the inherent defects and inefficiencies of the Manchu and the Chinese traitor-bureaucrats who served them were responsible. The division of the farm lands into minute holdings resulted in uneconomic rural production ; the stripping of the lands for forage crops meant a decrease in the number of animals available to the farmers ; the falling into disrepair of the roads led to the economic and social isolation of districts ; the lack of repairs to canals, dykes, and water conservancy works spelt famine from drought and flood throughout the length and breadth of China. All these things found their background and causes in the political and social system maintained by the Manchus and their henchmen—a system which was really a throwback to feudalism.

Dr. Sun Yat-sen grew to manhood in a village community in which all the decadence of the Manchu regime was evident, accentuated by the contradictions imposed by the advent of Western political and economic forces to this country. He saw a system of poverty which made the lives of the vast majority of his people seem a hopeless burden.

The third trouble was weakness. The reason for the weakness of the people must also be studied in the light of the domination by the Manchus, and the blow struck by Western political and economic forces against the outer fabric of Chinese sovereignty. During the years of Manchu rule the Chinese people as a whole appeared to have shrunk back into their inner selves. There was no direct contact between the masses of the people and the ruling house. The only contact maintained was that with the Chinese traitors and sycophants who served the Manchus, and who formed the corrupt mandarinate. These men developed into a powerful and self-perpetuating group. Their interests became those of a new class. From the very fact that they were ready to be the willing tools of the alien conquerors, they were inclined towards, and later committed to, a policy of rule whereby the power of the Manchus was enhanced and maintained. This could only be done by frustrating the people, thereby reducing them to a state of despondency and weakness.

The people were rendered effete, intellectually as well as politically, for centuries ; as a result, the country became degenerate, stagnant and inert. It was only the potential energy of the massive body which had been built up by our ancestors in the ten centuries before the Manchus, under our native Tang, Sung, and Ming Dynasties that enabled China to maintain her position of supremacy, until the first contacts with the West showed her power to be fragile and illusory.

When we were drawn into the ambit of international power politics a little more than a hundred years ago, defeat after defeat was suffered by our country, and the people became accustomed to regard the nation as naturally weak. " Others act as knives and cutting board, while we serve as fish and meat," was the usual effeminate complaint.

For these three maladies China had to be given a radical cure. Dr. Sun Yat-sen probed our national pathological condition to the depths with his keen political sense. He formulated and later advocated the San-Min-Chu-I as the best formula to meet the situation. But his principles to-day have taken on a deeper content. Looking at the world situation, we are able to understand more clearly how the San-Min-Chu-I can be applied to world affairs in order to bring order out of seeming chaos.

3

We have seen two World Wars taking place within a quarter of a century. Why should it be so, when the people in every country involved want peace? But peace is hard to secure; it is little more than a respite between wars. Why cannot harmony and goodwill be maintained for long? The primal cause is deeply seated in the multiple inequalities among nations; because of them there can be no peace. Only international justice can lay the foundations of world accord.

During the first European War, both the Allies and the Central Powers were vehement in claiming the justice of the cause which compelled them severally to take up arms. Both sides called upon God and man to witness that they fought for justice and peace. England and France also accepted the slogan that they were waging war for the defence of democracy. Later, when the United States entered the combat, President Wilson proclaimed that Americans were in the war " to make the world safe for democracy."

For four years, from 1914 to 1918, the war raged with prodigious fury. After the close of the struggle the Treaty of Versailles was signed in June 1919. It was thought all the world over that henceforth a new reign of peace would be established. From the signing of the Treaty to September 1939 only twenty years and a few months elapsed. Again a feast of carnage and gore has been set before the peoples of Europe, and world peace is completely destroyed.

The causes of this World War II are complicated, but the kernel of the trouble is to be found in the inequalities among nations. Among these the following stand out in bold relief.

First of all there were the inequalities imposed by the victors on the vanquished. The defeated Powers were saddled with heavy loads of war guilt. The Peace of Versailles stipulated in unequivocal terms that the criminal party was Germany, and the German delegates to the Peace Conference had to sign an admission of their country's guilt. The value of that document, the judgment of partial judges, will always be viewed with reserve by history in the light of the morality of the leaders of those nations who disposed of Shantung Province, relegating the territory of one of their allies to the safe-keeping of Japan, another so-called ally. The German delegation signed this document under duress. This effrontery against international justice gave Hitler a rallying-cry by which to mould the German people into an avenging host.

Next, Germany was obliged to pay a stupenduous amount by way of indemnity. The leading financial experts of the victorious countries, as well as those of the vanquished, vainly declared that the burden was too great for Germany to shoulder. Liberal world opinion argued a case to show that modern war paid no dividends to anyone. The reactionary elements retorted that it was possible to get blood out of a stone. With great ingenuity the German financial experts turned the situation to their advantage. Germany asked for and received loans to the amount of some two billion pounds sterling from the victor Powers, principally America. The Governments of these countries thought that financial shackles were being securely fastened upon Germany in addition to the political fetters forged at Versailles. Half of this money was used for payment of reparations and the other half was ultimately diverted to rearmament.

Leaving aside the vexed question of colonies, the physical inequality brought about by non-fulfilment by the victor nations of the promises of general universal disarmament supplied Germany with an additional grievance, and from 1919 to 1932 the Weimar Republic was helpless to deliver the country from the humiliations attendant on her defeat in war. The Government was looked upon by large sections of their people as being a traitor to the cause of the fatherland. Making full use of that situation Hitler rose to power in 1933. The National Socialist Party, composed of political and social charlatans, declared that their chief aim in acquiring power was to free Germany from the bonds of the Versailles Treaty. But their true aim was to match violence with greater violence, and substitute injustice by more injustice. So after the Nazis had firmly entrenched themselves in Germany they embarked on a tremendous and thorough-going plan of rearmament which was ruthlessly pushed forward to its ultimate end, a new war.

Until his aggression against little, defenceless Austria, Hitler's watchword—freedom for Germany—was very appealing. In China, bound hand and foot for a century by unequal treaties, there was " the compassion of a fellow-victim for Germany." Of course, things are different now. But it is allowable to conclude that it was owing mainly to the unfair treatment of the defeated by the victorious after the last war, that peace in Europe lasted only for some twenty years before a new catastrophic clash broke out.

In the second place, the inequalities imposed by great Powers upon small and weak nations also contributed to the breakdown of peace in Europe. Nor did Germany, after the first European War, serve as the only example. Weak nations are scattered all over the world, and what Germany had gone through has been, more or less, their daily experience.

In the third place, the inequalities imposed by the culturally or materially advanced nations on the comparatively backward peoples form another source of friction, strife, and bitter feelings that often result in wars. The former class, by bare-faced, oppressive measures, or subtle exploitation, exerts its will upon the latter class. Colonization, the opening up of natural resources, the selling of goods, etc., are practised by means of high-handed or crafty methods to the injury of the defenceless. It is needless to dwell on the two latter causes of international conflict at length, for as a nation we have had ample experience to remind us of their existence.

4

The question may be asked, why there are inequalities? The answer can thus be given : International injustice is due to the growth of imperialism, which in turn originates from the expansion of capitalism. The so-called democracies, standing for peace and justice two decades or so ago, were all capitalistic States, even as they are now. Therefore, after victory was won in 1918, what they took most to heart was naturally the private interests of their capitalist class, those of the governing caste, and then the interests of their own respective countries. The welfare of other individuals, classes, countries, and the world at large, were nothing to them. For being unmindful of the common good while seeking selfish advantage, which inevitably leads to the world disorder of injustice and oppression, England, France and America should be rightly held responsible.

Germany's slogan in 1933, that she set out to annul her unequal treaty, should have won, and did win, our sympathy then. But now she is allied to our enemy Japan, and has changed her original rôle from an object of aggression to that of an aggressor. A great many smaller States in Europe are now mercilessly ground under the heels of the Nazis. Yesterday's opposition to injustice has founded a reign of injustice of its own, the fighter against oppression has turned his coat and become a new slave-driver. That is what I mean by the statement that to substitute violence by greater violence and injustice by more injustice will create worse inequalities.

As regards Japan, her war-cry has been to build a " New Order of Great Asia " or " Greater Asia's Co-prosperity Sphere," just as her Axis partners want to establish a New Order in Europe. Such an ominous combination is, of course, all for self-interest at the cost of others. So, if the Axis countries were to win in their present gamble, what would be the complexion of that New Order promised by them? There would in all likelihood be imposed a peace more unjust, more oppressively unequal and inequitable, than the last one dictated at Versailles.

5

From whence is this conclusion drawn? We have to look into the Axis policy with respect to Europe to answer this. The ambition of Germany and Italy is to conquer the Continent and partition it between themselves.

Toward the end of 1938, a weekly periodical in Canada published a map for the ten-year plan of unifying Europe which was used by the Nazis for domestic propaganda. At the time people simply dismissed the thing as a fantastic dream. But before long the plan was being put into action step by step. In January 1939 the *News Review*, a London weekly, reproduced the map. According to the Nazi blue-print, Germany had planned : (1) The annexation of Austria in the spring of 1938 ; and (2) The annihilation of Czecho-Slovakia in the autumn of the same year. These two aims were successfully accomplished in the spring of 1938 and 1939 respectively. (3) The absorption of Hungary in the spring of 1939 ; that country has become one of the Axis satellites ; though in appearance an independent State, she is practically an appendage to Germany, whose orders are divine laws to her ; so this part of the plan also has been carried out. (4) The incorporation of Poland in the autumn of 1939, which was accomplished in September that year, according to schedule, and marked the formal opening of this second European War. (5) The liquidation of Jugoslavia in 1940 is being carried out at present (April 1941). (6) The overwhelming of Rumania and Bulgaria in the autumn of 1940, both countries having been coerced into submission between January and March 1941. (7) The conquest of Switzerland, France, Belgium, the Netherlands and Denmark in the spring of 1941. This part of the plan was successfully accomplished more than six months earlier than scheduled, for in June 1940 all was over. The only exception was Switzerland, which is still a neutral. (8) The occupation of the Soviet Ukraine and Caucasus in the autumn of 1941.

The initial steps of Hitler's ten-year plan for unifying Europe were precisely those which I have enumerated above.   My impression when I first saw the map was to treat it as Westerners treated Tanaka's memorial.   The rulers of England and America also treated it as unauthentic, but events have proved that it was a methodical scheme, intended by Hitler in deadly earnest.   The definite time-limits fixed in this plan range from 1938 to 1948.   In 1948, Europe is to be entirely under Axis rule.   The portions Hitler proposes to dominate include Northern Spain and Portugal, the major half of France, the Netherlands, Belgium, Denmark, Norway, Sweden, Britain, Ireland, the three Baltic States, Finland, Switzerland, Austria, Hungary, Poland, Czecho-Slovakia, Jugoslavia, Bulgaria, Rumania, Western Turkey, and the whole of European Russia, with the entire Near East thrown in for good measure.   The rest, comprising the main part of Spain, Southern France, Greece, Albania, Eastern Turkey and North Africa, is to be ruled by Italy.   This is the Axis plan for the partition of Europe.   The job is all but finished, except that England still stands defiant, Soviet Russia has not yet been conquered, and Switzerland, Sweden and Turkey still remain neutral.   The only serious obstacles left now are England and Russia, with Turkey as a possible lesser third.

As soon as Germany had succeeded in her Balkan campaign, the next move she would take would be to control Turkey.   After that, the Near Eastern states would be swallowed.   Then, Soviet-German relations are sure to be worsened, a Soviet-German war would take place.   If these conjectures are correct, it is easy to understand why a pact of neutrality was signed between the U.S.S.R. and Japan.   A German invasion of Soviet Russia was supposedly prevented by the non-aggression pact signed between them.   So long as time was not yet ripe for the former to take action, the agreement would be regarded as still valid ; but once she was ready to go ahead, of what avail would be a scrap of paper !

6

How about Axis ambitions in the Orient ?   What does the enemy's " New Order of Greater Asia " or " Asia's Co-prosperity Sphere " comprehend ?   I think even Japan herself would find it difficult to define it : whenever the time is auspicious, the flexible sphere can be expanded at will.   Probably, the enemy hopes to start from our North-east right down to Indo-China, Siam, Burma, the Strait Settlements, including Singapore, and all the British and Dutch dependencies, not excluding the Philippines, New Zealand

and Australia. The first big stride in her programme is evidently to knock out China, after which the rest of East Asia, its south-eastern islands, and the entire Southern Pacific should be hers for the taking.

From the above, it may be concluded that if the Axis will have won the war, Europe would be divided between Germany and Italy, while Asia belongs to Japan alone. Could this kind of world rebuilding maintain peace for long? Certainly not. The Axis countries declare, on the one hand, that they are fighting against injustice and inequalities, yet, on the other, are creating new and worse ones. This is irrevocably in conflict with the spirit of the San-Min-Chu-I, and therefore cannot be accepted by us.

What I have just said goes to prove that the "New World Order" planned by the Axis is nothing but a "Disorder," since it is to be built on injustice and oppression ten times worse than those to which we are accustomed. If this Great War should be ultimately won by Britain, America and ourselves, what then would be the result? From our standpoint, the new world should be reconstructed along the lines of the San-Min-Chu-I.

There are, however, critics who might demur. They would say it is well and good to practise these principles in China, but since conditions differ in all the other countries, the guiding principles for dealing with the local situation must also vary from place to place and from China's. It is to be feared, they might argue, that these doctrines could not be exported to foreign lands. This I believe to be utterly mistaken.

7

Let us make a brief survey of the views and ways thoughtful people in England and America have put forward for rebuilding the world, and then compare them with our Three People's Principles.

First, on the British side there is Harold Laski, secretary of the Parliamentary Labour Party and professor of political science at London University. He has lately published a book entitled *Where Do We Go From Here?* which may be summarised as follows :

(1) The inequalities in the life of the British people must be done away with. By their incomes, Britons are divisible into three classes. Those whose individual annual incomes exceed £2000 form the ultra-rich group. Of the total population of 47 millions in Britain, only half of 1 per cent. belongs to this class, but their aggregate annual income totals 17 per cent. of the whole nation's. Next is the middle group, comprising 10 per cent. of the entire

population, and enjoying 30 per cent. of the national income. These two groups, 10·5 per cent. of the British people, together possess 47 per cent. of the national income. The third group is the poor, making up 89·5 per cent. of the total population, having only 53 per cent. of the national income. From these statistics, it is obvious that the wealth of the English people is very unevenly distributed : a small minority has a lion's share in the nation's income, while the great majority is rendered so poor as to be unable to have a decent living. Therefore, according to Laski, Socialism should be put into practice in order to wipe away inequalities among the people, strengthen national unity, and encourage the common man to contribute his share toward ultimate victory.

(2) The British Government should immediately declare that India will be given independence soon after the war. To get full-hearted support from the Indian people in the present struggle, Britain's plans for their future must be made known to them. Though this kind of news is not published in the daily papers, the Indian problem is none the less a grave one. It is to be remembered that when the Viceroy of India declared that India was at war with Germany soon after September 3, 1939, Indian Nationalists publicly denounced the war declaration. They contended that whether or not India was to be at war against another country must be decided not by the Viceroy acting for the British Government, but by her own people. On account of the conflict, members of the National Congress and their leaders, ten thousand odd, are still imprisoned in gaols. They want the British-controlled Indian Government to give them instant independence and the establishment of a National Government. If these were granted them, they would be willing to take part in the war by helping Britain in her Herculean efforts to defeat Hitler. They know full well that if ever the Axis had its way, their sufferings could only be increased and aggravated ; so, their sympathy lies with England rather than with Germany and Italy. But, since England is fighting for the cause of freedom, why is this very freedom, they ask, denied to them ? Therefore, Laski advocates giving freedom to India as soon as this war is over. Such a declaration will react favourably in increasing Britain's fighting chance to win the war, if for no other purpose.

(3) The British Government should immediately announce the main points of a plan for reconstructing the new world on the basis of justice and equality after the war, and thus to rally Europe's conquered peoples and encourage them to rise in open revolt against the aggressors.

Another point of view is presented by a Mr. Davenport, a radical liberal. To untie the complicated knot of livelihood for the British people, he proposes the immediate adoption of State capitalism. The State is to be the only owner of capital : properties such as lands, buildings, factories, means of production, banks, etc., are all to be nationalized. After the process has been carried out, when the State has in hand all the work it can do, lands and tools of production left over could be rented to individuals. Other kinds of private property may be enjoyed by the individual, provided that private fortunes do not exceed £100,000 for each person. Acquired fruits of labour whether mental or manual, above this limit will be contributed to the State during one's lifetime ; after that, all the accumulation will revert to the nation, inheritance being positively prohibited.

By these measures it is thought economic inequalities between the rich and the poor among the British people could be abolished and the burden of the national debt removed for ever. Before the current war, Britain's national debt amounted to £8000 million. As long as the war lasts, the national debt will increase by £2000 million a year, so that at the end of four years, her pre-war obligations will be doubled. This £16,000 million require an annual interest payment of £500 million. With such heavy interest, itself a staggering burden, the British people and their future generations would never be able to pay off the original debts. All labour and production of the nation would be exclusively enjoyed by the holders of Government bonds and their descendants. In this way, the great majority of the people would be bond-slaves for ever. If State capitalism is put into practice, or the means of production become State-owned, not only would the menace of national debts be averted, but the ill-effects of manipulations by bankers could also be stopped for good.

A third suggestion is made by Sir William Beveridge. According to him, if Britain were to win this war, a great federation of European democracies should be organized, among which post-war Germany should be included. The nations incorporated in it should comprise Britain, France, Germany, Denmark, Norway, Sweden, Finland, Belgium, the Netherlands, Switzerland, Ireland and the British Dominions of Australia, Canada, New Zealand and South Africa— East European and the Balkan States being excluded from the scheme. This union of democracies would have a population of 235 millions, and a territory of 8,822,000 square miles, twice as great in both respects as the United States of America. All member nations of this union are more or less alike in culture and manners of living and close in economic relations in the past. Germany is the only country without a democratic tradition ; but if she is beaten, her form of government would, of course, undergo a radical change. Without her participation peace in the future cannot be guaranteed.

This Federation of Europe would have a federal government to take care of diplomatic affairs, national defence and common colonies over-seas, as well as to establish a uniform currency and facilitate inter-state trade for the sake of political integration and economic harmony among the constituent members. Within each State, democratic government should be the rule. The federation should have a Constitution. Its administrative organ would be responsible to its legislature. The latter is to be made up of two chambers, one elected by the people of the various states, and the other representing the states themselves. Finally, there should be federal judicial organs to ensure the people's rights, both civil and political, for the sake of social security and political equality. With the permanent peace of Europe as an end, internal affairs of the states on the one hand, and external or inter-state affairs on the other are to be separately handled by the states and federal government.

From studies in history, Beveridge found that the form of social security usually underwent four stages in its evolution, viz. self-protection of the individual, alliance, joint defence, and the public police. If members of civilized society have to go through these four stages to get protection from lawlessness, there is no reason why States should not get theirs through the same processes. The first two stages have long been a matter of experience among countries ; the third one we reached in the League of Nations after the last Great War. To attain collective security for countries it is now necessary to establish an international police system for safe-guarding peace. Hence such a union of nations. But Beveridge's plan is confined to a number of European countries only. According to him, great States of the world other than this union of European democracies are, if his plan is actually launched forth, the United States of North America, the Union of Soviet Socialist Republics, and the Republic of China.

8

The New Republic, an American journal, has lately advanced the following ideas for the post-war reconstruction of the world. The Anglo-Saxon nations should lead the world forward thus : (1) Co-operation of the two countries' planning and of technological minds

in improving the economic, productive and cultural status of the
whole world.   (2) The universal elevation of men's standard of
living by means of modernizing production and socializing distribution.   Economic life of all humanity should be on a par with that of
the American people.   (3) Opening up and developing national
resources of backward countries with only the benefit of the peoples
concerned in view.   No capitalists or business men of any one of
these two or other nationalities will be permitted to exploit the
common people of the new nations.   (4) Rationalizing the agricultural and industrial productions of all lands, which should be
self-sufficient.

The American journalist Edgar Snow, for long a traveller in
China, has published an article in *Asia* on the same subject.   He
calls for the immediate abandonment of British and American
imperialism, so as to form a common democratic front and cripple
Axis propaganda.   The Governments of these two countries should
openly admit that so long as there were enslaved peoples not
liberated, there could be no peace and order in the world.   (1)
America should sign new treaties on an equal footing and of mutual
help with China to aid her recovery of full sovereignty.   She
should also abrogate all her unequal treaties with the latter, give
up extra-territorial rights, recall her Army and Navy from Chinese
soil and waters, renounce her part in Shanghai's International
Settlement, and give up all special privileges obtained in the past
through political and economic coercion.   This would undermine
Axis machinations in Asia and lead to winning Soviet co-operation.
(2) Meanwhile, Britain and her Dominions should (*a*) make a
declaration for the liberation of colonies and the formation of a
world union of democracies ;   (*b*) promise independence to India
and Burma as soon as the war is over, and carry out immediately
compulsory education and training in self-government in these two
lands ;   (*c*) do the same in other colonies to prepare them for independence ;   (*d*) promise to help other victims of imperialism, such
as Korea and Indo-China, in winning freedom after the war ;   (*e*)
promise to render financial, technological, medical and other aids
to all soon-to-be-liberated colonies in their post-war efforts at
industrialization and collective and co-operative enterprises ;   and
(*f*) announce the conditions for emancipation of the colonies, such
as, that they should, when free, be members of the world federation
of democracies, participate in tariff agreements, pacts of mutual
help, disarmament treaty and the arbitration of international disputes, contribute men and materials to the international police

force, adopt the democratic form of government, and use a common currency.

9

From what has been advocated by contemporary thinkers in Britain and America, we may draw the following conclusion : their hopes for the solution of economic inequalities in the domestic life of all nations conform in broad outline with our Min-Seng-Chu-I ; their universal application of the democratic polity agrees with our Min-Ch'uan-Chu-I ; their wholesale liberation of colonies and the grant of independence, freedom and equality to weaker nations accord with our Min-Chuh-Chu-I ; and finally, their proposals for the formation of a world federation of democracies to prevent war and ensure peace and security for human existence are in conformity with our ideal and vision of the state of *Tatung*, the World Commonwealth of the future.

The San-Min-Chu-I: Its Universality*

I

MODERN wars are divisible into two kinds : (1) Wars due to rivalry between Great Powers for natural resources, colonial space and markets, which may be branded imperialistic wars ; (2) Wars due to aggressive acts against weaker nations on the part of the Great Powers with the aim of exploitation and enslavement, breaking out when resistance is offered by the weaker side. Some States have not scrupled to resort to violence for the sake of imperialistic expansion ; the victim-nations have got to be ready, on the other hand, to hit back and oppose the invaders to preserve their national freedom and independence. So, for the latter, these kinds of war are recognized as wars of liberation ; while for the aggressors they are wars of cold-blooded conquest, pure and simple.

World War I in Europe belongs to the first class. The outcome was that, for a measure of magnanimity on the part of the victors, seeds of vengeance were sown deep in the hearts of the defeated and, also because of unequal distribution of war spoils among the former, the interlude of peace was broken, after twenty years, as soon as Germany was ready to attack again. Japan's invasion of China comes within the second category. Her object was to put an end to our existence as a nation. The present European conflict, however, though of the first class in its initial stages, has now developed into part of a global war of liberation as it changed its nature, and has actually become merged with our long-drawn-out War of Resistance against Japan. Twenty-eight nations, including the U.S.A., Britain, the U.S.S.R. and China have come together to defeat Axis aggression.

Britain declared war against Germany to check the latter in her attempts at dominating Europe and, ultimately, to threaten the British Empire. So, at the very outset, it was imperialistic. Before long, however, as the conflict developed, freedom and liberation became the battle-cry of the enslaved peoples as well as that of their liberators. For instance, erstwhile free nations such as Czecho-Slovakia, Poland, Norway, Belgium, the Netherlands, France, Jugoslavia and Greece all fought Germany, one after another, not

* A lecture delivered at the School for Diplomatic and Consular Service, Chungking, July 2, 1942.

for natural resources and markets, but to preserve their own freedom and independence. Since its outbreak, this European struggle for liberation has been led by Britain, who, fighting for her own existence, cast off, as it were, her former rôle and stood valiantly in the rank of the defenders of freedom. Again, a year ago, Hitler, in spite of the Soviet-German Non-aggression Pact, started his attack upon Russia. Confident of success, he believed that while everything was safe in the West, it was the time to ensure victory by destroying the U.S.S.R. by one overwhelming blow. The U.S.S.R., having no imperialistic ambitions, and observing the terms of the Non-aggression Pact, was not ready to meet the onslaught. Still she took up the challenge and defended her land and her people with vigour and resolution. Since the outbreak of the Soviet-German War, the anti-imperialistic struggle among the European peoples has increased in intensity and bitterness. In the East, Japan's teacherous blow at Britain and America last December for grabbing the Orient and the Pacific all to herself has decided the two Western democracies to fight against her side by side with us. Britain's clashes with Germany might have been imperialistic in intention at the beginning, but that she is on our side, together with America, has now put her definitely in the camp of the anti-imperialistic group.

2

The cause of war, in the final analysis, may be traced to inequality between nations and peoples. Conflicts due to rivalry between the Great Powers, or arising out of resistance of the weaker nations against the strong are all traceable to this one cause. To stamp out war for ever it is absolutely necessary to establish a universal reign of equality. The most thorough-going doctrine on this subject is the San-Min-Chu-I, which is rooted in the very idea. It behoves us believers in these principles to devise a scheme for solving the problem of world peace.

Our principle of nationalism is built upon the equality of all nations. From the past even till now, it has been the custom for the stronger to prey upon the weaker Power, with the result that the oppressor and the oppressed stand in hostile opposition. While no one denies the strong their lawful rights, it is equally true they have no justification whatsoever for depriving the weak of theirs. Germany was plainly within her rights, some ten to twenty years ago, to ask for the removal of the bonds imposed on her by the Versailles Treaty, but when she trampled her neighbours under her feet, as old violence was replaced by new, and fresh inequalities were created, war became inevitable. During the American Civil War more than four-score years ago, when the Southern landlords insisted on negro slavery for their cotton plantations while the industrial North demanded free labour all over the country, President Lincoln made a memorable remark worthy of our recalling to-day. He said the nation cannot remain half free and half slave, as the two halves cannot co-exist in accord. This saying may well be applied to the world, for the world of to-day also must not remain half free and half slave. President Roosevelt declared in his broadcast not long ago that, if there is one nation in the world without freedom, it means no less than that the freedom of the people of the United States is threatened. Liberty, the dear privilege of all humanity under the sun, is as much cherished by the backward and weaker as by the more advanced and stronger peoples. Nobody in the world takes delight in being a slave. That there are the free and the enslaved bespeaks beyond a doubt inequalities among nations.

Thus, it falls upon us as a bounden duty, after the dark forces are beaten, to see to it that all enslaved nations will recover their freedom. We could not rest satisfied if only ourselves shall have fully re-established out birthright while Korea, Indo-China, Burma and India remain under alien rule against their own free choice. That would be grievously inadequate as measured by the obligations laid on us by the principle of nationalism.

The difference between our nationalism and that of most other countries lies just in this. Hitler also stands, to quote an extreme case, for nationalism, since his Nazis are called National Socialists. But his brand, narrow, bigoted and chauvinist, strives only for the self-interests of the German nation at the total expense of others. This sort of nationalism can never serve the cause of peace, as it is unreservedly committed to one nation's ego. Our nationalism is rooted in our traditional political ideal several thousand years old : our " wang-tao," the " king's way," consists in commanding respect with virtues, not with force.

3

The time has come for us to make known our attitude and policy in regard to the post-war world. It is our conviction that China's neighbours, such as Korea, India, Burma and Indo-China, should some day all have restored to them their freedom and independence. This is as much implicit in the nature of things and of this crusade of liberty as it is explicitly recognised by Britain herself, who will have to redeem her pledge of giving freedom and home rule to both India and Burma after the war. The American Under-Secretary of State, Mr. Sumner Welles, said in a recent speech that to lay the corner-stone of permanent peace it is imperative to root out the remnant forces of imperialism. We, on behalf of our fellow-continentals, must insist that the causes of injustice and future armed conflicts between nations be uprooted once for all from the Asiatic region.

The logical sequel of our nationalism is *Tatung* or world commonwealth. This is the culmination of all political thinking. When that state is realised, boundaries between countries vanish and the whole world becomes one body politic, employing its sovereign authority to assure public safety. While this lofty ideal will not come true in a day or two, it is nevertheless imperative that all the European nations subjugated by Hitler within these few years, as well as those in Asia who lost their freedom during the past century, should recover their sovereignty when peace is restored. A new Union of Democratic Nations shall then be organized by the free States, on the basis of equality, to settle disputes among themselves by arbitration or other pacific means. If resorting to arms is outlawed for good, there is no reason to doubt the possibility of *Tatung* in the not too remote future.

Nor is the conception of universal brotherhood the product of our own thinkers alone. Karl Marx's Communism shares it with them, although it is doubtful whether the methods proposed by him are suitable to our times. Even the Communists in Soviet Russia are yet far from their goal. But with the founding of the new State, the original name of that country has disappeared. In the full name of the Union of Soviet Socialist Republics, there is not a word of geographical description. Not so are the United States of America or the United States of Brazil : America and Brazil being both place-names. Thus, another U.S.S.R. might be formed elsewhere, and herein dwells the hope that world commonwealth or universal brotherhood may come to the world some day. Marx and Lenin's ultimate end points, in another word, at the world federation of communities, which would be possible only when all national boundaries are removed.

In the above, we have said that if our nationalism is universally applied, inequalities among nations will disappear. At the same time, if our People's Right and People's Livelihood, two principles of political and of economic equality respectively, were simultaneously carried out within the various nations, all internal as well as international strife and disputes would cease for ever, and permanent world peace would be a reality. Among American and British thinkers not a few are working on this same line of thought, that inequalities must be removed so as to eliminate the basic evil leading to war ; what they have in mind is entirely in accord with our convictions.

4

The present generation will have gone through two disastrous wars within thirty years. If nothing effectual is done, we shall most probably be caught in another one before long. Needless to say, the havoc wrought by modern warfare is incalculable. British public men, when they have occasion to talk about fundamental questions with their foreign friends, sometimes refer to their inability, between 1919 and 1939, to extinguish the latent flames of war or to find remedies for their own economic ills, and would attribute this failure to the fact that more than a million young men of great promise had been killed in the last war. These men, the flower of the nation, if still alive, would be all men in their fifties to-day, in the prime of life and capable of doing vast good for their own country-men and the world generally. Their death is thus an irreplaceable loss, not only to the British nation, but also to the world. Germany's case was more tragic ; had that country not lost her more than two million war dead, the rise of Hitler might have been prevented.

In the present war the cost is even bloodier. In opening her eastern front, Germany sent several million troops to attack the Russians, who have inflicted on them tremendous casualties. German losses were reported around 10 millions dead, wounded and missing. Soviet Russia's losses were placed at 4·5 millions. From this computation, the total casualties in the East Europe battle-fields for the first year have amounted to well over 10 millions. This is considerably worse than in the last war. Material waste and damage must be accordingly much heavier too. For instance, the year's expenditure of the U.S. Government from July 1941 to the end of this June, the major portion of which is appropriated to her Army and Navy, comes up to the huge sum of $32,000 million, also dwarfing last war's four-year total. Britain's daily cost of arms is now £13 million, as compared to £2 to £3 million over two decades ago. Meanwhile, regions mown bare by fire and steel were formerly limited to Belgium and North-east France, other places being little touched. But the last two years, Germany sent hundreds of bombing planes in repeated raids to ravage England,

and the latter is now despatching bombers, a thousand at a time, to make havoc of Cologne, Essen and Bremen, hurling down thousands of tons of death and destruction, and blasting whole cities from the surface of the earth. If this is to continue, all big German towns will be blotted out one by one.

After 1918, people in Europe and America were fed up with war ; pacifism saturated the whole society among former friends and foes alike. Remarque's *All Quiet on the Western Front,* fully reflecting the prevalent anti-war feeling then, ran into scores of editions. Students of Oxford and Cambridge even took mass oaths never to fight for king and country. America refused to join the League of Nations and became isolationist, swearing to have no more ado with European affairs, for she had incurred some bad debts in addition to contributing 50,000 lives. Into such a world, Hitler came. He tore the Versailles Treaty to shreds, while Britain and France, dazed, could not lift a finger. In six or seven years, Germany had many times more than recovered her former strength. Before the invasion of France, the U.S. Congress instituted a Neutrality Act to prevent new loans to Europe and prohibit U.S. merchantmen sailing in belligerent waters. Later, as the holocaust spread all over Europe, and as far-sighted Americans saw every day how impossible it was for their country any more to avoid being drawn in, America began seriously to prepare for the inevitable. At long last, after Japan's unexpected treacherous attack on Pearl Harbour on December 7, war was formally declared by her against the Axis aggressors.

5

As people have everywhere suffered from war, thoughtful minds, dwelling on how permanent peace can be attained, have come to the common conclusion that predatory imperialism, already the cause of two world wars, must be eradicated from the post-war world. Weaker and smaller nations must be freed from bondage ; colonies must no longer be given over to imperialist exploitation. Those whose cultural development does not yet measure up to self-government should be placed under international tutelage and guidance. Economically, we have the American proposal for the sharing of natural resources of the whole world by all, including victors and the defeated, or the newly freed ; while with the removal of pre-war trade barriers, international free trade is to be restored to the world.

America has lately signed Lend-Lease agreements with China,

Britain, Soviet Russia and others. These agreements of economic mutual aid are founded on a system of bartering arms for raw products. For instance, the United States supplies China with planes, guns, etc., and receives from her tungsten, tin, antimony, raw silk, *tung* oil, pig bristles, etc. What America supplies us is certainly worth more than what we can send her during this period. So, it has been agreed upon by both parties that the obligations we are not able to meet at present will be redeemed in future without prejudice to our post-war economic development. At the same time, we have undertaken not to do anything which may be detrimental to the world's economic interests.

When we come to carry out our promise, difficulties are bound to arise. Thus, the removal of tariff walls has a lot to do with our future development. The United States, a highly developed country industrially, can well afford to practise free trade. But for China, just about to start on her industrialization after the war, this may prove a great handicap and disadvantage. For a country to industrialize herself the old method is, by means of erecting a tariff wall, to protect home manufacturers and infant industries from too keen outside competition. If we are not to adopt a protective tariff after the war, it means that China will have to leave her doors wide open for foreign, and especially Japanese, dumping of cheap goods, which in turn means that our own infant industries will be swamped and left to die prematurely. Let us cite the cotton goods industry as an example. We are a cotton producing country ; if we cannot, under the free trade agreement, withstand Japanese penetration in cotton goods trade, our spinning mills will never increase and develop to such extent as to consume all our cotton crop, actual and potential, and will not produce enough cloth to meet our own demands. As a result, our raw cotton will have to be exported to Japan for her to turn it into cloth for sale back to us. In this way, we will for ever be saddled with a purely agricultural economy, and our market become the object of foreign rivalries. Such a situation cannot be conducive to world peace.

6

I have said the erection of tariff walls is an old method. Now what is the new one proposed ? The new method is this : national ownership and State operation of industrial production. This would imply State control of foreign trade ; foreign goods would not be allowed free entry, no matter what high custom duties importers are willing to pay. It would also mean that both domestic and international trade are under State operation and management according to a planned policy. Since there would be no free imports by private traders naturally there need be no tariffs. Soviet Russia has been conducting her foreign commerce according to such method. We can do likewise if we think it necessary. As to whether we shall or not, it depends upon our own policy, foresight and determination. Thus, if Japan wants to buy from us a certain quantity of raw cotton, our Government will demand from her in exchange a certain amount of goods we need. The Government will handle the exchange of merchandise, private merchants not being permitted to do so. When imports and exports are so regulated, cheap, undesirable Japanese goods cannot be dumped on our markets. However, this would call for a modification of the policy advocated in other countries, for such international trade would no longer be free, but would be State controlled and operated.

The principle of *laissez-faire* applied to international trade is a traditional concept of capitalist economy. Before the last European War, free trade was virtually the accepted national policy of Western countries ; but after 1918, there began a radical modification of this policy of free trade everywhere. In the British Empire, there was introduced the policy of Empire Preference. Japanese goods could not enter Canada, for instance, freely to compete with British goods. After the devastation in the present war, rehabilitation of national economy may mean that commerce and industries will, in most likelihood, be planned and controlled, and perhaps directly conducted by States. Such a situation may conceivably bring about the elimination of private enterprise in international trade.

Some days ago the British Government announced the nationalization of coal royalties and State control of all coal-mines. Coal-mining is, we know, the backbone of British industry. Britain's coal-fields are abounding ; but the pits, many of which are worked on a small scale, were all privately owned and managed. Competition among them was keen, so that when the general business depression came over the land, a great number of them were forced to close up and the miners had to go unemployed. Throughout the two decades after 1918 this had been an unsolved problem. The Labour Party, agitating for national ownership and management of the mines for years, failed in their attempts. Now that the nation is involved in a life-and-death struggle, such a measure has become unavoidable for maintaining coal production and the livelihood of the colliers ; hence the Government's act. It seems now that, even after the war, nationalization will continue. Nor is this all. There are signs that the banking business, the dome of British capitalism, may also be brought within the sphere of State enterprise. The shape of things emerging during these critical times is that institutions of Socialism are being gradually, imperceptibly established in Britain and, as they may have come to stay, private free competition in large industries will probably be more and more curtailed after the war. This economic metamorphosis amounts, in fact, to a step toward the practice of our Min-Seng-Chu-I. By going on, step by step, peacefully in that direction, Britain will ultimately achieve Socialism.

7

Now we have come to what we set out to prove at the beginning of this lecture, that San-Min-Chu-I not only can deliver China, but also redeem the world. The world-wide implication and universality of these teachings have become every day more evident with the turn of events.

On the score of nationalism, Britons and Americans are agreed upon the equality of nations, from which the liberation of the weak and small is a logical conclusion. On the subject of democracy, the Anglo-Saxon countries being original democracies, will naturally want to see the same, or even a modified system of democratic government, practised in all other countries. With respect to the livelihood, which was regarded in the past as the hardest problem seeking solution, which took Russia a great revolution and much bloodshed to achieve, it has become clear now that it could be brought about by legislative procedure instead of by resorting to class struggle and violence.

This proves beyond doubt the catholicity and universality of the San-Min-Chu-I. After this purgatory of fire and blood, therefore, social and economic changes of the world can all be introduced peaceably : the theory of class war is refuted, and its methods are rendered unnecessary. According to orthodox Marxism, wars should be turned into civil wars of social revolution within the various countries. This phenomenon is to-day not to be found anywhere. The Labour and Communist Parties of Britain are in complete accord with the Government. In America, the two great labour organizations have given their word to refrain from strikes for the duration. The only conflicts are those between the oppressed and the oppressor—the battles of civilization against barbarism, of freedom against enslavement. The greatness of the San-Min-Chu-I, their superiority over other systems of politico-economic doctrines, is borne in upon us with ever greater force.

PART TWO

To Democracy

China Marching Toward Democracy

At its eleventh plenary session in Chungking, early in September 1943, the Central Executive Committee of the Kuomintang, the highest executive power of the ruling party in China, passed unanimously a resolution of the greatest importance for the political future of the country. This resolution reiterated the determination of the Kuomintang to institute and enforce a government of the people, by the people, and for the people at the earliest possible date, in accordance with the doctrines bequeathed by Dr. Sun Yat-sen, Father of the Chinese Republic. It specifically called upon the National Government of the Republic to convene the National Constituent Assembly within one year after the conclusion of the war, for the avowed purpose of adopting and promulgating the permanent Constitution of the Republic and fixing the date for its enforcement.

The convocation of the National Assembly will mean the automatic and formal termination of the period of Political Tutelage under the Kuomintang, and the inauguration of the final stage in China's political evolution, that of Constitutional Democracy. Herein lies the fundamental difference between Kuomintang tutelage, or party rule, in China and dictatorship in the Fascist states. Mussolini and his Fascist Party never had the slightest intention of giving up or restoring political power to the Italian people ; they had to be forcibly overthrown by their own Sovereign and the Italian people before their regime was ended—and ended in chaos. The Nazi Führer and his dictatorship will most probably follow in the footsteps of his Axis partner after final defeat in war and revolutionary upheaval at home. Dictatorship in the Fascist countries is an end in itself, while Political Tutelage in China is a transition from monarchical despotism and war lord tyranny to constitutional democracy.

That the revolution to transform China into a modern democracy must undergo three successive stages was originally foreseen by

6   77

Dr. Sun Yat-sen in 1905, when he successfully amalgamated the diverse anti-Manchu revolutionary secret organizations into a cohesive group under the *Chung-Kuo Kehming Tungmenghui* or the Sworn Brotherhood of the Chinese Revolution. The three successive stages were to be Military Government for the overthrow of the Manchu Empire and the liquidation and complete suppression of all remnants of the imperialists, feudalists, anti-republicans, and armed reactionaries, and later, the lawless war lords who came after Yuan Shih-Kai ; Tutelage Government under the Revolutionary Party, which then was the Tungmenghui, and later the Kuomintang, who became trustees, so to speak, and exercised political power on behalf of the people, to guide them in the practice of self-government, and to lead them in the march toward democracy ; and finally, Constitutional Democracy, when the trustee ruling party will restore complete sovereignty to the people, who will, through their elected representatives sitting in the National Assembly, adopt and promulgate the Constitution and elect and organize the Government of the Republic as provided for by the Constitution. When this final stage is achieved, the Kuomintang will be just an ordinary political party. It will then have to appeal to the people as the electorate for support of its party policies, and to elect its nominees to office in the local and national governments, just as any political party in Britain and America would do.

2

The three-stage programme for the political development of China had not been carried out during the first decade and a half of the Republic. Soon after the October Revolution in 1911, which gave birth to the Republic, Dr. Sun Yat-sen, who was provisional President when the Republic was proclaimed in Nanking on New Year's Day, 1912, had resigned power to the northern war lord Yuan Shih-kai, because of divided counsels in the ranks of the revolutionaries and their inexperience and incapacity to carry on the Revolution to its logical conclusion. Dr. Sun Yat-sen realized that the Revolution had achieved success too easily, albeit it was only apparent success, and the revolutionaries were really too unprepared to retain power and build up a genuine democratic republic. He therefore relinquished power willingly and abided his time.

Yuan Shih-kai, who had organized and trained the modern army in North China during the last days of the Manchu Empire, succeeded to the presidency ; a republican Parliament with a

Kuomintang majority sat in Peking. Conflict between President and Parliament was inevitable. Yuan forced the issue by ordering the dissolution of Parliament, and the killing and banishing of recalcitrant members, finally issuing decrees for the dismissal of all military governors who were members of the Revolutionary Party. The so-called Second Revolution of 1913 broke out in the Yangtse Valley when the dismissed military governors rose in revolt. Dr. Sun Yat-sen was then in Japan. He rushed back, trying to save the situation. It was too late, for civil war had started, and soon afterwards the revolt was crushed by the superior forces of Yuan Shih-kai. In 1915, while the war in Europe was in its second year, and Japan was having a free hand in the Far East, Yuan Shih-kai was misled by his flatterers into subverting the Republic and proclaiming himself Emperor of the Chunghua Empire. Revolts again broke out in the southern provinces, and Yuan died soon afterwards, in the summer of 1916. From then until 1928 the country was ruled by successive war lords under a regime of successive private wars for supremacy between them.

While the war lords were contending for dominance, Dr. Sun Yat-sen returned to Canton for the third and last time in 1923 to reorganize the Kuomintang and resume the much interrupted National Revolution, which, after his death in 1925, culminated in the rise of the National Government in Canton as the recognized Government of the Republic, and the successful conclusion of the revolutionary war with the capture of Peking in the summer of 1928.

With the preliminary unification of the country, achieved by military action under the brilliant leadership of Generalissimo Chiang Kai-shek, the nation was ready to begin the second stage in its political evolution toward democracy. To discuss and work out measures for the introduction of Political Tutelage or provisional party rule, a plenary session of the Kuomintang Central Executive Committee was convened to meet in Nanking in the middle of August 1928.

The late Mr. Hu Han-min, the late Dr. Chao-chu Wu, Dr. Wang Chung-hui, Dr. Li Yu-ying, and the present writer, all members of the Central Committee, were then sojourning in Europe. On the proposal of the late Mr. Hu Han-min, and at the invitation of Dr. Li Yu-ying, the group met in a suburb outside Paris one summer morning, and began an all-day session to exchange views and prepare a proposal to be submitted to the Central Committee in plenary session. As a result, a proposal calling for the setting up

of the Five-Yuan system in the National Government was drafted
by the writer and telegraphed to Nanking in their joint names.
The plenary session approved and passed the proposal *in toto*.   In
the fall of the same year, the five Yuan, as a first attempt at the
development of the Five-Power Constitution, were severally inaugurated.   Each and all derived sanction and power from the
party and were made responsible to the party.   The period of
tutelage had begun.

3

Political Tutelage is really a system of planned political development, akin to planned economy.   To be successful, it requires the
authority of a strong central government, without which it will not
work, especially in a sprawling, loosely organized country like
China.   It was this fundamental need for a strong centralized
administration that initiated steps toward the curtailment of the
semi-independence of the military rulers in the outlying provinces.
A military conference for the disbandment of superfluous troops and
demobilization of the revolutionary armies, aggregating more than
two millions, was convened in the winter of 1928.   Plausible and
elaborate plans were submitted and adopted by the conference,
attended by the leading commanders.   But the effort was fruitless.
A series of disastrous fractricidal wars began almost as soon as the
disbandment conference rose.

Another and a greater obstacle to be overcome before political
reconstruction in accordance with Dr. Sun Yat-sen's programme
could be put into practice was the rise of the Chinese Communist
Party as a separatist and rival military power.   While the fratricidal campaigns were going on, the Communists were entrenching
themselves in South-central Kiangsi Province and rapidly spreading
out in other parts of the country.   This had become a greater
menace to the Government and the party in power.   No political
solution was at the time possible.   A sustained military campaign
had to be undertaken to suppress the Communists in the southern
provinces.   It was only after years of hard fighting that the Kiangsi
and Hunan Communist bands were driven from their lair.   Since
then they have relocated themselves in North Shensi, after their
much publicized so-called 10,000 *li* march through West and
North-west China.

With the approaching end of the period of internal dissension
and civil strife, there came the greatest menace and crisis the nation
ever had to face.   This time it was the threat of foreign aggression

in the shape of the Japanese invasion of the metropolitan provinces of North China. The three Eastern Provinces of Manchuria had already been lost for some years—since September 18, 1931. Jehol was next grabbed by the Japs, whose aim was the conquest of intramural North China.

The years from 1931 to 1937, when total war was finally forced upon us, were extremely difficult times. With the enemy ready to move in and the whole country in a state of sustained alarm, there was little attention and energy left for either Government or populace in the provinces to devote themselves to peaceful preparation for self-government and constitutional democracy. The hue and cry throughout the length and breadth of the land was for resistance to the death against encroachments upon the national territory. But the state of our national defences was deplorable. The Army was neither trained nor equipped to oppose a mechanized enemy of proved power and fighting ability. The Government had to play for time to prepare for the inevitable showdown. In the meantime, in order to strengthen solidarity and further unite the nation behind the Government and the party, it was thought necessary to institute immediate measures leading to the termination of one-party rule and the hastening of constitutional government. One of these measures was the writing of the Draft Constitution by the Legislative Yuan under my presidency, and another was the preparation to hold elections throughout the free provinces for the formation of the Constituent National Assembly.

4

These measures originated in a comprehensive proposal which I submitted to the third plenum of the fourth C.E.C., which met in Nanking in the middle of December 1932. This proposal of mine is known as " Project for the Concentration of National Strength to Combat against the Menace Threatening Our National Survival." As revised and adopted by the plenum, section 3, on preparations for constitutional government, reads as follows :

SECTION 3. ON PREPARATIONS FOR CONSTITUTIONAL GOVERNMENT

(1) For the purpose of concentrating national strength to combat the foreign menace and to ensure national survival, be it resolved that the measures for instituting self-government as stated in the General Principles for National Reconstruction be put into practice at the earliest moment, as preliminary

conditions for the preparations leading to the inauguration of Constitutional Government.

(2) Be it resolved that the National Constituent Assembly be convened to meet in March 1935, to pass and adopt the Constitution and to decide on the date for its promulgation.

(3) Be it resolved that the Legislative Yuan be directed to proceed immediately with the writing of the Draft Constitution, and to cause it to be widely published in order to facilitate its discussion and study by the people generally.

Early in 1933 the Legislative Yuan started work on the drafting of the proposed Constitution. A Yuan committee of 37 members was appointed to undertake the task, with myself, President of the Legislative Yuan, acting concurrently as chairman, and Dr. John C. H. Wu, a well-known jurist and a new member of the Yuan, as one of the two vice-chairmen. It is needless to recount here in detail the work of this special committee and that of the Legislative Yuan as a whole in the writing and final adoption of the Draft Constitution, as the subject is treated in a special article elsewhere. It took nearly three years of continuous work and discussion before the Legislative Yuan completed the drafting. Late in October 1935 the third reading of the draft was completed and passed.

The completed draft was then submitted to the Fifth Congress of the Kuomintang, which met in Nanking on November 12, 1935. The Yuan draft as a whole was accepted by the Congress, with certain reservations which were referred to the newly elected Central Executive Committee for final action.

Since the convocation of the National Assembly in March 1935 did not materialize, owing to incomplete preparations for the election in the province, the Kuomintang Congress resolved that it should be convened within 1936 at the latest. The date was later fixed by the C.E.C. as November 12, 1936, the birthday anniversary of the Father of the Republic, and the official version of the Draft Constitution was published by National Government decree on May 5, 1936. A year later, on May 18, 1937, the draft was again revised by the deletion of one article. This now stands as the final and official draft of the future Constitution of the Chinese Republic.

Holding a national election in China is no simple matter. The primary machinery for carrying out the electoral process is defective, and sometimes entirely absent. There is no census of the population in the provinces and districts to guide the local officials. There is certainly no register of qualified voters in the villages and towns.

All these missing links had to be devised and provided for at short notice before an election could be properly conducted. Hence the repeated delays and failure to comply with the decisions of the central authority. November 1936 passed with no National Assembly in session. So in February of the next year the Kuomintang C.E.C. again fixed a date—a year from the date last decided upon, November 12, 1937—when the much-postponed National Assembly was to meet to adopt and pass the Draft Constitution.

But on July 7, 1937, there was the Lukouchiao or Marco Polo Bridge attack by the enemy, signalling the outbreak of war throughout the country. What has happened since then is world history. Electoral campaigning and all such activities were stopped at once. Early in November the Government evacuated Nanking and moved up the Yangtse, first to Hankow and later to Chungking. So, after repeated delays, and further successive changes of date, there was to be no convocation of the National Assembly for the duration of the war.

5

The period of Party Tutelage, beginning with the reorganization of the National Government and the institution of the Five-Yuan system in October 1928, has now lasted for fully fifteen years. This is certainly far beyond the time-limit assumed by Dr. Sun Yat-sen when he mapped out the three-phase plan for China's political evolution from absolute autocracy to constitutional democracy. It has lasted longer than even our party leaders had wished when the question of the duration of Party Tutelage was brought up. On June 15, 1929, the second plenum of the third C.E.C. had resolved that the period of Tutelage Government be fixed at six years, to be completed by 1935. At the same time it was also resolved that a detailed time schedule for the execution and fulfilment of the tutelage government programme be drawn up by the Political Council. But this schedule has become a dead letter, and is virtually forgotten, for no one in the Government now can even recall what its provisions were.

This failure to live up to good resolutions and to materialize the high-minded decisions of the party was partly due to inexperience and incompetence on the part of the rank and file of the party membership, who were entrusted and charged with such responsibility. But a more important cause existed. This was the die-hard attitude of certain party members who consciously reject the party dogma that party rule during the period of tutelage should be subject to any limit. What they want is indefinite prolongation of the one-party regime in order to build up a strong and unshakable political machine of, by, and for themselves. These people fear that once the period of tutelage terminates, opposition and rival groups outside the Kuomintang, such as the Communists, will seize power, and the San-Min-Chu-I will be scrapped, to be replaced by something else. What they could not understand is the fact that the San-Min-Chu-I must be put into practice in order to prove its worth as a body of guiding principles for the upbuilding of the nation. And to be really successful, a constitutional democracy must emerge from the present party trusteeship. There can be no really democratic government in China if the party in power should hang on to power indefinitely without reference to the wishes and desires of the people. Such an attitude has been responsible for the failure of the Kuomintang to achieve greater results in the political development of the nation during the past decade and a half.

But despite our shortcomings and sins of omission, Kuomintang leadership has done great things for the country. This, even our most severe critics must admit. First of all, the good things we have accomplished is the growing power of the national consciousness and national solidarity of our people. The San-Min-Chu-I has infused in them a strong sense of national dignity and a deep conviction of our national destiny. Our friends abroad sometimes cannot understand how the Chinese people can hold on against such overwhelming odds for so long, resisting the total might of our enemy. Some think that we are just fatalists, accepting and suffering whatever punishment and bad luck may come our way without murmur and complaint. Some may even think that we are sub-human, enduring suffering and pain which no other people can put up with. The truth, I think, lies in the inherent greatness of the Chinese people, roused to consciousness by the National Revolution, and inspired with the faith and hope of a bright future by the teachings of the Three Principles.

In spite of the war, the Chinese Government has done wonders in promoting and spreading public education throughout the country. Colleges and universities were moved bodily from the great cities and coastal areas to the remote up-country fastnesses in the West and South-West. Adult illiteracy is being tackled with a view to its eventual liquidation. In the four and a half years since 1939, some 1·4 million persons have passed through special training courses in the training establishments operated by the central, provincial and local authorities. Seventy per cent. of the trainees have been personnel actively connected with local self-government, the average age of whom is around thirty years. These men will return to their various localities to serve as organizers of the self-government units in the villages and towns. They may become chairmen of the village and town meetings, or members of the *hsien* and city councils. Not a few of them will rise to responsible positions as mayors and administrators of the several thousand *hsien* in the country.

Another good thing that the years of the tutelage have developed is the complete working out of a new system of local self-government for the country. In the early days there was no generally accepted criterion for the institution of self-government. Dr. Sun Yat-sen had laid down, in his General Principles for National Reconstruction, the *hsien* as the unit for self-government. But he left us no exact blue-print as to how such self-government was to be organized and conducted. As a result several theoretical systems were being advocated and put to trial in the provinces. General Yen Shih-shan has his own plan in Shansi, and Generals Li Tsung-jen and Pai Chung-hsi had another system introduced in Kwangsi. There was also the Ting-hsien experiment in Hopei and the Chou-ping model in Shantung. Kiangsi, Kiangsu, Chekiang and Kwangtung also have other systems under experiment.

The *Hsien* Organic Law passed by the Legislative Yuan was officially promulgated by the National Government on June 5, 1929. This law attempted to bring all the experimental systems into harmony by embodying the best features of each. The Shansi idea predominated, because it was the best known and had been tested by the longest experiment. But the subdivision of local units was found unsuitable to conditions in the Southern Provinces. As a result, a new provisional set of regulations governing the organization of local government was issued by the military authorities of the Bandit Suppression Command, at the time engaged in the campaign to liquidate the Communists' armed bands in Kiangsi. These interim regulations at once superseded the *Hsien* Organic Law, which practically became a dead letter. Under these regulations, the old *pao-chia* system of the Sung Dynasty was revived with modifications to suit modern conditions. It has taken ten years to work out the present system of local government, now known as the New *Hsien* System.

6

The new system was embodied in a new set of regulations published by the Government in September 1939. It has now been in force for four years. A report covering its enforcement and operation from 1939 to 1941 has been made public by the Ministry of the Interior. It is stated that of the 1469 *hsien* located in 18 provinces in Free China, 944 have been reorganized under the new system, which is 64 per cent. of the total area. Under the new system, each village or town is to have a " centre-school." In the *hsien* enumerated 21,306 such centre-schools have been established, or just under 85 per cent. of the possible total. Each *pao* comprising about 100 households, more or less, is to be provided with one " citizen-school " of the primary grade. Already 142,595 such citizen-schools have been opened, representing just under 38 per cent. of the total number of *pao*. Each *hsien* is to have a " health-centre " ; 783 *hsien* health-centres have been established, or 83 per cent. The organization of co-operative societies is proceeding more slowly than planned. In the first two years, only 5548 *pao* co-operatives, 1444 village-town co-operatives and 122 *hsien* joint co-operative societies have been started.

The smallest subdivision in this system of local government is the *chia*, comprising some ten households ; the next higher unit is the *pao*, about 100 households. Then comes the village or market town, which may comprise 20 or 30 *pao* ; when all the villages and towns within a certain administrative area are organized, they become the *hsien*. The competent executive and legislative organ in these divisions is the meeting of the household heads in the *chia*, the meeting of all adult citizens in the *pao*, the meeting of representatives in the village and the town, and finally the *hsien* council for the whole *hsien* composed of members elected from the villages and towns. In each unit there is a man responsible for the local administration. When the system is completely organized and functioning according to plan, these public officials are elected by their respective constituencies. During the first stages, before they function properly, such local functionaries are appointed by the higher authorities in the province.

This system of local self-government is the foundation upon which constitutional democracy in China will be built. Much work remains to be done, and diverse, difficult and vexed problems have to be adequately worked out before its success can be claimed. As it is, it presents a great promise for the future.

The origin of the *hsien* as the basic territorial subdivision in the central administration of the country is very ancient, dating back to 211 B.C., when China was unified for the first time under the First Emperor of Tsin. The national territory was then divided into 36 Chuen or provinces, and subdivided into smaller administrative units called the *hsien*. Thus, in its origin, the *hsien* was not an autonomous unit. It has remained a territorial subdivision of the central administration up to the present time, until local self-government was attempted during the last few years. Being merely a subdivision of the Central Government, its administration was directly appointed by and made responsible to the Central Government or its principal agency, the Provincial Government. Under the *ancien régime*, only in the village and the market town, beyond the pale of the walled centre in which the magistrate sat, was some form of indigenous self-rule permitted to exist. This local autonomy usually took the form of patriarchal rule by the village elders or the clan elders, if the whole village was populated by the same clan. Frequently these elders, who composed the village council by virtue of seniority through popular acclaim—the only form of election known—were dominated by, or at least under the influence of, one or a few wealthy landowners, or retired mandarins who had returned to their native villages, to enjoy the respect and homage accorded them as ex-officials, in the twilight of their careers. Such a group of village rulers is collectively known as the " Shun-Ch'i," or " men of honour and age." Not infrequently these " men of honour " degenerated into " men of dishonour " when they became corrupt and oppressive as owners of the village lands or keepers of the village pawnshops, which served as usury banks. Then they would become objects of unpopularity and hatred. But usually the villagers could do nothing about it, since these men were influential with the *hsien* magistrate, who would confirm and maintain them in their positions as village rulers.

With the introduction of local autonomy, the position of the *hsien* is changed. It is being raised as the highest self-government entity. At the same time it still retains its age-old functions as local agency for the central administration, as far as national and provincial affairs are concerned. This dual capacity has brought with it added responsibility as well as new and difficult problems for the *hsien* local government. The mayor or administrator—popularly known to the West as the magistrate, because in the old days he served also as a judge in both criminal and civil adjudication—in addition to his old duties as subordinate to the central authorities responsible for the administration of national laws and the execution of Central Government orders and regulations, now has to carry out the wishes and decisions of the district council. When the new system is in full operation, he will not only be elected by

the council, but may also be dismissed by the same popular organ.
This means that to be a successful *hsien* administrator the official
henceforth will require to be a man of high qualities. The achievement of local autonomy democratically instituted will require the
introduction of expert and efficient management of public affairs.
These two must go hand-in-hand. Otherwise the new system will
not function in the way it is intended to. Hence the emphasis on
trained personnel.

It is the policy of the Kuomintang to develop a corps of trained
and qualified personnel to fill the elective offices in the hierarchy of
local government. Laws are being enacted and enforced to require
all persons who may aspire to public office to qualify themselves
by passing the necessary public examinations, or having their
previous records in official service scrutinized and approved by the
authorities of the Examination Yuan in the National Government.
This applies not only to all local administrators, but to all candidates
for election to local bodies, such as town and *hsien* councils. This
is to ensure that local government shall be not only democratic in
its nature and origin, but also efficient in its functioning. In other
words, the goal for our immediate political evolution may be
summed up in the slogan : Democracy and efficiency must be
achieved simultaneously.

7

As a war measure, and pending the convocation of the National
Assembly and the nation-wide enforcement of the new local self-
government plan, certain interim arrangements were adopted by the
Kuomintang Government for the gradual widening of the basis for
the erection of democratic government. In the spring of 1938 the
special Kuomintang Congress at Hankow passed a resolution calling
for the creation of the People's Political Council to form a united
national front to prosecute the war to ultimate victory. This P.P.C.,
for short, was accordingly organized, with leading personalities from
all active political groups besides the Kuomintang invited by the
Government to sit in its meetings, which were held periodically to
hear reports submitted by the administrative heads of all Government departments, to ask questions for specific information and
clarification of policy, and to present proposals and resolutions for
debate and decision. Since its formation, membership in the
council has been increased from the original 150 to the present 240,
the majority of whom are now elected by the provincial councils,
with the remainder nominated by the Supreme Council of National

Defence and formally confirmed by the National Government. When the full council is not in session, a resident committee of 25 members, representing all participating groups, is elected to reside in the war-time capital, to carry on routine business, and act as liaison between the P.P.C. and the Government. This resident committee also meets at intervals to hear reports presented by the Government ministries.

All resolutions and decisions passed and adopted by the P.P.C. in session are submitted to the Supreme Council of National Defence for final approval and action. Although the P.P.C. is advisory in nature, and its decisions are by no means mandatory, yet practically all its important resolutions so far submitted have been approved and acted upon by the Government. In this respect it is in fact a National Assembly in embryo. Ministers in the Government have more and more to pay heed to the P.P.C. Not a few of the important and otherwise powerful ministers have found themselves in uncomfortable positions when P.P.C. members indulged themselves in straight talk and outspoken criticism. This is a hopeful trend in China's march toward democracy.

Acting immediately upon the Kuomintang C.E.C.'s recent resolution to convoke the National Constituent Assembly within one year after the conclusion of war, the Preparatory Commission for the Enforcement of Constitutional Rule has been appointed by the Supreme Council of National Defence. This commission is composed of 35 to 49 members, divided into three groups according to origin of the members : Kuomintang C.E.C. members, P.P.C. members, and other members, besides the first two groups. This is concurrently a fact-finding and advisory body. Its functions and terms of reference are stated in the organic law in the following provisions :

(1) To submit to the Government proposals concerning preparatory measures for the enforcement of Constitutional Rule ;

(2) To inquire into the working of various representative bodies of local public opinion, and to report its findings in current reports to the Government ;

(3) To investigate the manners and circumstances in which all laws and regulations relating to preparation for constitutional government are being enforced and carried out, and to report its findings to the Government accordingly ;

(4) To serve as a liaison organ between the Government and public bodies in matters concerning the Constitution and related political questions ; and

(5) To examine and discuss all matters concerning the enforcement of Constitutional Rule in accordance with the Government's instructions.

It is expected that sub-committees will be appointed and sent out by the Commission to tour the provinces and to gather information in accordance with the above terms of reference. Such public inquiries and fact-finding missions will serve not only to stimulate public interest in preparations for the forthcoming convocation of the National Constituent Assembly, but also to speed up the nation-wide enforcement of local self-government, as the necessary basis upon which Constitutional Rule must be erected.

Among the membership in the Commission, two well-known Communist leaders are included : Chow En-lai, Communist spokesman in Chungking and liaison representative for the Communist 18th Army Group Command, is a member appointed from among the third group of non-P.P.C. and non-Kuomintang members, while Tung Pi-su, Communist P.P.C. member, is concurrently designated a member of the supervising committee.

8

This leads me to deal briefly with the Communist problem in China. As it is, the Communist power, organized separately as a Government functioning in a certain area of the national territory, and maintained in power as the ruling party in the occupied region by military forces answerable to the Communist Party alone, is nothing less than an *imperium in imperio*. It pays lip service to the National Government of the Republic, but the so-called " Shen-Kan-Ning Border Region," which encloses some 24 *hsien* located in an irregular area in North Shensi, East Kansu, and South-east Ninghsia provinces, has a Government of its own, organized and administered in contravention of the national laws governing provincial and local administration. National Government decrees and Executive Yuan and ministerial orders have no effect or validity within the Communist districts. The Border Government collects its own taxes and prints its own paper money. Banking and trade with other parts of the country are carried on as Government monopolies. There have been unconfirmed reports current from time to time that illicit trade is being conducted with Japanese-occupied and puppet-ruled areas.

The Communist armies as incorporated in the National Army in the early days of the war numbered only three divisions, with a number of auxiliary units, totalling some 40,000 to 50,000 men.

These were reorganized as the 8th Route Army, and later renamed the 18th Army Group. This army has now grown to enormous proportions. Its numbers are generally accepted as being about 500,000. Such expansion is effected without reference to the orders of the Supreme Command. In fact, for some years now, the operations of this army in Shansi, Suiyuan, Hopei, Honan, Shantung and North Kiangsu provinces have been entirely independent of the High Command. The Communist troops under their own leaders act on their own responsibility, without the least concern about the wishes and orders of G.H.Q. Nominally they are still part of the Chinese National Army, but in fact they are an independent and separate army.

The Communist 8th Army was originally assigned North Shensi, East Suiyuan, Charhar and North Hopei Provinces as its designated war zone, within which it was to operate against the enemy and puppet forces. Honan, Shantung, Anhui and Kiangsu Provinces were assigned to the other Chinese armies. But instead of acting according to orders, the 8th Army went ahead with its own expansionist plans by recruiting and organizing irregular units within the zones of other commands. Friction was inevitable, and sometimes fratricidal outbreaks occurred. One by one other central Government units were edged out of South Hopei, North Honan, North Shantung and North Kiangsu Provinces. Irregular units claiming to be 18th Army men were found as far south as Hupei and Anhui Provinces.

Then there was the New 4th Army, organized out of remnants of the various Communist bands south of the Yangtse River for guerrilla warfare to the south of Nanking. In the autumn of 1940 orders of the High Command were issued to the 18th to move back to the north bank of the Yellow River, and to the New 4th to cross the Yangtse to North Kiangsu. The dates fixed for execution of the orders were repeatedly postponed, but to no avail. The New 4th, instead of going north to cross the Yangtse, turned south against orders and came into collision with other units. The consequences were unfortunate. The commander of the New 4th was captured and his troops dispersed and disarmed. The High Command ordered their liquidation. Yenan Communist Headquarters countermanded the High Command's order by appointing a new commander to the New 4th. This incident has caused much bad blood and brought about a situation between the Government and the Communists which so far has failed of an adequate solution.

In the spring of 1941, Communist members of the P.P.C., as a gesture of protest against the dissolution of the New 4th Army, refused to attend a session of the Council. This ill-advised behaviour was severely criticized by political leaders of independent groups. They have resumed attendance at subsequent sessions.

There can be only two solutions to the Communist problem in China. The forcible or military solution has been ruled out as undesirable, especially at a time when the nation is still unitedly fighting to expel the invaders. But even if the war were over, it would be equally deplorable to resort to force for bringing about the desired military and administrative unification of the country. Outside of a few hotheads in the Kuomintang or the Army, opposition to a military solution of the problem is wellnigh universal. The Kuomintang C.E.C. in plenary session has repeatedly resolved, in 1942 and again in 1943, to bring about a satisfactory termination of the deadlock by political and peaceful means.

The following resolution passed at the 11th Plenary Session of the Kuomintang Central Executive Committee explains in full the official attitude on this vexed problem :

"Having heard the general report on the Chinese Communist Party's activities, subversive of the State and detrimental to our war efforts, we realize with deep regret that the said party, instead of showing the slightest sign of being moved by the generous and tolerant attitude taken by the 10th Plenary Session held last November, has actually intensified its activities of endangering the security of the State and sabotaging our war efforts.

" Our patriotic war against aggression having passed through its most critical stage after six long years, the victory anticipated by the whole nation is already in sight. In order to ensure lasting freedom and welfare for the country and final triumph over aggression, the Government is firmly convinced that unless national unity is placed on a solid foundation, it is next to impossible to carry out successfully the programme of resistance and reconstruction. Bearing in mind this guiding principle, the Government sincerely hopes that the Chinese Communist Party will refrain from committing acts undermining national unity and obstructing the prosecution of the war. It is with this purpose in view that the Government has consistently taken an attitude of forbearance towards the said party. Animated, now as ever, by the same spirit, we do hereby resolve to entrust the Standing Committee with the task of settling this matter and of persuading in an appropriate manner the Chinese Communists to realize their past mistakes and honestly redeem the pledge made in their declaration of September 22, 1937, namely,

" ' (1) To struggle for the realization of the Three People's Principles ; (2) To abandon the policy of creating disturbance and propagating the Communist movement ; (3) To dissolve the present Soviet Government, thus helping to bring about the political unity of the whole nation ; (4) To disband the Red Army by incorporating it in the National Army under the direct command of the Military Council of the National Government.

" ' In this way, national interests will be safeguarded, military orders and government decrees carried out, victory in the War of Resistance and success in our reconstruction work assured, so that the fervent hope of the people may be fully realized.

" ' As the Plenary Session has resolved to convoke the Constituent National Assembly within one year after the cessation of hostilities to make and promulgate a Constitution, all other problems can be discussed and solved in the assembly.

" ' The present session of the Central Executive Committee, while resolutely striving for the consummation of its fixed policy of unifying the country and safeguarding the victory of war, hereby reiterates to the Chinese Communist Party its most earnest sincere expectations.' "

The above resolution represents not only the liberal and tolerant attitude of the Kuomintang and the National Government of the Republic, but also expresses the fervent hopes and aspirations of the entire Chinese nation.

With a democratic system of government on the way to realization, and with the convocation of the Constituent National Assembly definitely pledged to take place within the first post-war years, the hope of a political solution to the Communist problem is brighter now than ever before. The Kuomintang, as the ruling party, has formally and solemnly made public its pledge to the nation that convocation of the National Assembly will mean the termination of party tutelage, and the restoration of sovereignty to the nation. Generalissimo Chiang Kai-shek, as Leader of the Kuomintang and President of the Republic, has unequivocally declared to the world that China will be a democracy in the full sense of the term. He has unmistakably stated in his opening speech before the 11th C.E.C. Plenum that when constitutional rule is inaugurated in this country with the meeting of the Constitutional Assembly, the Kuomintang will retire to a position of equality with any other party in China.   Let me conclude by quoting his own words on this point.

" After the enforcement of Constitutional Government, our party should hand over the Government to the people. . . . After the enforcement of Constitutional Government, our party should be on an equal legal footing with other ordinary parties and the common citizens, and should enjoy equal privileges and rights, fulfil equal obligations, and receive equal treatment from the State under the principles of freedom of assembly, organization, speech, and publication in accordance with the law."

Writing China's Constitution

I

THE story of China's movement towards constitutional government is as old as that of her movement towards democracy. Indeed, one cannot conceive of a democracy working without a Constitution of one form or another. Since the story of China's march toward democracy is told elsewhere in this book, it would be unnecessary repetition if I should write another story of her constitutional movement. So in this article I shall confine myself to a discussion of the Final Draft Constitution, which may be regarded as the latest fruition of the whole movement, and to answer such questions as to how the draft was written, and what is written in it. Inasmuch as this Draft Constitution, worked out by the Legislative Yuan after three years of assiduous labour, was officially promulgated by the National Government, and will be submitted as the Chinese Government's formal draft to the Constituent National Assembly for adoption, it may be properly regarded as China's Constitution *in potentia*. A clear understanding of the draft is, therefore, of key importance to the clear understanding of the future democratic China.

To go back a little into history, we may take as our starting-point that memorable date, December 18, 1931, when the three Eastern Provinces (Manchuria) were forcibly occupied by Japanese troops. Far-sighted statesmen of the Kuomintang realized then that to cope with such a serious national crisis, all the forces, military, economic, intellectual and otherwise, both in and outside the party, should be consolidated. To check the powerful and ruthless aggressor, China must be truly and effectively united. Many felt that a constitutional government, instead of party rule, would be the best means of bringing about such an unification. In the National Emergency Conference held in April 1932 at Loyang, a resolution was passed that the Kuomintang should wind up its party rule— that is to say, put an end to the so-called period of Political Tutelage —as soon as possible. In the Third Plenary Session of the Fourth Central Executive Committee of the Kuomintang, held at Nanking in December 1932, another resolution, drafted and proposed by myself, was passed to the effect : (1) that the National Assembly should be convened in March 1934, and (2) that the Legislative Yuan should be instructed to draw up a Draft Constitution as soon as possible.

Acting on the basis of the latter part of the resolution, the Legislative Yuan began immediately to devote itself to the task of Constitution drafting. A Committee was formed with myself as chairman and Dr. John C. H. Wu and Mr. Chang Chi-pen, two eminent jurists, as vice-chairmen. The Committee met several times, and twenty-five fundamental principles in regard to the draft were agreed upon.

Dr. John C. H. Wu's labours deserve special mention here. He was commissioned by the Committee to produce, single-handed, a preliminary draft on the basis of the above-mentioned principles. This draft, consisting of 214 articles, since popularly known as *Dr. Wu's Tentative Draft*, he was authorized to publish under his name. The publication of the draft had two purposes in view : (1) to sound public opinion regarding the Constitution, and (2) to use it as a basis for the drafting of a permanent Constitution. Its reception by the public, though very critical, was on the whole more favourable than one could have expected under the circumstances. When one compares it with the later drafts, noting how far they have been influenced by it, one realizes at once how essentially right Dr. Wu has been, at least, as regards the fundamentals of Constitution drafting.

Using *Dr. Wu's Tentative Draft* as a basis for discussion, and numberless criticisms thereon from various quarters as reference material, the Constitution-Drafting Committee proceeded to draw up another draft which consisted of 160 articles, and was formally published on March 12, 1934. This was the first draft drawn up by the Legislative Yuan. It is usually known as the *Preliminary Draft of the Constitution of the Republic of China*. The main purpose of its publication was, as in the case of Dr. Wu's draft, to invite public discussion and criticism. During the two and a half months that followed its publication, 281 dissertations containing opinions on and criticisms of the draft were received by the Legislative Yuan. This showed that the public was greatly interested in the Constitution. To examine the merits of the opinions and criticisms contained in these articles, I appointed a Committee of three, with Dr. Foo Ping-sheung, a veteran diplomat and able jurist, now Chinese Ambassador to the Kremlin, as its chairman.

The achievement of this little Committee is noteworthy. It carefully analysed and classified all the opinions and criticisms received and then produced a compendium entitled *The Compilation of Opinions on the First Draft of the Constitution*. The book was of great service to the Constitution-Drafting Committee. After more than a month's discussion and deliberation, the Committee produced a revised draft, which was the second published by the Legislative Yuan. This second draft is known as the *Amended Preliminary Draft Constitution of the Republic of China.*

The second draft, a few months after publication, underwent another revision, Dr. Wang Chung-hui, a jurist of international fame, formerly President of the Judicial Yuan, and then Judge of the Permanent Court of International Justice at The Hague, who happened to be back in China at the time, also participated in this revision in an advisory capacity. Criticisms and suggestions from other quarters were, of course, also carefully considered. The revision was finally completed by October 16, 1934, after three readings and many lengthy discussions in the Legislative Yuan. This draft, containing twelve chapters and 178 articles, was the third drawn up by the Legislative Yuan, and was for a time considered to be final.

But this supposed final draft did not, however, prove to be final. It was first submitted to the Central Political Council of the Kuomintang, which in turn submitted it to the Fifth Plenary Session of the Fourth Central Executive Committee, held in December 1934. The latter, in one of its resolutions, expressed only general principles by which the Standing Committee of the Central Executive Council was guided in its examination of the contents of the third draft. The Standing Committee did not, however, take upon itself the task of actual revision, but simply drew up some specific instructions, which, together with the draft itself, were again sent back to the Legislative Yuan for further deliberation. The latter, acting upon these instructions, which favoured simplicity and elasticity, amended the draft once more. Two chapters on Finance and Military Affairs were struck out, and three chapters on Provinces, Districts and Municipalities were combined in one under the caption of Local Government. Thus the draft was greatly simplified and reduced in length, consisting of only eight chapters and 150 articles. This draft, the fourth one, was submitted to the Sixth Plenary Session of the Fourth Central Executive Committee of the Kuomintang, held in November 1935, which readily expressed its general satisfaction and approval. To give the draft a finishing touch, the Central Executive Committee addressed itself to its work, and as a result of its labours, instructions containing three specific points were drawn up, which in turn were again sent to the Legislative Yuan. The latter, interpreting the instructions, amended the draft for the last time, and thereby gave it its final form.

The final draft, containing 148 articles, was formally published by the National Government on May 5, 1936. On account of the date of its publication, it is popularly called the *Draft Constitution of Double Five* or the *Double Five Draft*. In a later amendment one article, Art. 146, was struck out. Apart from this slight change, the *Double Five Draft* has remained up to the present exactly the same as when it was proclaimed.

According to the original scheme, the Constituent National Assembly with the special mission of enacting the Constitution was to be convened at the end of 1937. But the increasingly tense relations between China and Japan in the first part of the year, followed by the actual outbreak of the Sino-Japanese War on July 7, has completely prevented the original scheme from being carried out. With the war continuing at its height, it is, of course, impossible to convene such a Constituent Assembly now or in the near future. However, it is gratifying that in the Eleventh Plenary Session of the Fourth Central Executive Committee of the Kuomintang, held in September 1943, a resolution was passed to the effect that the National Assembly should be called for the purpose of enacting a permanent Constitution in not later than one year after the war. The problem of enacting a Constitution will therefore be the first important thing to engage the attention of the Chinese people as soon as peace is restored to them.

2

If I were asked, " What is *the* outstanding characteristic of the Final Draft Constitution as a whole ? " I should unhesitatingly reply, " It is its permeation with the principles and teachings of Dr. Sun Yat-sen, especially his San-Min-Chu-I." Even a cursory glance at the draft will not fail to convince one of the truth of my statement. Although the method used by Dr. Wu in his *Tentative Draft* of naming the chapters according to the three principal headings of the San-Min-Chu-I has not been adopted in the final draft, yet we find the spirit of San-Min-Chu-I present everywhere. It pervades every chapter, every article.

Let us look at the Preamble of the Draft Constitution. It reads as follows :

" By virtue of the mandate received from the whole body of the citizens and in accordance with the bequeathed teachings of Dr. Sun Yat-sen, Founder of the Republic of China, the National Assembly of the Republic of China hereby ordains and enacts this Constitution and causes it to be promulgated throughout the land for faithful and perpetual observance by all."

Here we must note that the words, " in accordance with the bequeathed teachings of Dr. Sun Yat-sen," are by no means put there for euphonic or rhetorical purposes. They are there in letter and in spirit.

Article I of the *Draft Constitution* reads as follows :

" The Republic of China is a San-Min-Chu-I Republic."

The provision of this article had caused some serious misgivings on the part of those who failed to understand the real meaning of San-Min-Chu-I. To clarify their doubts, I gave an explanation in an article published several years ago. " To understand why we should provide in our Constitution that our Republic is to be a San-Min-Chu-I Republic," I said, " we must first grasp what San-Min-Chu-I really means. The so-called San-Min-Chu-I consists of three principal parts, viz. Min-Chuh-Chu-I, Min-Ch'uan-Chu-I and Min-Seng-Chu-I. The purpose of Min-Chuh-Chu-I is to make China a free and independent State, free from the control of any other country or nation. The purpose of Min-Ch'uan-Chu-I is to make China a really democratic State, in which the sovereignty will be vested in the body of its citizens. The purpose of Min-Seng-Chu-I is to improve our social and economic conditions, so that all the people will be able to find means of achieving their livelihood and asserting their right to existence. Although this is the simplest and most rudimentary interpretation of the San-Min-Chu-I, yet it is precisely what this great doctrine means : and, we may say, it is also precisely what we want China to be. . . . When thus understood, should we object any more to the constitutional provision that China should be a San-Min-Chu-I Republic ? "

I have more recently evolved a better definition of the San-Min-Chu-I as national freedom for the nation-state, political freedom for the citizens within the law, and economic freedom for all the people to attain a higher and better livelihood. San-Min-Chu-I, therefore, may be called the three freedoms : freedom from foreign slavery, freedom from political tyranny, and freedom from poverty and economic exploitation.

Indeed, San-Min-Chu-I is both an idealistic and practical expression of modern democracy to the fullest extent. A San-Min-Chu-I Republic means nothing more or less than a Commonwealth " of the people, by the people and for the people." I remember, in the course of the drafting, some of the members of our Committee did suggest the wording as follows : " The Republic of China is a State belonging to the people, controlled by the people and enjoyed by the people." That suggestion was not adopted because it means practically the same thing as San-Min-Chu-I, but expresses it in rather abstract and clumsy language.

In the early days of the Draft Constitution some critics outside the Kuomintang also looked upon this article with misunderstanding and suspicion. They thought that by such a provision the Kuomintang's Party-Rule in China would be continued indefinitely, since, in their eyes, the Kuomintang alone was publicly identified with the San-Min-Chu-I. This was a misconception of the Kuomintang's programme ; it also did injustice to the San-Min-Chu-I. According to Dr. Sun's doctrine, the sole mission of the Kuomintang is to make the whole body of the Chinese people believe in and practise San-Min-Chu-I, and to transform China into a San-Min-Chu-I Republic. In the process of so doing, i.e. during the so-called Period of Political Tutelage, the Kuomintang is to be regarded as both the " tutor " and " trustee " of the people. But as soon as that is done and China advances into the Period of Constitutional Government, the Kuomintang's position as the people's " tutor " and " trustee " will come to an end. It will retire from the privileged position of *the* ruling party to a common position of *one* of the political parties. From thence onward, the San-Min-Chu-I, which really means democracy in all its aspects, national and political, as well as economic, will be a national legacy of the Chinese people. Organizations and activities of all kinds will be allowed, provided they are not subversive of the San-Min-Chu-I Republic. It goes without saying that in a San-Min-Chu-I Republic, there should be no place for dictators, anarchists, traitors, usurers, exploiters, or oppressors of the poor. As Dr. John C. H. Wu has aptly put it, " San-Min-Chu-I is like heaven in that it has many mansions ; but there could be no room for those who are bent upon turning the world into a hell."

3

Rights and duties are correlative. In the eyes of a certain school of jurists, duties stand even before rights. Some of them go as far as to deny completely the existence of rights. It is not my intention here to enter into problems of legal philosophy. What I want to point out is the fact that in our Draft Constitution we have specifically provided for certain duties of the citizens along with their rights. These duties are three, viz. the duty of paying taxes, the duty of performing military service, and the duty of rendering public service.

But from the standpoint of citizens in general, the most important function of the Constitution is the protection of their rights. Historically speaking, the struggle for constitutional government has been but a struggle for the protection of personal rights. For it was the desire of the governed to be free from the rule by arbitrary will or personal caprice of the governing authority that had germinated the whole movement towards constitutional government.

In drafting our Constitution we have never lost sight of this important fact. In Chapter II of our draft meticulous care has been taken in enumerating the rights and liberties of the citizens as well as in providing the means for their protection. In the case of protection of the liberty of the person, we have not only followed the spirit of the English Habeas Corpus, but have also provided the procedures for its enforcement in more or less detail. In view of the fact that illegal arrest and detention have been traditional forms of oppression against the Chinese people, the wisdom of this provision is self-evident.

Besides the liberty of the person, the Constitution provides that every citizen has freedom of domicile, freedom to change his residence, freedom of speech, writing and publication, freedom of assembly and association, freedom of religious beliefs, the right to private property, the right to present petitions, lodge complaints and institute legal proceedings, the right to exercise the powers of election, recall, initiative and referendum, the right to compete in State examinations, and all other liberties and rights not detrimental to public peace and order and public welfare. This is as complete a list of the liberties and rights of the people as one can find in any Constitution in the world. But some critics have raised a point of doubt on account of the fact that all the liberties and rights are made subject to the rule of law. Take, for instance, Article 16 : " Every citizen shall have the freedom of assembly and of forming associations ; such freedom shall not be restricted except in accordance with law." They seem to think that a provision like this would mean to give people freedom with one hand, and take it back with the other. My answer to these critics is as follows : In the first place, what the Constitution aims to secure is a government by laws as against a government by men. Just because the people's liberties and rights " shall not be restricted except in accordance with law," they are therefore protected from the arbitrary interference of the Government or its functionaries. In the second place, legislators are by no means free to enact laws restricting the citizens' liberties and rights. Article 25 clearly provides : " Only laws imperative for safeguarding national security, averting a national crisis, maintaining public peace and order, or promoting public interest, may restrict the citizens' liberties and rights." Thus, unless it is of imperative necessity the legislators are incompetent to make laws of this kind. If they should do so, laws so made would be declared unconstitutional, hence null and void, according to the procedure provided in Article 140.

Lastly, we must not forget to mention another significant provision under this Chapter, and that is Article 8, which reads : " All citizens of the Republic of China shall be equal before the law." It means, of course, that every citizen, irrespective of sex, race, class or profession, will enjoy the same rights and be subject to the same duties under the law. Here, we see, the equality of women with men is constitutionally guaranteed.

4

The National Assembly is a unique institution provided in the Chinese Draft Constitution. It occupies a place of peculiar importance in Dr. Sun Yat-sen's political theory and system. Its powers and functions as prescribed in Article 32 are as follows :

1. To elect the President and Vice-President of the Republic, the President of the Legislative Yuan, the President of the Control Yuan, the Members of the Legislative Yuan and the Members of the Control Yuan.
2. To recall the President and Vice-President of the Republic, the President of the Legislative Yuan, the President of the Judicial Yuan, the President of the Examination Yuan, the President of the Control Yuan, the Members of the Legislative Yuan and the Members of the Control Yuan.
3. To initiate laws.
4. To hold referenda on laws.
5. To amend the Constitution.
6. To exercise such other powers as are conferred by the Constitution.

From the above, we see at once that the National Assembly is the holder of all the " political powers " and the *source* of all the " governmental powers." It must be recalled here that one of the greatest and most original contributions of Dr. Sun Yat-sen to political science is the demarcation between " political powers " and " governmental powers." The former are the people's powers, while the latter are the powers or functions of the Government. The political

powers are four in number : Election, Recall, Initiative and Refer-
endum. In the districts and other local units of self-government,
these powers are to be exercised directly by the people. As to the
Central Government, these powers are to be exercised by the
National Assembly for the people of the whole of China. The
" governmental powers " are five in number : Executive, Legislative,
Judicial, Control and Examination. Hence the so-called " Five-
Power Constitution," as against the ordinary " Three-Power
Constitution " of the West. These governmental powers, being
really functions, are entrusted by the nation to the hands of the
National (Central) Government. Thus, the people in whom the
sovereignty of the State is vested (Article 2) create the Government
and hold it in potential control through the National Assembly and
by means of the exercise of the four " political powers." It is easy
to note that, being the creator or source of the Government, the
National Assembly could not be regarded as a part of the Government, although, as we have seen, every department of the Government is responsible to it and subject to its control. In the ordinary
course of things, its principal function is to get the right personnel
for the Government by election. The other three powers will be
exercised only on rare occasions, thereby giving the Government a
free hand in performing its functions. It is the idea of Dr. Sun to
combine democracy with the highest possible degree of efficiency,
to reconcile the idea of popular sovereignty with a functional theory
of government. It is gratifying to see that our Draft Constitution
has embodied the ripe fruits of his political thinking.

The National Assembly shall be constituted of delegates elected
directly by the citizens of the *hsien*, the principal self-governing
units, and the municipalities. Each *hsien*, municipality or area of
an equivalent status is entitled to send one delegate ; but in case its
population exceeds 300,000, it will be entitled to one additional
delegate for every 500,000 people. As to the election of delegates
from Mongolia, Tibet, and the oversea Chinese, it will be determined by special laws. The National Assembly will number approximately 2000 delegates. The term of office of the delegates is
six years. The Congress meets every three years, and its session is
to last one month or at most two months. On important occasions
there may be extraordinary sessions.

It has been suggested by some writers that during the adjournment of the National Assembly there should be created a smaller
body to act as its representative. It seems to me that such an
institution is not only unnecessary but positively harmful. It is as

untenable in theory as it is undesirable in practice. It is not only in contravention of Dr. Sun's political theory and system, but would create in practice a sort of oligarchy which may usurp the powers of the people on the one hand and meddle with the functions of the Government on the other. In fact, as I remember, in the course of our drafting, an institution of this kind had found its way into the provision of one of our preliminary drafts. But after careful deliberation it was dropped. We concluded that the National Assembly, large though it is, is already the smallest possible body which can represent the whole people, and can no longer be made smaller. Moreover, the National Assembly itself is already a representative body with delegated powers; and it is utterly indefensible for delegated powers to be delegated again to a smaller body.

5

According to Dr. Sun Yat-sen's theory, the five " governmental powers" are to be exercised by the five Yuan of the Central (National) Government. In our Draft Constitution, it is provided that the Executive, Legislative, Judicial, Control and Examination Yuan are the highest organs through which the Central Government exercises its executive, legislative, judicial, control and examination powers respectively. But over and above them is the President, who, besides being the Head of the State and the Representative of the Republic in foreign relations, is also the Chief of the Executive and the " co-ordinator " of the five Yuan. He holds some measure of check and supervision over all the Yuan, but has complete or direct control over none except the Executive Yuan, whose President is appointed by and directly responsible to him, and also subject to his removal. The Presidents and Members of the Legislative and Control Yuan are appointed directly by the National Assembly, and subject only to its recall. The Presidents of the Judicial and Examination Yuan, while appointed by the President, are not subject to removal by him, but to recall by the National Assembly. With the exception of the President of the Executive Yuan, the Presidents of all the Yuan are directly responsible to the National Assembly. Complicated as it might seem at first sight, the system really secures a certain degree of independence for each of the governmental departments, and provides a kind of check and balance amongst them.

The President of the Republic exercises many and various powers besides those of appointment. He commands the land, sea and air forces ; he may issue emergency orders and take other necessary steps when the country is confronted with a grave danger, or when its economic life meets with a serious crisis, subject to the duty of submitting his action to the ratification of the Legislative Yuan ; he may request the Legislative Yuan to reconsider a legislative measure before its promulgation or enforcement, and only a vote of two-thirds of the members present can save the measure from being killed. One of his most significant functions is to serve as a kind of co-ordinator between the different departments of the Central Government. Article 45 provides : " The President may call a meeting of the Presidents of the five Yuan to confer on matters relating to two or more Yuan, or on such matters as he may bring up for consideration." If the President exercise this power discreetly and wisely, he can contribute enormously to the smooth co-operation and proper functioning of the different parts of the machinery of the Central Government.

Students of political science who are familiar with the Western system of government might ask whether our Draft Constitution follows the Presidential System or the Cabinet System. Our answer is : It follows neither, but adopts something of both. *Vis-à-vis* the National Assembly, by which it is elected and to which it is responsible, our Government looks like a Cabinet System, of which the President is the Prime Minister, with the Executive Yuan as his Cabinet. But the National Assembly is not a Parliament ; it is more like an electorate and constitutional assembly in one. *Vis-à-vis* the Legislative Yuan, our Government looks like a Presidential System, for the President is neither elected by nor responsible to it. But unlike the President under the Presidential System, the President under our Constitution is responsible, not to the people in general, but to a definite body ; that is, the National Assembly, which is always watching him and may check or even recall him when necessary.

Something must be said about the local institutions, especially their relationship with the Central Government. The local institutions as provided in the Draft Constitution are of two grades : (1) the Provinces ; (2) the *hsien* and municipalities. The latter are " units of self-government," while the former are rather administrative areas of the Central Government. The status of the Provincial Governments has raised serious doubt, but viewing the Constitution as a whole it is probably more proper to say that they are agents of the Central Government, and serve as kind of *liaison* between the " units of self-government " and the Central Government.

Historically the Chinese provinces have never been self-governing entities like the states of U.S.A. or the cantons of Switzerland.

The *hsien* and municipalities, being units of self-government, are endowed by the Constitution with extensive powers. In the General Meeting, the people of each *hsien* or municipality elect directly their Magistrate or Mayor and members of the *hsien* Council, or the Municipal Council, as the case may be. Besides election, they also enjoy the other three political powers, viz. recall, initiative and referendum, as far as elected local officers and local matters are concerned. In Article 104, it is provided that " all matters that are local in nature are within the scope of self-government." But, on the other hand, it is also provided that " the scope of local self-government shall be determined by law," and it is to be borne in mind that only the Legislative Yuan can make " law." Thus, while the powers of local government derive directly from the Constitution, they are subject to legislative restriction and control of the Central Government.

Students who are familiar with the political systems of the West might again ask whether our government is federal or unitary. Again, our answer is : It is neither, but has something of both. The usual criterion by which political scientists decide whether a government is unitary or federal is whether the Central Government or the local government has the residuary power. In our Constitution, neither has it. It does not enumerate the powers either of the Central Government or of the local government. It entirely discards the idea of enumerated powers and residuary power, and adopts what may be called a functional distribution of power, which is expressed by Dr. Sun Yat-sen in his " General Principles for National Reconstruction " as follows : " All matters that should be uniform throughout the country should be given to the charge of the Central Government, while all matters that require local adaptations should be given to the charge of the local government ; thus striking a happy medium between unitary and federal systems."

6

As we have seen in our exposition of the San-Min-Chu-I, Min-Seng-Chu-I, the Principle of People's Livelihood, ranks the first in importance, though it is treated last in order. In his " General Principles for National Reconstruction " Dr. Sun Yat-sen writes : " The people's livelihood is of prime importance in the programme of national reconstruction." Indeed, nowhere does Dr. Sun Yat-sen show his candidness and sagacity so fully as in his treatment of this problem. His method of treatment is a thoroughly practical one. "We must base our method not upon abstruse theories or upon empty learning, but upon facts, and not upon facts peculiar to foreign countries, but upon facts observable in China." So he brushes aside all foreign theories, and tackles the Chinese economic problems in a realistic manner. He does not want to see China blindly follow the course either of absolute private capitalism or of undiluted Marxist Communism. He would prefer an intermediate course between the two, and this he advocates in his own Min-Seng-Chu-I.

In Chapter VI on National Economic Life an attempt is made to realize the leading ideas of Dr. Sun's Min-Seng-Chu-I in a concrete, practical, legal form. A perusal of this chapter will not fail to impress one that it has succeeded at least in tackling two vital factors in the economic life of the nation, viz. Land and Capital.

In regard to land, I would like to cite a few provisions which illustrate how closely we have followed Dr. Sun Yat-sen's land principles. "The land within the territorial limits of the Republic of China belongs to the people as a whole. . . . Every landowner is amenable to the duty of utilizing his land to the fullest extent" (Art. 117). "All subterranean minerals and natural forces which are economically utilisable for public benefit, belong to the State and shall not be affected by private ownership of the land" (Art. 118). "The unearned increment shall be taxed by means of a land-value-increment tax and devoted to public benefit" (Art. 119). "In readjusting the distribution of land, the State shall be guided by the principle of aiding and protecting the land-owning farmer and the land-utilising owners" (Art. 120).

In regard to Capital, I shall call the reader's attention to three articles which may show the nature and kind of capitalism that China is going to adopt. Art. 121 : " The State may, in accordance with law, regulate private wealth and enterprise when such wealth is considered detrimental to the balanced development of national economic life." Article 122 : " The State shall encourage, guide and protect the citizens' productive enterprises and the nation's foreign trade." Article 123 : " All public utilities and enterprises of a monopolistic nature shall be operated by the State ; except where in case of necessity the State may specially permit private operation." It is evident from the above cited articles that China has no intention of abolishing at once the institution of private capitalism. On the contrary, private enterprises are constitutionally guaranteed, encouraged and protected, subject, of course, to regulation by law.

Chapter VII on Education contains eight articles. The provision in Article 137 seems worthy of special attention, as it is the most concrete and the most judicious. It reads as follows : " Educational appropriations shall constitute no less than 15 per cent. of the total amount of the budget of the Central Government, and no less than 30 per cent. of the total amount of the provincial, *hsien* and municipal budgets respectively." On this article, Mr. Wen Yuanning, the Editor of the well-known *Tien Hsia Monthly*, remarks : " The wisdom of such an article no one in his senses can dispute. It is possible for other forms of government to exist with an illiterate population. But illiteracy goes ill with constitutionalism. The proper functioning of a constitutional government, especially in China, depends upon an intelligent and educated public. The more intelligent and educated the governed in a constitutional state, the smoother the wheels of government will run. Anything, therefore, which will forward the cause of education in China will also help the cause of constitutional government here." This observation of Mr. Wen's I heartily endorse. I believe that it is on education more than on anything else that the successful working of our Constitution will depend.

7

The power of amending the Constitution is given to the National Assembly. But the procedure required in the matter of constitutional amendment is different from ordinary acts or enactments of the National Assembly in two important respects : (1) An amendment to the Constitution may be made only when it is proposed by over one-fourth of the delegates to the Congress and passed by at least two-thirds of the delegates present at a meeting having a quorum of over three-fourths of the entire Assembly. (2) A proposed amendment to the Constitution must be made public by the proposer or proposers one year before the assembling of the National Assembly. It goes without saying that the last provision is made in order to give the people of the whole country ample time to deliberate on and discuss the wisdom of the proposed amendment, thereby enabling them to express their opinions and instruct their delegates to act accordingly. In practical effect it will amount almost to a general referendum or plebiscite.

The question of interpreting the Constitution is a more difficult and complicated one. What organ is to be given this power ? In the course of our drafting, various suggestions have been brought up for our consideration. In Dr. John C. H. Wu's draft, a particular court, to be specially elected by the National Assembly from among persons of definite qualifications, is introduced. In a private draft of one of our members of the Constitution-Drafting Committee, the power of interpretation is to be exercised directly by the National Assembly. In the Preliminary Draft of the Committee, it is left to the Judicial Yuan to submit its tentative interpretation to the National Assembly for a final decision. In the so-called Amended Preliminary Draft, it is left to the Supreme Court to submit its tentative interpretations to the National Assembly. In the draft of the Legislative Yuan, it is simply provided that the interpretation of the Constitution shall be given by the Judicial Yuan. Finally, in the *Double Five Draft*, a distinction is made. As a rule, " the interpretation of the Constitution shall be given by the Judicial Yuan " (Art. 143). But as " laws in conflict with the Constitution are null and void," the draft sees fit to provide a special procedure by which the " power of constitutional review " is to be exercised. Thus, in Article 140 it is provided : " The question whether a law is in conflict with the Constitution shall be settled by the Control Yuan submitting the point to the Judicial Yuan for interpretation within six months after its enforcement." That is to say, if the Control Yuan does not raise the point, the Judicial Yuan has no right to pass judgment upon the constitutionality of any law. The system may seem a bit complicated to some, but it undoubtedly serves as a check on the Judiciary, which might otherwise become too powerful.

In this article I have attempted to present only the salient points of the Final Draft Constitution for the consideration of the reader. As the draft is the result of years of labour and collaboration between the drafters and the general public, and as it is the formal draft that the Kuomintang and the National Government are going to submit to the first National Assembly to be convened within one year after the war, it is reasonable to expect that the draft will be adopted by the Congress without much radical change.

It must be understood, however, that I am not claiming finality for the Draft Constitution, nor am I of the opinion that there should be no changes at all. As a matter of fact, in a speech before the People's Political Council three years ago, I explicitly declared that no Constitution can be made for all time, for no human institution is perfect. A Constitution, to be living, must march with the times and be open to revisions. It is altogether probable that salutary changes will be introduced by the National Assembly in the Final Draft, especially those necessitated by the bitter experience of, and lessons gained from, the present war.

8

PART THREE

To Better Livelihood

War-time Economic Problems, Their Solution and Bearing on Post-war Reconstruction *

THE Chinese people, while engaged in a life and death struggle for their national existence, are to-day confronted with grave economic problems. As time goes by and the war is prolonged these problems become more and more aggravated, and therefore demand our immediate and serious attention for their early solution.

Owing to the rise in consumption of commodities and the enormous increase of national expenditure, the issue of bank-notes, which are legal tender, must perforce be increased to meet budgetary demands. Hence the prevailing rise of prices. This rise will occur in any country engaged in a long and large-scale conflict. After the last Great War, not only Germany, after her defeat, and Russia, during her revolution, but even Britain, France, and the United States, after their victory, had all suffered to a greater or lesser degree from the ill-effects of inflation. The three victorious Powers were fortunately in a better position to take necessary measures successfully to combat the inflation danger. If proper remedial measures, such as efficient price-control and proper rationing of essential supplies are adopted in time by a Government, it is not altogether impossible to avoid the pitfalls of currency inflation.

The present war in Europe has been going on now (1940) for a year and a quarter, and the difficulties arising out of inflation there are not yet evident. Britain and Germany, the two main combatants in this struggle, must have learned from past experience and taken precautionary measures to forestall and render innocuous the impending danger. Inflation may not be avoidable, and prices must rise to some extent, yet its worst effects can be warded off. However, what others do in this respect may or may not be applicable in our case : this is for us to consider.

We have fought for three and a half years. The last seven or eight months have witnessed a steep climb in living costs. To-day our national economy is beset with grave difficulties. The trouble

* Address to the Legislative Yuan, Chungking, November 30, 1940.

has been traced to four major causes : first, as the over-burdened and inadequate lines of transport and communications have increased their charges on traffic by more than ten times, the pre-market costs of production have as a result been going up also ; secondly, since the removal of the seat of Government to Szechuan, consumption in this part of the land has been considerably increased with the sudden growth of population, thus rendering it hard for the supply to keep up with the demand ; thirdly, war-profiteers, taking undue advantage of the situation, are buying and hoarding large quantities of materials, thereby forcing prices up still further ; lastly, with the masses of able-bodied young men in the Army, the productive man-power in the rear has badly shrunk, causing the supply of goods to dwindle out of proportion to the growing demand. But the real, fundamental cause of the general price rise is decidedly attributable to currency inflation, made necessary by the mounting war expenditures.

2

No country at war can make both ends meet. The common makeshifts are : to raise loans in the shape of victory bond issues ; to increase the rates of existing taxes, and institute new ones ; to issue more currency notes than at ordinary times, etc. In such ways, the living standard of the nation will be lowered and its remnant earnings gathered into the hands of the State for stopping up the gap. The revenues of this country, inadequate for national defence and administrative functions even in normal times, fall grievously short of the requirements of war. No other country has been so light of hand in levying taxes or in contracting national debts as China. Whenever there is a deficiency, the practice has been to borrow from the banks, which have to print more and more legal tender notes. But these, once in circulation, cannot be withdrawn by the banks in any appreciable quantity. We have, therefore, a swollen outflow and a trickling influx, and the balance of payment and receipt is thereby upset. With the increasing output of paper currency, prices and wages rise accordingly. Meanwhile, the people, to guard against the growing costs of commodities, store up goods rather than accumulate money. This is a two-edged blade, cutting both ways : on the one hand, the accelerated demand depletes the already diminishing supply of goods, and hence causes the rise of prices ; on the other, the circulation of currency is speeded up, which is in effect equivalent to a fresh issue of paper money, and still further cheapens its purchasing value. Both these panic situations gather momentum as the process goes on, doing great damage to individuals and the State alike. The unwholesome effects of inflation on prices when it runs out of control are not to be made light of, though we are fully conscious of the Government's dilemma, and would give them our sincere sympathy.

Before the war, the total volume of bank-notes in circulation was $1400 million. With national expenditure steadily increasing, and the people hoarding goods instead of depositing money in the banks, for fear of loss, or with a view to profit, the national banks are forced to issue floods of bank-notes to defray the expenses of the war. When food prices go up, the indices of all other things, including wages, are bound to follow suit. For instance, the farm labourers, who formerly asked for only a few dimes a day for transplanting rice-seedlings, must now be paid many dollars per working day per person. This prevailing rise of prices casts its shadow not only on social economy, but also on the nation's finance, for the budget, after it has been ratified by the legislature, is rendered inoperative before many months have elapsed.

3

Judging from current conditions, the nation's budget must continue to mount as the years go by. Since the outbreak of this war, the budgetary estimates of national revenue and expenditure have been repeatedly rendered ineffectual, owing to changing circumstances. But however difficult the financial situation may be, we have got to go on with the war and, at the same time, carry out the great task of national construction. No one has yet suggested that because of lack of funds we should cease fighting the enemy-invader and abandon the work of building up our country into a unified, democratic modern State. Despite all obstacles, we must go on with it unless we decide upon national suicide as the lesser evil, which is, of course, preposterous.

This year's budget of $17,000 million may sound alarming, since its size is unprecedented. But when measured by the price level to-day there is nothing extraordinary about it. A banker friend told me the other day that prices have already risen eight to ten times. That is to say, the budget figures given above must be reduced by a decimal, if assessed in terms of the pre-war value of the dollar. When converted into foreign currencies, the sum amounts to only about £100 million sterling or U.S. $500 million. According to the Parliamentary report of the Chancellor of the Exchequer,

Britain's daily war expenses are £9·1 million; if our estimated spendings were intended for Britain's use, they could only last some ten or eleven days, while we have to spread them thin over 365 days. Again, if we take an American instance, the annual administrative funds of New York City alone are greater than our national expenditure, including war expenses. Furthermore, if we push on full blast with our gargantuan plan of national construction, the figure will prove to be quite insignificant.

4

After victory is won, what will be the approximate yearly cost for State construction and maintenance of national services? First, military readiness for national defence and local security will be indispensable. Even the minimum maintenance for these two items would not be inconsiderable. At present, the regular Army on the front and in reserve numbers well over 5 million men. When the war is over, the disbanded troops can be easily absorbed by the local militia and police force. Supposing the total enlistment of the standing Army and these two forces to be also 5 million, with pay at $60 each a month, plus 300,000 officers at $150 each on the average a month; the lowest yearly maintenance cost will be $4140 million. Arms and equipment, uniforms, barracks, motor transport, etc., which are highly expensive, are not included in this figure.

Next come educational expenses. It goes without saying that if we want to construct a modern State illiteracy must be wiped out, the general cultural level raised, and technical ability inculcated in great masses of the nation. If each average family of five sends one child to a grade school, 90 million families, which make up our total population of 450 millions, must have as many children. If every grade school takes care of one hundred children, 900,000 schools would be needed. Granting each school three teachers, doing also clerical work, there would be 2·7 million teachers. If each of them were to be paid $100 a month, the total for salaries would come up to $3240 million a year. Besides, there are the middle schools, technical schools, colleges, and universities. If one-tenth of the boys and girls coming out of grade schools enter middle schools, and one-tenth leaving the latter are enrolled in technical schools, colleges, and universities, there will be 9 million inter-mediates, and 900,000 technical and advanced students, in all about 10 million. If every twenty of these 10 million were to have one faculty or staff member, paid an average monthly maintenance fee of $200, the year's total would be $1200 million. Thus, the salaries of all classes of teachers, when scraped to the bone, would amount annually to $4440 million. This, be it noted, does not include the construction cost for school buildings, libraries, laboratories, playgrounds and dormitories, which must come to a considerable sum.

Thirdly, officials of the central and local governments will number more than a million. At present, every ten households form a *chia* or *pao ;* so the whole nation ought to have about 900,000 *pao*. If each of these employs a clerical worker, who is to be paid $100 a month, the total monthly pay-roll would be $90 million. And to carry on the functions of the district, township, village and *hsien* ruling bodies, as well as those of the provincial and central governments, another large amount is necessary. Altogether, $3500 million would be a meagre sum for just the salaries of all the public servants, exclusive of the cost of office buildings, fixtures, etc.

Fourthly, our future public health service should be an important feature in State construction. We are now paying only $6 million odd for it, a ridiculously low sum when compared with the expenditure of other countries. The United States have a general medical practitioner for every four or five hundred people, and still there are plenty of complaints that the majority of the population is not getting proper medical care. We should at least have a general practitioner and an assistant per thousand to begin with. In that case, 900,000 physicians, with an equal number of assistants, would be wanted. If each of them is paid an average of $200, a minimum outlay of $180 million every month, or $2160 million a year has to be provided for their services. Of course, hospitals and medical and surgical equipment and supplies, etc., are to be provided for outside of this sum.

As regards the management of communications and transportation, it is taken for granted that such enterprises must be self-supporting. The above-mentioned four main services, i.e. defence and police, education, government and administration, and health and medical services are, however, without revenues, and yet must be somehow provided and maintained. Add them together, and we have to pay out $14,240 million a year. Add another $5000 million or so for running expenses (exclusive of salaries) and for countless varieties of buildings and equipment—military, educational, government and medical—and the total expenditure of $20,000 million is not at all excessive. With respect to the nation-wide construction works of all sorts and kinds, let it be set down at

$10,000 million for post-war annual investment, when a five-year plan will be pursued in earnest. The grand total of $30,000 million, an astronomical figure, but one actually to be reduced by a decimal in terms of the pre-war dollar, is the least budgetary expenditure for which the nation must be prepared if a modern State is to arise out of the ashes and ruin of our country.

5

Since post-war reconstruction requires such a tremendous amount of money, many people are inclined to shake their heads in disapproval, as if a modern State could be realized gratis by the wave of a magic wand. But since we are determined on the importance and urgency of our task, surely nothing should daunt us. Our annual total national income is tentatively estimated at from $80,000 to $135,000 million ; thus, a budget of $30,000 million is only about 30 per cent. of the whole. If the people, after having done their duties for the general good, could have the remaining portion of the national income justly distributed among themselves for maintaining a rather even and tolerable living, the demands of the State could not be regarded as exacting.

Take the conditions in Britain, for example. From September 1939 to April 1940, the daily war expenses averaged £6 million. According to the British economist Maynard Keynes, this, in the course of a year, will have taken half of the nation's total annual income. The British war expenditure is now estimated to have risen to £9 million per day. It seems to me that, counting all other necessary spendings, the daily expenditure of the British Government cannot be much less than £12 million : in other words, the yearly fiscal outflow must reach £4300 million or more. The annual total national income of Britain in normal times has been estimated at £4850 million. At present, because of war-time full employment, and the prevalent rise of prices and wages, a rise in the national income say of £2000 million may be added. Even then, the war is costing Britain well over 60 per cent. of her national income, the people living on the remaining 40 per cent. or thereabouts.

The United States (in 1940) had not yet declared war, but are only preparing for it. In their budget for the fiscal year July 1, 1940, to June 30, 1941, the mere estimated increase for national defence is listed at U.S. $15,000 million. According to the original plan, the yearly expenditure on this item was set at U.S. $20,000 million, which is also 30 per cent. of the annual total national income.

Therefore, if we want, as no doubt we do, to carry on the two-fold campaign of national resistance and State construction, 30 per cent. of the nation's gross receipts, to be spent on these two heads, must be regarded as a very light burden indeed. However, gauged by the financial conditions of the Government at present, that huge sum is, of course, not available for spending.

6

On the problem of monetary circulation, it is interesting to recall that in 1912, soon after the launching of the Chinese Republic, Dr. Sun Yat-sen published an article under the title, "The Monetary Revolution," in which he advocated the abolition of the "tael" and the withdrawal of silver dollar coins from circulation. In their stead, he proposed the emission of paper bank-notes as the exclusive legal tender currency. This paper currency was to be issued by the State Bank, and put into circulation by the Government of the Republic for the payment of all services rendered to the State, and for Government purchases of all goods and produce from the people. In this way, the bank-notes would constitute evidence of indebtedness by the Government to the people. In their turn, the people were to use them for payment of all taxes, duties, fees and charges which they must render to the Government. These notes, having been collected by the Government as taxes, etc., were to be withdrawn from further circulation and forthwith destroyed. The process would then be repeated, when new notes were to be issued for use.

When this proposal was made public some thirty years ago, its author, the Father of the Republic, was ridiculed by all the gentry and intellectual class as a practical joker. Theoretically, they argued, it was very well, but the good old people of China, the "lao-pai-shing," were too much habituated to the use of hard, silver money, and could therefore have no confidence in the proposed fiat money printed on paper. Such people had forgotten their own national history—forgotten that China had invented paper currency, which was first introduced and circulated a thousand years ago, in the time of the Sung Dynasty. Nor could they have imagined that twenty-three years later, in 1935, when economic conditions the world over were badly upset, and the enemy, taking advantage of the situation, began to lay hands on our silver dollars * in order to

* The economic branch of the Japanese secret service sent hundreds of trained ruffians, armed with daggers, iron rods and pistols, to smuggle out thousands of cases of Chinese silver dollar coins.

stir up financial troubles for us, as well as to fatten himself with illicit profits, our Government in self-defence proclaimed and successfully carried out its currency policy by the issue of " fapi " legal tender. All silver and gold, coins and bullion, were nationalized and withdrawn from circulation.

Thus, what was thought impracticable came to be quite natural. For during these last several years we have been using this very paper money to develop and mobilize our economic resources, to concentrate our human and material power toward the prosecution of this terrible war. Had we not adopted this legal tender paper currency, we should have been unable to carry on our great struggle against the enemy. To-day, all the more, we should maintain the effectiveness of this paper legal tender policy. However, according to the principle of the People's Livelihood, this policy is only a means to an end ; it is not by itself sufficient. From this point we are led to think of the problem of food.

7

Dr. Sun Yat-sen advocated the public distribution and sale of food on the basis of meeting the four prime demands of life, which are food, clothing, lodging and movement, as expounded in his Min-Seng-Chu-I. Since there is public management of public utilities, such as railway transport, telegraph and telephone services, electric lighting, and city water supply, against private monopoly, there is no reason why the same evil should not be prevented in the case of food. By public management and control of this principal means of livelihood, private exploitation of the public by a few individuals for their own profit can be eliminated in one masterly stroke. This policy can, I am convinced, solve our present problems, caused by a regime of rising prices and scarcity of goods. At the same time, it will also help to alleviate the financial stringency facing the Government. I have mentioned before that State expenses are for ever multiplying, and funds must be found to meet them. The unrestrained issue of paper currency by the Government banks is surely not the best method of grappling with the situation.

Now, let us take the food problem under consideration, and let us see whether the public distribution and sale of rice, our staple food in this part of the country, can solve for us the problem of food and commodity prices, reduce the volume of currency in circulation, and find a solution for the financial worries of the State. The three-fold problem posed here can, I think to some extent, be met successfully, for the following reasons :

First, if rice is distributed and sold by the State, its price can easily be cheapened. If the price of publicly distributed rice be reduced, none but fools will choose to supply themselves with privately sold rice at a much higher cost. If the reduction could be as much, say, as half of the current market price, who would want to pay the inflated price for the benefit of profiteers ? The lowering of the staple food price must react favourably on the general price index by bringing down prices all along the line.

Secondly, it is possible, I think, to employ this measure to reduce the volume of currency in circulation. These bank-notes are daily flooding the market as the Government authorities pay them out to finance the war. Not more than 10 per cent. of the emitted paper will flow back to the treasury. The influx could, however, be considerably increased by the Government's selling of State rice to the extent, say, of 100 million piculs, which amount, let us assume, is available for State trading.

Thirdly, this policy, if effectively carried out, will not merely strengthen our present financial position, but may prove to be a source of State revenue for the future, which could be turned to good account in our post-war construction. I hear that the total rice harvest in the free areas this year is estimated at 750 million piculs. If a proper scheme is contrived by the Government to buy up the available supply, the State can, under efficient and honest management, without injury to the people, earn a handsome profit of some $10,000 million with which to carry on the war. Our customs duty receipts are now only $500 million, while the salt tax yields another $100 million which, compared with the prospective rice profits, are really insignificant sums.

Therefore, as regards the State monopoly of rice, its first function is to reduce the price of rice and, with it, the general cost of living ; its second, to recall currency notes over-issued in the past, which deflation will also exert a salutary influence on commodity prices ; and its third, to provide a new source of revenue for our war-time exchequer.

8

After much deliberation I have thought out a way for putting the policy into practice. We can take Szechuan to begin with. The tillers of land in this province are mostly tenant farmers ; rents are as a rule paid in kind, from 60 to 70 per cent. of their rice harvest, to landlords. This year's crop is from 70 to 80 per cent. of normal, yielding about 80 million piculs in all. So the minimum total intake of the landlords should be no less than 45 million piculs of unthreshed grain. How, then, are we going to round up this mountain of rice and convey it into the hands of the State? We do not propose confiscation, though, as a revolutionary measure in an emergency, this could well be done. The Government can peacefully buy the rice for the State. An order may be circulated to the tenant farmers to the effect that, beginning from next year, their harvest rent should not be delivered directly to their landlords, but should be taken to the offices of the national grain collection centre. When the landlords ask for their rent grain, all that the tenant farmers need to do is to hand over the receipts given them by the rice collection offices ; the Government will see to the rest. A landlord, whose grain rent is, say, one hundred piculs of unhusked rice, will be paid, when he claims his due from the Government, the full market price, half in cash and the other half in State Construction Savings Certificates. This is no confiscation, and yet the staple food of the nation would be conveyed into public granaries.

It is known that this province has still 100 million piculs of unhusked rice in private storage. The State should buy them up in ten transactions. For the first 10 million, the Government will pay the full market price of $120 a picul, half in currency notes and the other half in Savings Certificates. When putting this grain on the market for public sale soon afterwards, the Government will charge only $100 a picul. Consumers buying it with cash, the State can obtain a cash profit of $40 a picul. In the second month, a second transaction of 10 million piculs is to be made with the grain owners. As the market price has now fallen to $100 a picul, the Government's cash and bond payments will be $50 a picul in cash and $50 in bonds. When this grain is sold, the official price can be fixed at $80 a picul, the Government reaping a cash profit of $30 for the State. The cutting of the price will go on as the process of buying and selling is repeated, until a reasonable level is reached, when an even balance will be maintained between the buying cost and the selling price. Thus prices, that of rice first of all, will go down, and the circulation of paper money on the market will be contracted in volume and reduced in velocity.

As regards tenant farmers and owner cultivators, their excess grain should also be bought up by the State. Private selling to private parties should be prohibited ; violations of this rule to be treated as illegal. In buying grain from the owner cultivators,

80 or 90 per cent. of the cost should be paid in cash, and the rest in bonds, to encourage production. To secure the surplus produce of the tenant farmers, something even more than the market price, and all in cash, could be paid them in order to stimulate rice planting. In such wise the superfluous earnings of landlords and land-owning farmers could be canalized and conveyed into the hands of the State.

This is a way of mobilizing the excess wealth and purchasing power of the land and the landowners, and of compelling them to do their share of duty by means of enforced savings. Thus, by pooling individual savings, the State will derive a source of hitherto unused wealth for public expenditure. As things are going now, the landlords, with too much money, which they cannot properly spend, will continue to acquire land and to hoard rice, so as to grow richer and richer, without a thought of contributing their share to the war effort. It seems to me that nothing could be more rational than what I have set forth here as a means of dealing with our present difficulties as well as of planning for reconstruction after victory.

9

People may object that this might be good theory, but questionable practice. Take Szechuan again, for instance ; they would say : But all the big landlords here are ex-war lords who fought in our past civil wars ; some of whom are still quite powerful, though subject now to the Government. What they took from the people when they ruled the country was all invested in landed properties ; while the millionaire-profiteers of this war have also acquired large estates. The Government could not mobilize their surplus wealth without meeting with serious resistance. Such fear is apparently reasonable. But we would ask, how does the strength of these strong men, landlords and capitalists, compare with that of the enemy who has mobilized 3 million men to crush us, and fought us for three years now, with no conquest yet in sight ?

Another objection is, that this method of buying and selling grain is fraught with difficulties, so that not only the landlords, but also the farmers, would object to it. My answer is best put in a question : the Government, in enforcing conscription for the Army, has encountered innumerable difficulties ; is it conceivably more difficult to conscript wealth than to conscript men for the war ?

There is a third objection : for grain collection the Government will have to employ a host of public servants, and in the end corruption will inevitably be rampant. This is no argument either. The enforcement of conscription has also disclosed numerous abuses, yet we cannot abandon the system because of them, as one cannot "forswear eating for fear of being choked." The present system of military conscription may not work out as well as could be wished, but we can improve it. The same is true of grain collection. As to the vast increase of public servants, the grain collectors, that is no fatal obstacle. The question is : would they or would they not perform a useful service to the nation ? Since this War of Resistance began, 5 million men have been mobilized for military service. In order to provide the means for carrying the war to a victorious end, it would not be too burdensome for the nation to mobilize one-tenth to one-fifth of a million of public servants to enforce the grain collection programme.

If the policy advocated is successfully adopted, equalization of land ownership, as prescribed in the Min-Seng-Chu-I, will not be so far away. For the landlords, seeing that the acquisition of landed estates could yield them no exorbitant profits, would then cease to buy up more and more land. When the times are opportune, the State can issue land bonds to buy back all privately owned land for redistribution to the peasants who till the soil.

Compulsory saving is applicable not only to owners of farm lands, but to holders of urban sites as well. The way of enforcing it is the same. By order of the Government, house tenants are to pay their rents to the city Government against receipts ; when the house-owners ask for rents, the tenants simply hand over these receipts to them ; armed with these, the owners go to the municipal treasury offices to claim their money. Suppose a house-owner has $1000 to collect there : on presenting the receipt, he will be paid $500 in cash and the rest in Savings Certificates. To enforce savings thus is not too difficult a process.

10

When Dr. Sun Yat-sen first propounded his ideas about the equalization of land ownership and the public sale of food, people were incredulous as to their feasibility. If the same reasons for scepticism are used to argue against my stand for these two policies, I will cite a foreign example to prove my point, for there is the concrete example of Soviet Russia to dispel doubt and refute our opponents.

From the outbreak of the Revolution in 1917 to the eve of her first Five-Year Plan in 1927, Soviet Russia was still an agricultural country. Beginning from 1928, when the first Five-Year Plan was initiated, the annual total investments of the State ran into tens of billions of roubles. The enormous capital invested for giant under-takings was amassed entirely out of land-produced wealth extracted from the peasant-farmers who, shortening their coats and tightening their belts scraped and saved by the sweat of their brow. So, while in 1913 Russia's production was 40 per cent. industrial and 60 per cent agricultural, in 1936, before the termination of the second Five-Year Plan, the ratio had been reversed to something like 80 per cent. industrial and only 20 per cent. agricultural.

During the first European war, Russia's casualties were over 10 million, and close on the heels of that came the internal struggle and the intervention of the Powers, with the result that not a single mine or factory escaped ruin. In 1921, when the revolutionary campaign was wound up, the new-born State began to salvage whatever could be reclaimed from the heaps of wreckage ; by 1927, the restoration work was done. Commencing from the next year, the first Five-Year Plan went on in full blast, costing the nation in all hundreds of billions of roubles, more than a hundred times my tentative estimate of our post-war budget.

Where did the Soviets get the means to finance such gigantic plans ? To put it in a nutshell, from the nationalization of land. The Government distributed land among the peasants, with a heavy levy of 60 to 70 per cent. on their produce ; after collection, the grain tax was exported to exchange for machinery from abroad. While the plan was proceeding, the Soviet people were still at grips with poverty, shivering in the cold and cowering in squalid houses during the long Russian winter, and half-hungry all the year round. The British and American Press concluded then that the Revolution was a flat failure, since in Czarist days the people had been some-what better off. But the Soviet people did not lose heart ; they were, instead, full of fervour and confidence, putting up with momentary sufferings as matters of course. With the whole nation battling against hardships and tribulations innumerable, the first Five-Year Plan was accomplished before schedule time.

The second Five-Year Plan was carried on in easier circum-stances. I have visited Soviet Russia twice ; the impressions I got from these two occasions, in 1938 and 1939, especially the sharp contrast in material improvement, were most favourable. The first time I went there, the people, all workers and peasants, were still rather poor, but imbued with a new faith and actuated by a grim determination ; their life was hard, though everyone had work to do and something to eat ; women's dresses were uniformly shabby and slovenly. In my second visit, just a year later, the atmosphere was quite different : the people had become much more cheerful, their living generally was improved, and women were considerably better dressed. The people were the same people, but because of their outstanding achievement, their means of enjoying life had undergone an almost magical change for the better.

,The moral to be drawn from the Soviet example is that what they have done could also be done by us. Only they did the thing with a heavy hand, while we can do it more peacefully and less violently.

Before the current war, the Government budget of this country never exceeded $1200 million. Our Generalissimo once said that if we continued on these lines State construction must become an impossibility. I agreed with him. Though our new budget is some $17,000 million, yet because of the sharp rise of prices the sum is still equivalent to our pre-war budget. We must have our own industries, first heavy and then light, and we must have education, common as well as technical, to build up a modern State. The burden for State construction must be borne by all of us. Therefore, mobilization of wealth for solving our pressing difficulties and paving a way to future ease is a step which the country, sooner or later, must be ready to take.

Fundamental Problems of China's Economic Development *

I

CONCERNING China's economic development there are, roughly speaking, six fundamental problems demanding our attention and study. The first is the problem of our object—what we aim at achieving by economic development. The second is that of time —when is the opportune moment to pursue the task, and how much time is needed to accomplish the work ? The third is that of the nature of an economic development. The fourth is that of our financial resources. The fifth is, whether the work should be done by the State or by private enterprise. The last is that of how the work should be planned and executed.

There is a practical consensus of opinion about the object of our economic construction, especially after the painful experience of these last five years (1942). We want to be both rich and strong above all other things. Because she has been weighed down by poverty, China has been unable, for the past century, to assume a world position to which she is rightfully entitled. Our economic development must aim, therefore, at removing the causes of this poverty. We have had no industries worthy of the name. For thousands of years the nation has been vegetating in an agricultural economy, which cannot support the country and the people at a standard of living requisite for their existence in a modern State. When victory and peace have come, we shall have to speed up the process of industrialization so as to assure ourselves as a nation of security from foreign attack, and as individuals of a general abundance of food and clothing. If we fail in that, the nation is doomed to perish. All are agreed on this point.

2

The problem of time calls for deep thought. The Republic is thirty-one years old now ; seventeen years have passed since the National Government was founded in Canton. From 1911 to 1927, at which latter date the Government was reorganized at Nanking, there was no sustained effort at planned construction.

* A lecture delivered at the Section for Party and Political Training of the Central Training Institute, Chungking, September 8, 1942.

During those sixteen years, petty war lords ran amuck, ravaging the land and plundering the people. 1925 found the revolutionary Government busy uprooting the provincial militarists. In 1927 the country was unified. From then on, several years were spent in suppressing rebellion and consolidating unification. So, actually before the current war broke out, there were only five years during which the Government had the chance to do any work toward building up a modern State. Before July 7, 1937, the Government had to make hasty preparations for the impending emergency. For the last five years, although reconstructive activities have been carried on side by side with the War of Resistance, whatever constructive effort there has been was strictly limited in its nature and scope, primarily as a war measure for meeting the most pressing needs. Work of great importance, but not indispensable to the war, was ruled out. Thus, any full-scale economic development can begin only after victory, when world order will be restored with the resumption of peace. But as to how long we shall have a peaceful world in which to push on with our plans for economic development is a question that merits our serious consideration.

There are thinkers and economists who often neglect this vital point of opportunity and availability of time in their discussions of post-war reconstruction. They think that when peace comes, it is bound to be a durable peace, lasting a century or more, so that we can do our job in unhurried ease, without having to rush onward as we do now. This is really a mistaken view. The ancients have a saying : " Think of dangers while in safety ; take precautions by being ready." No one can foresee now what the world will be like when the common enemy is beaten and the war ended. We hope for the best, of course, wishing that peace may be permanent. But hopes and wishes are not realities. For the good of the nation, it is safer to be on our guard lest peace should not be of long duration. No one can guarantee that five or ten years after the end of this war another war will not break out. It is highly probable that the enemy may seek his revenge. It would do us all good and no harm to suppose that the period of our peace-time reconstruction will be quite short. With such an idea in mind, we can take time by the forelock.

Here I must digress from my subject to condemn the vicious habit, current in our society, of wasting valuable time without return. Most of us are easy-going, happy-go-lucky good-for-nothings, bent on ephemeral pleasures and silly amusements, as if there were perpetual peace in the world. What takes people of other countries one year to accomplish, we are usually unable to do in five years. In private life, the shameful habit of unpunctuality is common to all strata of society. Our Party Leader Chiang tried, among other things, to eradicate this habit by starting the New Life Movement, but after some years there is still little improvement. Even among civil servants and party workers, there are numbers who choose to fritter away their time in *mah-jong*, domino and poker games. This is positively criminal in war-time. We have so much to do and so little time ; how can we afford to kill time in such a stupid manner ? The British empire-builder, Cecil Rhodes, once exclaimed, " There is so much to do and so little done ! " The British people are noted as hard workers, yet he urged them on with these words. Compared to them, our country is far poorer, and our ability greatly inferior ; why do we waste our spare moments in idleness, instead of putting them to good use ? Men in the higher positions are often the worst offenders in this respect ; those drones of the nation should be rigorously punished !

Since the opportunity for our national reconstruction is so fleeting, and our bad habit of wasting time so deep-rooted, it behoves the youthful elements of the party to be all the more alive to the situation, and to make redoubled efforts. The only chance of rejuvenating the race, which may come once in a thousand years, should not be missed for one moment. Every minute in those vital five or ten post-war years is precious beyond estimation. Within that period, our economic development must be well on the way to completion. In case the world situation should suddenly change for the worse, and our country be threatened by another invasion, we should then be able to get along without depending wholly on outside assistance.

During the last five years, our friends, now our allies, have rendered us both moral support and material aid, for which we are, of course, grateful. But our ability to hold our ground during these hard, critical years is 95 per cent. due to our own efforts. In these nine months since the outbreak of the Pacific War, foreign help has been extremely limited. The American aircraft sent to help us are surprisingly few. The American air force in China is small. Lately, British bombers, up to a thousand at a time, have been sent to attack German cities ; their losses on the average amount to 5 per cent., which may be as many as fifty planes in each expedition. This latter figure is about the number of planes in the American air force in China. After the war, we must be self-sufficient in respect of all weapons for our national defence—in aircraft, guns and tanks—if we are to enjoy national security.

It should not be thought that five or ten years is too short a period. In fact, the shorter the time limit we set ourselves for the task ahead, the better it will be for its accomplishment. If we were to give ourselves only five years, we should be forced by the period set to strive all the harder and, consequently, an adequate amount of work would be done in the end. If we imagine that the peace will last fifty years after the war, so that all will want to return to Shanghai, to have a good time there seeing the latest films and going to dances, nothing much will have been done by the end of half a century.

Can we hope that our basic economic construction will be fairly achieved in five or ten years ? I believe we can. The example of Germany is highly instructive. After the Versailles Treaty she lost virtually everything. Political upheaval and economic crisis made it almost impossible for the Reich to survive. But in seven years, from 1933 to 1939, she became much stronger than she had been formerly. She has now fought for three years, and still it takes the combined strength of Soviet Russia and Britain barely to withstand her. The fact that her industrial basis was left intact after 1918 has immensely helped her recovery ; and we can in this way compare our economic situation with hers. But although her inordinate ambition of world conquest is sheer madness, and to be abhorred by us, yet her magnificent mastery of time, and supreme efficiency in doing things, together with her people's fanatical devotion to their country, cannot but command our admiration and attention.

Another instructive example is afforded us by Soviet Russia. In November 1917 came the great Revolution, which gave birth to the Soviet regime. In March 1918 the new State was compelled to sign a peace treaty dictated by Germany. Foreign intervention followed in the wake, and finally, a great famine swept over the land. But beginning from 1928, Five-Year Plans were successfully launched, to such effect that in ten years a new, rich and powerful State has reared its mighty stature across two continents. If the Soviet people had not wrestled with time in their factories and mines, and on their farms, putting forth titanic efforts, the country could not have withstood the present German assault, nor remained free. If others have done it, why could not we do the same ? In short, it must be insisted that not only the young, but the elderly generations as well, should live to see a new, vigorous China rising in all her glory amidst the ashes of this war and the ruins of the past.

3

As regards the nature of our economic construction, views are divergent as to whether we should have light industries or heavy ones first. There are people who think that light industries are easier to start with, while the heavy require too much capital and technically trained specialists. Again, it is argued that light industries are quickly productive of wealth, while heavy industry yields no immediate profit. These people point at industrially advanced nations, such as England, America, and even Japan, saying that all of them built heavy industries when enough wealth had been accumulated for capital after the full growth of their light industries. England began with spinning and weaving woollen and cotton textiles ; America with producing goods for domestic consumption, and Japan with textiles and paper-making. Ergo, China also should, they argue, start in the same way.

The great mistake in this line of reasoning is that it overlooks the elements of time and opportunity. The English industries had a history of one and three-quarters of a century, the American of a century and the Japanese of at least seventy years. If we also could have the next century secure from foreign attack, such a slow development might not be fraught with dangers. But if we have only five to ten years' respite, to proceed at such a snail's pace would be certain suicide. Besides, even if peace could be ensured to us for the next century, modern industrial technique waits for none, and we either have to catch up or to lag behind, following at a leisurely pace with out-of-date methods and technique. In that event, we should always be vulnerable to superior forces.

As time is vital, and the opportunity propitious, we must industrialize our country in the shortest possible time. All industries are interlocked. Agriculture and industry also are interwoven ; the basis of all industry is heavy machine production, so the heavy industries must be established first. The very machines for the light industries are, in fact, produced by the heavy industries, without which economic construction is but an illusion. Now, if we cannot produce those machines by ourselves, we shall have to import them all from abroad. Our industrial development will turn out to be dependent upon the heavy industry of other countries.

In building up heavy industries we should profit by the bitter experiences of the past. As I have said, the National Government at Nanking had five years to carry on its work of economic development under the menace of invasion. But not even a single large-scale iron-smelting plant was set up. The Ministry of Industry and the National Resources Commission each intended to build such a plant. The Ministry soon abandoned its project, to leave this field of work to the latter authority. After much projecting, studying, discussing and designing on the part of the Commission, five years were gone, with nothing done except a plan on paper and a chosen site levelled off for buildings. Since the war, transportation conditions have been in a bad way, so iron and steel, the very sinews of the war, are still lacking. It is common knowledge that the late Manchu Empire began to build its navy, smelting works, shipyards and merchant marine at the same time as Japan, but because time was wasted, practically nothing was accomplished. Taking the lesson dearly to heart, we must confine ourselves within a shorter time-limit and strive for more definite results.

Railway transport and communications must go hand in hand with heavy industries, since development of the former will quicken the growth of the latter. Resources in remote parts of the country, such as the Province of Sikang, and the vast regions on the north and south sides of the Tien-shan, cannot be exploited without railways. Dr. Sun Yat-sen's " Industrial Development of China " lays down a scheme for building 100,000 miles of railways. This is too gigantic a task for us to complete within ten years, but at least half the plan ought to be realized within that period. In the past sixty years we have built only 10,000 miles ! Even India to-day has over 40,000 miles, while America has about 250,000 miles ; and most European countries, if we take their populations and territories into consideration, have also many times our mileage of railways.

What I have said about economic development relates merely to State enterprise. While the Government authorities occupy themselves with heavy industry, the people, as private producers, can proceed with the light industries.

4

Next, it may be asked : where are the colossal funds necessary for this tremendous development to come from ? Among well-informed economists, it is generally conceded that the required capital can come from two main sources. The domestic source is to be derived by the Government through the increase of taxes and national bond issues. The other source is foreign capital loans and homeward remittances from our overseas compatriots.

It is relevant to our purpose to evaluate the relative importance and availability of these two sources for our capital funds. It would, of course, be an ideal situation were it possible to draw on both the domestic and foreign sources at the same time. But suppose this cannot be done! Suppose it happens that both foreign loans and overseas remittances are not coming through according to expectation! Immediately after the war, China will have to begin again as a much poorer country than before. Where, then, can the Government find the necessary wherewithal to carry out the plans for industrialization? We must seek an answer to this question before our problem can find a solution.

There are people who believe that foreign loans will be freely and abundantly available to us after the war. Such optimism is entirely unfounded. It must be borne in mind that post-war reconstruction will occupy the attention of all the European countries devastated and occupied by Germany, as well as of defeated Germany herself, to whom some of the victor nations will have to give help. Not only Germany and Italy, but Britain too, whose ports and cities, factories and residences and lines of communications have been badly damaged, will need money for rehabilitation. The damage sustained by Soviet Russia during this war is much greater than that which was experienced during the revolutionary war; so Soviet Russia, too, will be in sore need of reconstruction. The United States of America will probably escape the ravages of war, but her industries, mobilized at present for war production, will have to be reconverted to civilian production as soon as fighting is ended. Thus, an enormous mass of war production machinery will be dismantled and replaced by equipment to produce peace-time commodities. The switch-over will cost a vast sum of money. Yet the only country capable of giving loans in the post-war world will be America, to whom all others will turn for help. Under such circumstances, we cannot expect too much from her.

Judging from present Lend-Lease practice, we can form a good idea of the situation. About half a dozen countries are receiving Lend-Lease aid from America now; we have so far received less than 1 per cent. of the total. When the war is over, the countries now subjugated by Hitler in addition to Britain and maybe Soviet Russia, will all compete for American assistance. Without straining our imagination, we can easily see that American loans to us will probably not be available in very large amounts; at least, not commensurate with our potential needs.

Another possible difficulty in utilizing foreign capital is the difference between our own economic policy and that of the other countries towards us. This may prove to be a formidable obstacle to securing American loans. In the past, enterprises run with capital raised from foreign loans, such as the railways, were uniformly controlled by foreign business interests. That amounts to inviting imperialistic infringement of our sovereignty in the form of economic dictation by alien capitalism, reducing the country to an economic colony of the Powers, and draining the resources of the land to fatten alien exploiters. Foreign commercial firms in China were formerly all registered only in their own countries, beyond the pale of Chinese law. Furthermore, there were extra-territorial rights, leased settlements, gunboats, foreign garrisons, etc., to protect their investments, if necessary by force. That is the reason why foreign capitalists were anxious to do business in China, operating electric light and power plants, building municipal gas and water-works, running 'buses and tramcars, manufacturing cotton fabrics and cigarettes. If we were to extend the same special privileges to foreign business interests after the war, it might not be a difficult matter to obtain loans from them. But we do not choose hereafter to be the servile vassals of foreign banker lords. The unequal treaties must be abolished without reservations. Foreigners coming to China will have to observe Chinese laws. A beginning to our assertion of rights has been made recently by the promulgation stipulating that Sino-Foreign joint enterprises should at least have 51 per cent. of native shares. As we are going to carry out economic policies in conformity with Min-Seng-Chu-I, foreign capitalists may feel that under the circumstances the profits are not attractive enough to induce their investments. Thus, the prospect of foreign capital investment in China is not bright.

As foreign loans will in all likelihood be niggardly, and homeward remittances of overseas Chinese negligible in proportion to our requirements, we shall have to depend upon domestic sources. We are still an agricultural nation. Any considerable wealth readily accessible to us immediately after the war can only come from the land. Our only recourse is for the Government to husband this wealth and devote it to national reconstruction.

An initial step has already been taken in that direction by the Government's food policy, which last year introduced the measures for collecting the land tax in kind, and for the enforced buying of grain by the State. The estimate of this year's grain crop levied by the State as land taxes and bought from the farmers is in all 80 million piculs, which is by no means an exorbitant demand when

compared with the total produce of the country. At the present
market price of $200 a picul, the whole will be worth $20,000
million. This revenue, collected from the land, is now contributing
to the State's war expenditure. When the war is over, the proceeds
from such collections will form a part of the State's capital fund for
economic construction. At present, grain collection has not yet
reached its saturation point ; the system employed in levying and
buying needs to be much improved. The share contributed by
most of the land-owning class is still too light, while self-cultivators
and tenant farmers are bearing too heavy a burden. Land-owners
as a whole have reaped large fortunes these last few years ; those
who collect their rent in kind, and receive grain amounting to several
hundred piculs a year, are living lavishly. Great landlords are
proportionally much better off than in pre-war days. Such conditions are diametrically opposed to the Min-Seng-Chu-I. We must
determine to eradicate such an irrational situation, and introduce
the needed agrarian reforms.

There is an age-old saying that all lands under heaven are the
king's, meaning the State's. We are going to make the statement
not merely a hollow saying, but a true description of actual conditions. Individuals may enjoy usufructs over lands granted them
by the State—that is, the rights of use and improvement, such as
cultivating them, and building factories and houses on them—but
nobody should be allowed to deal with them in business transactions,
least of all to speculate in them and get huge, easy, quick profits.
At present the big landlords are acquiring real estate, with their
unused and unusable wealth, from the small land-owners, mostly
self-cultivators, so that the wealth produced on the land becomes
harmful rather than beneficial to the nation. If they were to invest
their money in industries, it would be quite a different matter.
But instead of doing this, they buy more and more farm lands.
Land values are thus bolstered up ten, twenty, fifty times, but the
agricultural products gathered therefrom cannot be increased in
any such proportion. Hence, nine-tenths of the money sunk in
such investments is lying idle from the nation's point of view ; and,
what is worse, the cost of rice, and with it the general cost of living,
is artificially raised to incredible heights in order to pay proper
interest on their uneconomic investments.

This vicious process can only be stopped by prohibiting the
private buying and selling of land, and carrying out an economic
policy under the guidance of the Min-Seng-Chu-I. When self-
cultivators want land, the State can rent it to them on long lease.

By proper regulation and control, the evils of large concentrations of farm land in private ownership will be eliminated, while with the immense profits accruing from the public ownership of these very lands, the State can acquire the means to do immense good.

In prosecuting her first Five-Year Plan, Soviet Russia adopted exactly this method. Some fifty or one hundred or more self-cultivators were organized into a collective farm, and the Government levied a certain percentage of the produce as tax-rent. Thus, the wealth which the landlords had been getting before the Revolution was now concentrated in the hands of the Soviet Government. The capital for the first Five-Year Plan was almost entirely raised in this way. Of course, during the first two Five-Year Plans the Russian people suffered severely. Farm and other natural products, such as wheat, butter, lumber, oil, etc., had to be exported in exchange for machinery. We, too, have numerous products which can be exported : to name a few, there are tea, *tung* oil, cotton, soya beans, raw silk, hides, wool, tungsten, antimony, tin, and mercury.

5

Our future industries are broadly divisible into those run by the State and those operated by private interests. More precisely, there are four classes : those both owned and run by the State, those owned by the State but run by private interests, those owned by private citizens but run by the State, and those both owned and run by private parties.

The first class and the last are self-evident. The second includes those industries which the people are incapable of establishing by themselves for the time being ; the State sets them up and then leases them for operation to private parties. The cement, cotton-spinning and sugar factories of the province of Kwangtung before the war are good instances of this class : the machinery, as well as the factory premises, all belonged to the Provincial Government. The third class of industries includes those whose capital is raised by private subscription, but for lack of experience in management on the part of the promoters, the State takes over the task of operation. Further, certain industries may be run by the State and private interests in co-operation, certain others may be owned and operated by social groups and organizations, and still others by the local public bodies.

What I have just said is in accordance with the Min-Seng-Chu-I. For with the exception of communications and large enterprises connected with national defence, the people are welcome to engage themselves in all other industries. In the past, the Government wanted to do everything all at once, but since it was impossible to carry out all such projects, very little was done at all. Hereafter, the State and the citizens should severally and jointly participate in the country's economic development. However, industries privately run must be regulated and controlled by the laws of the land and the policies of the government ; privately gained profits should be used for further investments for the benefit of the nation. Since the nineteenth century, the shortcomings of rampant capitalism have been glaringly conspicuous in free competition : all industries being owned and operated by private interests, with the Government blind and deaf to the many abuses and evils. Capitalism has been the foundation of Britain's and America's social structure. But since the outbreak of this war, the Governments of these two countries have been exercising increasing control. It is our belief that after this war, measures of State control and State planning for larger ends will tend to be more thorough, gradually culminating in some form of State capitalism or Socialism.

In Soviet Russia, all private enterprises are prohibited. During the first two Five-Year Plans the Russians devoted their attention almost entirely to the heavy industries, with great and speedy success. But because the State wanted to do everything and all things, industries producing daily necessities were relegated to the background. The result was that manufactured goods for daily consumption became scarce and could not meet the people's demands. Conditions since 1938 have not been greatly improved. Now, when war is raging on the European front of that country, the lack must be more acute.

Soviet Russia has uprooted the institution of private production for profit. People are forbidden to make use of their money for personal gain. Those having a million roubles can only deposit their wealth in the State banks ; they cannot build factories or open hotels. Under such an economic policy, industries vital to national defence have done very well indeed, but those indispensable to the people's daily life are still very backward. It goes without saying that such an all-inclusive State monopoly is quite unsuitable for this country. With proper regulation and control on the part of the Government, the system of private ownership, or operation, or both, can be easily prevented from producing the ills inherent in unregulated free competition.

In the sphere of controlled economy the most advanced country is Nazi Germany. When Hitler came into power he did not confiscate the existing private industries, but put all the large enterprises under his iron control. The quantity of production, prices, wages of workers, profits, and their utilization for further investment are all dealt with by governmental rulings. Nominally, industries are still privately owned and managed ; in practice, there is virtually State ownership and rigid Government control. In war-time Britain and America also, State planning and direction of private production is being extensively practised. In the post-war world, the economy of advanced nations will not, as far as I can see, return to unrestricted and unplanned free competition as in the past.

6

With respect to the technical problems of our economic construction, they are concerned with questions of planning, execution, administration, inspection, and personnel. As for the first, a detailed plan should be made ready for devoting the first five post-war years to industries of national defence. The backbone of such industries is certainly the production of iron and steel. Our current output in this respect is less than 100,000 tons a year ; less than the daily or weekly output of the Great Powers. India's annual production is now 1·5 million tons, Japan's over 5 million ; Britain's 20 million, Soviet Russia's about 30 million ; and America's approaching 90 million tons. If we cannot increase our output by many times after the war, there can be no industrial reconstruction to speak of. Five years after the war is ended, at least 2 million tons a year should be produced ; another five years later, it should reach 5-6 million tons.

Next, oil production. Following a prospecting survey by a foreign oil company some twenty-five years ago, it was generally assumed that we have no oil-fields. But the facts turn out to be otherwise. Oil-fields have been discovered in at least three provinces. The deposits at Yu-men are found to be very rich. In our Sinkiang Province abundant oil is believed to exist. Oil is indispensable in industry and defence. Germany's ultimate failure will most probably be due to her exhaustion of this life-blood of her war effort. In our post-war plan, exploitation of oil resources will be an important undertaking, calling for expert technical handling.

Our coal resources are also abundant, though production is now less than 10 million tons a year. How to increase the output, and how much it should be increased each year, are all to be specifically laid down in a plan. Our Economics and Communications Ministries have both started planning, each within its own sphere, but their plans are not well co-ordinated. For the immediate carrying out of economic reconstruction after fighting is over, a comprehensive plan, with its details carefully wrought out and in close mutual relation, is urgently required.

Last, but not the least, is the problem of personnel—the training of engineers, technicians, managers. Our lack of specialists is a handicap which has got to be overcome before we can proceed. We cannot do with those few we have now, for they are only too few in number. We should take full advantage of America's Lend-Lease policy to invite her specialists to come and train our men. When Soviet Russia started her first Five-Year Plan, she hired some 20,000 to 30,000 German and 5000 to 6000 American specialists to do the work, as well as to train their own skilled labour. Recently, the Ministry of Economics has been planning to send for American specialists, but the number decided on is too small. More should be invited to come, as many as we can get and as America can spare ; their salaries could be paid out of our American loan.

In conclusion, there is no more time to waste, no more opportunity to lose. We may hope for the best after this war, but we must be speedily prepared for the worst. Peace might last for five to ten years only. Therefore, a minute and comprehensive plan must be ready at hand in order to avoid further delay when victory is won.

PART FOUR

To Victory

The Pacific War and China*

I

TO-DAY I am requested to speak before this Weekly Memorial Service. First of all, I wish to make an analysis of the news we have just received regarding Japan's declaration of war on America. At one o'clock this morning, Japanese bombers raided Pearl Harbour —an American naval base in Hawaii—Manila and Hongkong in succession. Simultaneously, Japanese troops landed in Thailand for the attack on Singapore. After actual hostilities had already begun the enemy declared war on Britain and America at 5 o'clock on the morning of the 8th. Japan's desperate gamble against fate, staking her whole destiny with one throw of the dice by embarking on a new aggression, has now become a fact. We should make a careful survey and acquire a clear understanding of this new international situation.

The American-Japanese talks were initiated in the spring of this year. Some months ago, there were in this country not a few people who feared that America might be unable steadfastly to maintain her traditional policy toward the aggressors, and that there might be a likelihood of her compromising with Japan. Especially since the visit to America of Kurusu, who was to assist Nomura in the American-Japanese talks, the general public was worried lest Japan might for the time being withdraw her troops from China, in exchange for a relaxation of American pressure, in order to preserve her Navy, which has not sustained any serious losses in the four years of aggression against China. This apprehension is quite reasonable, because the enemy's Navy is relatively intact in comparison with his land and air forces, over half of which has been destroyed during these years by our armed resistance. However, even if the enemy should withdraw his troops from this country, we should at most have a quasi-victory instead of a total one. With his Navy afloat and powerful, the enemy can blockade

* Speech delivered at the Weekly Sun Yat-sen Memorial Service of the National Government, Chungking, December 8, 1941.

our sea coast and invade our territory again at any time he thinks opportune. We are still exposed to the serious threat of re-invasion.

In our bid to secure foreign aid, our foremost task is to win to our side Britain and America, particularly the participation of the U.S. Navy, which can be effectively used to annihilate the Japanese sea power. Only with the ruin of the Japanese Navy can we win a real victory and the chance to reconstruct our country in the next twenty or thirty years. This is not only in the interests of China alone, but also of Britain and America. Without the heroic armed resistance of China, carried on for so long, Japanese land and air forces would have been much more powerful than they are. As a matter of fact, the enemy's land and air forces have been much wasted and weakened by China. His Navy, the only weapon left intact, cannot, of course, stand up against the joint attack by Britain and America. Now Japan has gone mad and thrown down all she has in hand in one desperate move against Britain and America. This, indeed, means the beginning of the end for the Japanese aggressor. The apprehension we felt a month ago is now over. To-day America, Britain, China and Soviet Russia have, in fact, united to strike back at the aggressors with their mighty armed forces.

2

What new exertions should we make in view of this favourable international situation? We cannot just sit down and admire others while they carry on the fight for us. We must consider how to intensify our war effort. In my conversation with friends in Hongkong recently, some advocated our declaration of war on Germany and Italy in order to bring about the united world anti-aggression front. They deplored the fact that the world anti-aggression struggles were not yet amalgamated into a global war, with Britain and Soviet Russia fighting against Germany and Italy in Europe, and China alone resisting Japan in the Far East. If the anti-aggression wars are not coalesced into an integral war, China, they fear, cannot secure a seat in the future world peace conference, but will only be allowed a voice in the future Far Eastern peace settlement. Their argument is quite reasonable. But I felt that the time was still not ripe for such action. We are too far away from Germany and Italy. If we declare war and cannot engage in actual combat with them, it will be only a token war. Moreover, Britain and America, for their own part, might not have wished to see China declare war on Germany and Italy, in view of the international situation then prevailing. This was my opinion a few months ago. Now, in view of the fresh international development, and particularly of Japan's declaration of war on America and Britain, I think the hour has come for our declaration of war on Germany and Italy.

Furthermore, there are three other reasons justifying this action. Firstly, Britain and America are our allies, and are now being attacked by Japan, our enemy. Germany and Italy are allies of Japan. From the standpoint of the coalition against aggression, we should, therefore, declare war on Germany and Italy. Secondly, a few days ago Britain declared war on Finland, Rumania and Hungary. Militarily, Britain's declaration of war on them created no change in the situation at the moment. However, Britain is the ally of Soviet Russia ; and Finland, Rumania and Hungary are the enemies of Soviet Russia. From the standpoint of allies, Britain has taken upon herself the responsibility to declare war. The situation existing between China and Germany and Italy is comparable to the above. In addition, there is a further reason : the Soviet-German war may possibly develop in a direction seriously unfavourable to us. The Germans may penetrate southwards into Iran and Iraq through the Caucasus, and co-ordinate the Japanese move in Burma, Singapore and possibly India. By then the conflagration of war will have spread to the Near East and India, and China would come into actual armed conflict with the German aggressor. Under these circumstances, and in view of the present grave international situation, I feel that we should formally declare war on Germany and Italy, in addition to our close collaboration with Britain and America in the fight against Japan. We must unify the world anti-aggression struggles into a common war under a united front. I hope we shall seriously study and discuss this matter. In short, our cherished desire for years, for the close co-operation between America, Britain, China and Soviet Russia, in order to defeat the Far Eastern aggressor-nation is now being realized. America, Britain, China and Soviet Russia must collaborate closely to the end, until the total defeat of the German, Italian and Japanese aggressors is brought to pass. From now on, the world will be under the joint leadership of America, Britain, China and Soviet Russia. This, indeed, deserves the redoubling of our efforts toward the common victory.

In regard to our military move in co-ordination with this new situation, it is now, of course, under the serious consideration of our supreme command, and there is no necessity for us to discuss it here.

3

What should we do internally to improve our position, in addition to our diplomatic effort ?   There are, I think, two points to engage our attention.   Firstly, to speed up the realization of the Min-Ch'uan-Chu-I system of local self-government in order to lay the foundation for democracy.   Secondly, to build up the Min-Seng-Chu-I system of national economy.   Why do I emphasize these two points ?   It is because we have already accomplished 70 to 80 per cent. of the task as laid down in Min-Chuh-Chu-I.   And we have completed three-quarters of the task of armed resistance to-day. Not only the concrete basis for our ultimate victory has been secured, but also the ultimate victory will be won in a short time from now. Upon her ultimate victory China will fully achieve her independence, freedom and equality.   In addition to our task of armed resistance, we must perform simultaneously the work of State-construction.

The first task of State-construction is to establish the Min-Ch'uan-Chu-I system of local self-government ;   in other words, to enforce the new *hsien* system, as promulgated by the National Government, by constructive efforts.   Only through the establishment of local self-government can we achieve democracy.   We must remember that in the first year of the Republic we had Parliament and Provincial Councils.   But were the representatives really elected by the people ?   The so-called democracy we had then was, in fact, bureaucracy.   How can we call ourselves a democracy when we know it is only a make-believe ?   Such self-deception will do us no good, nor will it mean anything to the people.

Min-Ch'uan-Chu-I, in which Kuomintang has professed to believe for scores of years, is the only road to real democracy.   The materialization of Min-Ch'uan-Chu-I means the achievement of local self-government, or, in other words, the realization of the new *hsien* system as promulgated by the National Government.   This appropriate local system has not been established in the past.   There was no real local self-government as the basis for popular elections. So-called voters' registers, compiled by district officials, were fictitious and fraudulent, therefore worthless.   Democracy will be but an empty term if we fail in the establishment of local self-government, for only through local self-government can the spirit of real democracy be promoted in this country.   According to the stipulations of the new *hsien* system, a great number of workers must be trained to meet the need for competent personnel.   The training will, of course, encounter many difficulties and cannot be accomplished at short notice. But we are not to abandon our task on account of hardships. To-day the important task for loyal supporters of democracy is primarily the popularization of local autonomy.

The second task of State-construction is the establishment of the Min-Seng-Chu-I system of national economy. It is, in other words, to ensure that the benefits derived from the industrialization of the country shall be enjoyed by the whole people instead of by the few. For the attainment of this goal the Government must employ every method to prevent private capital from injuring the livelihood of the masses. Secondly, it must proceed with the industrialization of the country by the speediest means. This is of the utmost importance. It means the appreciation of time. We must have a correct sense of time. In the past, we have always appreciated money, man-power and material power rather than the importance of time. However, money, man-power and material power can be regained after they are expended ; while time will never return after it is past. The greatest defect of our people and Government, in time of peace as in war, is, it seems to me, the careless waste of time.

What methods should we employ to achieve Min-Seng-Chu-I economy ? This is the simultaneous operation of State enterprises, public enterprises and private enterprises. All of them can, in my opinion, go hand in hand without jeopardy to one another. Some enterprises can be run jointly by the State and private individuals. Those enterprises which are beyond the capacity of private interest will, of course, be run by the State ; but those which are outside the financial power of the State at the moment can be run by private capital. In the past, there were some enterprises which were beyond the then financial power of the State, and which were, however, not entrusted to private hands. As a result, years went by and nothing was done. This loss is indeed incalculable. To-day we must make our crucial resolve to accomplish, for instance, in three years the programmes which have been scheduled for completion in five years. If both the Government and the people will keep such a resolution in mind, China's industrialization will even be more rapid than that of the Soviet Union. In the favourable international situation which obtains to-day we all must redouble our efforts to materialize before schedule the reconstruction of Min-Ch'uan-Chu-I and of Min-Seng-Chu-I, so as to co-ordinate our ultimate victory. Thus will San-Min-Chu-I China be fully built up in the shortest time possible.

Insurance of Victory*

I

SIXTEEN years ago to-day (July 9, 1942), our National Revolutionary Army marched northward from Canton to rid the country of its war lords and end their regime of chaos. Five years ago (on July 7, 1937), we formally embarked on this War of Resistance to beat off a malignant foe whose ambition is our ruin.

The magnificent achievements of our armed comrades since the launching of the Northern Expedition have not only been hailed with gratitude and admiration by the whole nation, but have also won the esteem of the world at large. Their gallant stand against the enemy's powerful military machine since the outbreak of this war has been acclaimed the world over as something wellnigh miraculous. For five years, for justice and liberty, their life-blood has been shed. In the rear, the toiling masses, and in the occupied zones, our helpless and hapless countrymen under the heavy yoke of the invaders, are also paying their full share of suffering in sweat and tears. With the exception of a misguided few, who have forsaken their mother-country and have turned traitors for lack of faith in this war and in the future of this nation, the millions in Free and Occupied China are one in their confidence that victory will ultimately be ours.

Prior to the 8th of last December we clung tenaciously, for four years and five months, to the unchanging determination that come what might we would fight to the bitter end. As to when that bitter end would be reached, or what would constitute the ultimate victory, people had a rather hazy notion. That state of uncertainty was ended with the outbreak of the Pacific War. Since then, we are no longer fighting alone. Nations that love liberty, peace and justice, whose aggregate populations constitute four-fifths of the world's humanity, come to stand by our side on the battle-ground to face this brutal foe, for us the most heartless and deadly of the three enemy Powers. A new guarantee of ultimate victory was given to us. We have a firmer, more concrete grasp of the realities now.

When we were fighting alone, the situation was generally viewed

* A speech delivered before the Staff College, Chungking, July 9, 1942.

in two different ways. First, if we could only recover the *status quo* before Lukouchiao, victory might be said to have been attained. Secondly, it was felt that we should restore the pre-Mukden state of affairs and bring the four north-eastern Provinces back to our fold, before we could lay down arms. But whichever view was held, all were dubious as to whether the fruits of victory could be enjoyed for long after they had been gained. We were afraid that four or five years after apparent victory the enemy would attack again. To be candid, our lack of confidence in this respect was well founded. Even though the enemy might be compelled to, or might voluntarily, withdraw his Army, he could still at any time launch a fresh invasion if his Navy remained intact and his war industries undamaged. Our victory would be worth nothing.

This apprehension appears all the more well grounded in the light of our failure during the Revolution in 1911. At that time, when the Manchu Empire had been overthrown and the Republic nominally set up, members of *T'ung-Meng-Hui*, the predecessor of the Kuomintang, thought the Revolution was accomplished. A class of depraved politicians and literati, to weaken the determination of the Revolutinary Party, then raised the slogan that with the rise of the Revolutionary Army the Revolutionary Party had vanished. These unscrupulous elements besieged and urged the Father of the Republic to hand over all political power to Yuan Shih-kai, arguing that Yuan's military force was well capable of unifying China, whereas the Revolutionary Army was no match for him. Consequently, Yuan soon declared himself emperor, after killing and banishing members of the party by batches. Though he was almost immediately ejected from his throne, the seed of turmoil was planted deep by him in the soil of the land, and for fifteen years or so the country was torn by civil wars between rival war lords, each striving for political supremacy over the others. The Republic, nay, even the country, was almost ruined. The historical lesson is : that in spite of its apparent success, the Revolution was, in fact, a failure. The painful experience we are undergoing now warns us likewise that our ultimate victory must be real, not illusory. There must be no repetition of the same mistake.

2

The enemy is more developed industrially than we are. His energy might have been considerably sapped by us during these five years, yet he could still recover more easily than we can, since we are an agricultural economy. Take Germany, for example. After the Versailles Conference, all her arms and military equipment were destroyed. Her merchant marine was handed over to the victors. She was prohibited from building an Air Force ; her Navy was limited to 100,000 tons ; her standing Army was not allowed to exceed 100,000 men. After 1918, she was kept under these restrictions for thirteen years. But in 1933, when Hitler rose to power, he announced Germany's resolution to remove the shackles of the Versailles Treaty. He began by re-militarizing the Rhineland, and commencing a programme of rearmament. In seven years the Germans grew so powerful as to attempt to regain their former dominant position in Europe by resorting to war. When they set out on the warpath three years ago, in two weeks they annihilated Poland, which had an Army of more than a million men. No country has been able to threaten Germany so far ; she stands her ground unchallenged up to the present. That is because the industrial basis of Germany was left intact during the last war.

From 1914 to 1918 Germany's war dead amounted to several millions, and the numbers of her wounded and maimed were grievously large. The loss of lives and materials cannot be regarded as trifling. But her industrial equipment remained untouched ; her means of production and lines of communications survived the war practically intact. For instance, the Krupp works at Essen did not suffer any damage at all. When I visited Germany in 1928, that gigantic factory was indeed not casting guns, but fabricating farming implements and motor-cars. Yet, in a few months, as soon as occasion demanded, it was changed back into a great arsenal. What Germany lacked after 1918 was raw materials and capital. The latter she obtained by raising foreign loans. With these funds she imported raw materials and operated her factories.

Beside her unimpaired foundation of industries, Germany also carried on a camouflaged military training with redoubled zest. You perhaps all remember that there was, some eight years ago, an old German general in Nanking by the name of von Seeckt. It was he who supervised the training of the German standing Army of 100,000 after the last war. He formulated a plan for making all the privates under him the officers of a future, greater Army. As the Versailles Treaty forbade the use of heavy arms, he made use of trucks and automobiles, mounted with boards in the form of mock tanks, for field practice in panzer warfare. In the absence of flying machines, gliders were employed to train several million high school and gymnasium students for pilot service in future fighting aircraft. Such motorless gliders numbered tens of thousands. Last, but not the least, the German people, efficient in organization and obedient to their Government's orders, were enrolled and organized into apparently civilian but actually quasi-military bands.

As Germany, after the last war, could preserve her production to tools and equipment, and her prople were well organized and trained, she was therefore able to restore her armed forces within a short period when time was ripe. So, if any other industrialized country could have its heavy industries maintained in good order, even though it might be defeated, and might have sustained heavy losses in men and materials, it could still speedily recover its fighting power.

The industrial potential of our enemy is by no means comparable to Germany's, but it is certainly superior to ours. If towards the end of this war we were left to fight him alone, no matter how hard we might try, we could neither destroy his industries nor defeat his Navy.

3

The enemy has been persistently harping on his old theme of economic co-operation with China. If he were clever, he might have called off the puppet shows in Manchuria and Nanking, withdrawn his Army of Occupation from this country, and arranged a peace with us before the outbreak of the European War, or even before his Pacific venture. It would have been hard for us to have resisted the temptation. At the peace conference, he could have simply and good-naturedly proposed economic co-operation with us, offering to buy up our cotton, iron ore and coal, if we would be good enough to let him operate our mines and run our textile industry with his capital and his engineers. As we are industrially backward, iron and coal, which we cannot consume in large quantities, would have to be sold to him as a matter of course ; while he, in turn, could pay for these by selling us cheap manufactured goods. Thus, our resources would become his, and China his virtual colony. We should then have no prospect of industrialization, and even our existing small-scale industries would all have been squeezed out of existence in competition with his. If we had fallen into such a trap we should have been done for.

Again, the enemy has also constantly reiterated that he harbours no dark ambitions in respect of our territory. He wants, it is lamely said, to establish the " East Asia Co-prosperity Sphere " with our aid, and drive out all Western influence. He has promised us the abrogation of extra-territorial rights and the restoration of leased settlements, provided his subjects can settle down wherever they please in our interior, and enjoy all the rights given to our own citizens, such as buying and selling landed properties, opening up mines, and erecting factories. These same rights would be extended to our citizens sojourning in Japan, as evidence of " mutual benefit on an equal footing." Theoretically, there is nothing wrong in this, but in practice, where would our people in Japan get their capital to buy lands and put up factories? But the Japanese in China would have a firm economic foothold ; they could, without difficulty, acquire large tracts of our lands. Thus the " benefit " is not at all mutual, and the " footing " quite the reverse of equal. If we had bitten upon such a bait, the war and all we fought for would have been irretrievably lost.

4

The risk of carrying on the campaign of resistance single-handed, and thus being forced into a treacherous peace, was fortunately ended by the 8th of last December. We are now fighting together with twenty-seven other nations. The Sino-Japanese War has become an integral part of the global struggle against terrorism and rapacity. What we could not accomplish alone can now be put into execution, by joining our efforts with those of our allies. Previously, for instance, we could only wait for the enemy to bomb us ; but now America and Britain and, in the future, Soviet Russia, will most certainly despatch squadrons of bombers to pound Japan proper, smashing the enemy's industrial plants into smithereens. In the five years since we exchanged the first shots with him, we could do nothing to his Navy. When the Battle of Shanghai was raging his obsolete old cruiser *Idsumo* was anchored in the Whampoo River ; we sent dive-bombers to blow it up, but failed to inflict serious damage. That was because our Air Force was, as it still is, weak, and we have never had a Navy. But since he made his big blunder seven months ago his loss of ships has been rapidly mounting.

In the Coral Sea Battle, with more than a hundred naval craft and transports, he originally intended to effect a grand-scale landing on the north-east of Australia. On the high seas he unexpectedly encountered the combined Naval and Air Forces of our American ally. The result was that three of his carriers and a number of transports were struck and sunk. The enemy tried to conceal his crippling losses afterwards. It is plain, however, that despite his attempts to minimize the defeat, the fact stands out that whereas he had sent an offensive force to invade Australia, tens of thousands of his troops had gone to fatten the sharks, and his ships strew the floor of the sea.

Again, in the Battle of Midway, soon afterwards, he sustained further heavy losses. The plan was to attack and seize the Hawaiian Islands, and drive the American Navy out of the Pacific. Midway is the island in the Hawaiian archipelago farthest from America and nearest Japan. The enemy fitted out a great armada, including many transports, five brand-new carriers, each with a flight of fifty to sixty aircraft, battleships, cruisers, both light and heavy, destroyers, submarines and other supplementary naval craft. This was a formidable attacking force, but it was discovered in time by American scouting planes, before it contacted Midway. So, bombers of the American Navy, as well as Flying Fortresses of the U.S. Army based at Hawaii, went busily to work to stop its progress. The battle lasted three days. As a result, four of the enemy's carriers were sent to the bottom, together with their load of two hundred odd planes ; two battleships were badly hit, one heavy cruiser was sunk and one damaged, while transports, destroyers, and other vessels were sunk or knocked out of shape. After these two telling blows, though his main Home Fleet is still intact and formidable, his aerial power on the open seas is decidedly hamstrung, as two-thirds of his carriers have been eliminated.

Modern naval warfare is waged simultaneously with aerial warfare. When war broke out in the Pacific, two of Britain's battleships, the *Prince of Wales* and the *Repulse*, on guard at Singapore to checkmate the Japanese Navy in case it should attack, were sunk by enemy air action for lack of protection in the air. After Rangoon was lost, an enemy Fleet steamed into the Indian Ocean, where two of Britain's cruisers were for the same reason air-torpedoed in the Bay of Bengal. The Coral Sea and Midway Battles have accounted for two-thirds of his sea-borne air force. No matter how many more dreadnoughts he may still possess, it is not likely, at least in the near future, that he would venture to send his Fleet into the open seas for another offensive. We can reasonably presume that he would let it hug the shores of Japan for protection from a land-based air force, moving about, say, no more than five hundred miles from the coast.

That being the case, the enemy's ocean transportation must be greatly affected. It is known that the total tonnage of his merchant ships is five and a half million ; he has lost eight to nine hundred thousand tons up to now ; about a sixth of the whole. But his annual capacity for building ships is only about forty-five hundred thousand tons, which means that it would take him two years to replace the loss suffered in half a year. The sinkings and damage during these six months are, in fact, ample enough to handicap his ocean transportation. His Army in the Occupied region is not receiving a proper amount of supplies ; and the rubber, oil, minerals, and other products of Malaya and the East Indies are not being sent back home in sufficient quantities to meet urgent demand. It may be safely predicted that the enemy will fail first on the sea.

What we have hitherto been unable to grapple with is now being undertaken by our great and powerful ally, the United States. Our duty to ourselves and the world, however, is not thereby cancelled, though it is to a large extent relieved. It remains for us, as our Generalissimo Chiang has said in his recent manifesto to the nation on the fifth anniversary of the war, to exterminate the enemy on the continent of Asia. This we shall do thoroughly.

After the utter destruction of the enemy's Navy, thirty to fifty years would be required for him to rebuild it. His present Navy has had a history of over seventy years. Germany's land and air forces have become matchless, after a new lease of life, in a few years only, but her Navy has not grown to any size comparable to the Fleets of the great sea Powers. A capital ship costs several tens of millions to build. The personnel manning it must be trained over a long period. British naval officers, for instance, begin their schooling when mere children. Therefore, after the liquidation of the enemy's Navy, the complete victory of our cause would be ensured.

Besides, there is another guarantee : that when the enemy is overthrown, not merely China, but all the United Nations as well, will conclude a peace with him. Although, alone among the Four Great Powers, Soviet Russia has not yet participated in the war on the Asiatic front, it is probable that she will do so in the not too remote future, once Hitlerite Germany is defeated. Then, after his defeat, the enemy will have to submit to the terms of peace agreed upon by us all. When that time comes, we shall rightfully demand the implementation of the Atlantic Charter, especially the last part of it, which prescribes the international assurance of peace by means of world-wide disarmament, beginning with the defeated aggressor states.

When the Charter was first published, the war in the Pacific had not yet started ; conceivably, that particular clause was not meant for Japan. But from our point of view, since the 8th of last December, the sole culprit in the Far East, whose armaments should be taken away, is Japan. We should be privileged and empowered to draw up the details of the procedure for disarming the enemy, because we have offered the longest and most stubborn resistance to his aggression, and best know the extent of his cunning ambitions.

After the last European War, the Versailles Treaty imposed severe enough handicaps on Germany. Unfortunately, as the League of Nations was too feeble to apply international sanctions (first against Japan, when Manchuria was invaded), this second world war became inevitable. We must take that lesson to heart this time. The criminal aggressors must be effectively, thoroughly and permanently disarmed. Meanwhile, the peace-enforcing mechanism should be made much more effective and powerful than before. Victor nations must be granted fifty years' recuperation. For half a century the desperadoes should be prevented from rebuilding their land, air and sea forces and war industries. While these warlike nations have been denied the weapons of war, technique will necessarily have made vast strides, and the trained cadres needed for using new weapons will be lacking. Also, with an unchallenged prestige of five decades, the international peace mechanism will be firmly established. In case it should still be insufficiently powerful, our own national defence should be well equipped, so that even our Navy would be sufficient to protect our coasts from invasion.

5

Dr. Sun Yat-sen pointed out to us, years ago at Canton, that China was a " hypo-colony," not even a semi-colony, being one degree lower than such colonial states as Annam and Korea, for we were under subjection of not just one master-state, but of a great many foreign Powers. Any other country in the world which had a semblance of force wanted to lord it over us ; second or third class Powers in Europe treated us with haughtiness and contempt as an inferior nation. Italy and Austria had their settlements or concessions in China. But now, after five years' hard fighting, our international status is much improved. We are no longer the object of ridicule and contumely from all and sundry. It can be foreseen that after our victory over Japan, China will command even greater respect in the world.

On New Year's Day last, China was among the first Powers to sign the United Nations Anti-Aggression Declaration. After the signing, President Roosevelt shook Foreign Minister T. V. Soong by the hand, to greet China as one of the Four Great Powers. The day before yesterday (July 7, 1942), the fifth anniversary of the " Seven-seven," radio-telegrams sped through the air from America and Britain to congratulate us and express admiration for our long, heroic struggle against aggression. Professor Harold Laski said that people all the world over who love their fatherland and love freedom must feel grateful toward China. This is no mere compliment. If China had not made her great and bloody sacrifice these five years, the world's situation would not be as it is to-day, and the United Nations would be worse beset with difficulties. That is undoubtedly China's great contribution to mankind. At the same time, for our own sake, we have emerged from the status of a " hypo-colony " to that of a strong Power, sweeping away once for all the jibe that China is " a tray of incohesive sand," and the shame of being a *declassé* State. We have, in other words, rediscovered ourselves, and thereby have regained our self-respect.

The underlying cause of this transformation is, of course, the resurgence of our national spirit. A nation, regardless of its size. when inspired by its determined will to survive, will never die. Sooner or later it will achieve freedom and independence, and will be accorded a position of equality in the family of nations. During these three years no fewer than fourteen states have been overcome by alien force. Among them, France was the strongest of all on the European continent after the last Great War. Her Army and Air Force were both of the first order. After 1918 she built up a system of satellite small states around her, as planets around a sun. They followed where her wishes pointed the way. She was the motivating force of the League of Nations. But in this war she capitulated in less than two months of actual fighting. She has now become an appendage of Hitlerite Germany. Her several million troops, her armaments and her Maginot line of defence, were all of no avail. The reason of her failure, in a word, is the decline of her national spirit during these twenty years. After 1918 the French people became surfeited with pride, softened by pleasures, reluctant to exert themselves, and fearful of sacrifice. Consequently, an Army of over two millions surrendered unconditionally to the enemy, and now the whole nation is in the grip of the foreign conqueror. Early in the opening of our Sung Dynasty, a thousand years ago, Madame Blossom, royal concubine of the King of Shu at Chengtu, left us a short poem lamenting a similar fate. The quatrain runs thus :

Over the walls my lord raised his white flag in alarm ;
Deep in the shade of the harem, how could I comprehend ?
A hundred and forty thousand warriors were bidden disarm !
Was there no single man who his honour wished to defend ?

In our case, the national spirit of our forefathers throughout the centuries is still inspiring us. It is crystallized in the San-Min-Chu-I. Also, after the arduous struggle of the Father of the Republic and our revolutionary martyrs, and with the able leadership of Generalissimo Chiang, the whole country knows that to defeat and expel the enemy is the most pressing task of the nation. All these factors have united us as one man to resist the well-prepared enemy and, as a result, we are to-day regarded as one of the Four Great Powers. From now onward we should no longer think of ourselves as a weak, inferior nation ; rather we must straighten our backs and shoulder our duties toward the world.

6

In March 1938 I went from Moscow to Czechoslovakia and paid a visit to President Beneš. China had then been in the war for only eight months. The Czechoslovak President expressed his admiration at our gallant resistance, saying that he thought in the beginning that we could last two or three months at most, but now, as we were able to hold on, China must be a strong nation in the future. At the end of my call, as I rose to shake his hand, the President apologetically corrected himself, and said to me, " But you are already a great Power ! " In November 1939 I left Moscow for the second time, when the war in Europe was over two months old, and Czechoslovakia had already been crushed by Hitler. President Beneš was staying in the suburbs of London, where I went to see him. He appeared very sad, saying that in spite of her million troops and some two thousand military planes, Czechoslovakia was too small to make any effective stand against invasion, so that she had been compelled, without any resistance, to submit to German absorption. He opened a map, pointed at the great expanse of our territory, and then said that considering our perseverance in carrying on the war against overwhelming odds in equipment, he had nothing but respect and admiration for us. Beneš is a great statesman in Eastern Europe. He had done much valuable work in the League of Nations. The defensive network in the Sudeten mountain region, adjacent to the Czecho-German border, was almost as strong as the Maginot line, yet the Czechs did not dare to oppose the German invasion. The small size of the Czech state was the real cause of the failure. Half a day's drive by automobile could take one through the whole country. In the light of what Beneš said to me, how we ought to love the almost boundless space, the great land " embroidered with mountains and rivers " that we call China, given to us by God !

Here I have another episode to relate, as told by the late Tang Shao-yi, showing that China was quite a powerful State before the Sino-Japanese War in 1894. He told me that China had just had some new warships built in England, such as the *Chen Yuen* and the *Chi Yuen*, commanded by Admiral Ting Ju-chang, which paid a visit to Japan some years before the outbreak of war in 1894. After they had cast anchor at Yokohama, Chinese marines went ashore, sight-seeing in the city, without taking their arms. As they sauntered through the streets, some minor incidents occurred, for it was apparent that they looked down on the local inhabitants. Admiral Ting notified the Yokohama police authorities that while the Chinese Fleet was in port and our marines had their shore leave, it would be best if the local police did not carry arms, in order to avoid possible trouble. The chief of police promptly conveyed the message to the Ministry of Interior at Tokyo ; the Ministry submitted the matter to the Cabinet, which met for deliberation. As a result, the Japanese Government circulated orders all over the country that during the period of the Chinese Fleet's visit to Japan all policemen should carry no arms.

Before 1894 the subjects of the Chinese Empire enjoyed extra-territorial rights in Yokohama and Kobe ; when disputes arose between our people and the local populace, our consular officers were generally able to protect their countrymen from unfair treatment. I do not mean that extra-territoriality is a thing at all to be desired by ourselves, even in Japan, but what I have just said serves very well to illustrate the fact that we were not so insignificant as to be browbeaten by every foreign country fifty or more years ago. After our defeat in the naval battle of 1894, Japan began to follow in the track of Western imperialism at China's expense. However, it may be predicted that China will assuredly recover from her prostrate position after the war.

We shall not only regain our status of fifty years ago—that of the senior State in Asia—but we shall also regain the leading and stabilising rôle in the Orient that was ours for more than two thousand years. Annam was for centuries part of our southernmost territory, and Korea looked up to us as her suzerain State. Siam, Burma and Sumatra were tributary to China for the last thousand years and more preceding the last century of the Manchu Dynasty. China was not covetous of their tributes, accepting them, in fact, only as marks of respect. We, in our turn, sent back by the hands of the envoys of those vassal states, a good many precious gifts, as tokens of benevolence. To be brief, history tells us that China commanded great respect, but was kindly toward her neighbours, the weak and small states around her.

When we have won the war, our greatness will again be restored. Our countrymen should therefore no longer harbour an inferiority complex, or abase themselves before people of friendly nations. Nor should we, of course, be puffed up with arrogant pride. In intercourse with the people of other countries, whether official or private, friendliness and frankness must be our rule of conduct. If it happens that a country friendly to us should be misguided in its dealings with us, or with one or more of our other friends, it behoves us good-naturedly but firmly to point out its mistake, thereby resuming our ancient rôle of " making conquest not by force, but with virtue." Even toward the enemy after his defeat, apart from preventing any further attempt at aggression, we should be unstinted in our offers of help and instruction, so as to enable him to take his place in peace and amity in the international society. On the negative side, we should not run into the pitfalls of imperialism ; on the positive side, we must practise the basic principles upon which our Republic is founded, and help to build up a brave, new world of justice and equality for all peoples.

The Question of Korean Independence *

MEMBERS of the Korean Provisional Government in Chungking approached me two days ago (on March 20, 1942), with the request that I should speak on the question of Korean independence, in commemoration of the twenty-third anniversary of the declaration of Korean independence, and the formation of the Provisional Government of the Korean Republic in China on March 1, 1919. I gladly agreed.

I

Many among us, too busily absorbed with our own problems and privations, have almost forgotten the long connection which existed between China and Korea. It is necessary to remind ourselves that the relations between our two countries, as fraternal States, have had a history of nearly forty centuries. Through all the vicissitudes of this lengthy period, there has never been ill-feeling between us. This is because we have a common culture. In the recent past, Japanese imperialism, in its attempt to deceive the Chinese people and lull us to sleep, has often drummed into our ears that the Japanese are of the same culture and come from the same race as the Chinese. The assertion of common culture and common race can be made without pretence when it is applied to the Chinese and Korean nations, for when Korea was still independent her culture was identical with ours. Since the Japanese annexation, however, the original and indigenous culture of the country has been ruthlessly suppressed and nearly destroyed by the hated conquerors.

We all know that during the past few decades, while China was beset with perplexities in respect of her international relations with the West, she had at the same time to resist the pressure of Japanese imperialism in the Orient. Japanese aggression against China, and her ambitious attempt to swallow the whole of East Asia, both began with Korea as a bridgehead. The Japanese landed in Korea in 1894, to intervene in the domestic affairs of that country. This precipitated the Sino-Japanese War of 1894-5. The Manchu regime in China, feeble and moribund though it was, made a

* Speech delivered at the Problem-of-Korea Forum under the joint auspices of the Society of Oriental Culture, Chungking Branch of the International Anti-Aggression League and the People's Foreign Relations Association, Chungking, March 22, 1942.

belated attempt to support Korea and save her national existence. This attempt failed disastrously. China suffered ignominious defeat. But in the Treaty of Shimonoseki it was still solemnly written down that the two signatories would undertake to recognize and respect the independence of Korea. The enemy hesitated to destroy Korea at once, because he was wary of intervention by the Great Powers. A decade later, in 1904-5, Japan again went to war, and this time defeated imperial Russia on the plains of Manchuria. With the signing of the peace treaty at Portsmouth, Japan was conceded the position of a Great Power. Korea became a Japanese colony without a word of opposition on the part of the other Great Powers. A Resident-General, in the person of Marquis Ito, was sent to Seoul, to complete arrangements for the final absorption of Korea as a part of Imperial Japan. The so-called union of Japan and Korea was formally announced to the world in August 1910. The last sovereign of Korea was shipped to Japan and demoted to the rank of an imperial prince. Thus died Korea.

With Korea safe in his pocket, the enemy's next move was to entrench his position in our three Eastern Provinces, which he grabbed unceremoniously in 1931. From Manchuria his tentacles were wriggling toward our metropolitan provinces in North China. Then came the Marco Polo Bridge incident of July 7, 1937. China, goaded beyond human endurance, struck back at the invader as a nation, and launched our war for total resistance. The heroic fight which we have put up during these few years has brought about a new world situation and transformed the outlook in East Asia. We have not only exposed the cunning and overweening ambition of the enemy to conquer Asia and dominate the Pacific, but we have also smashed and shattered his well-laid plans for world dominion. This is the opportune moment for us to once more take up the question of Korean independence. The time for the revival of Korea is near at hand. The enemy started out on his career of lawless aggression with Korea as his spring-board ; he shall perish with his ambitions for ever with the resurrection of Korea as an independent nation.

That Korea must and will regain her independence, thus bringing to a conclusion the enemy's attempts at continental conquest and global hegemony during these last four decades, is a historical inevitability. It is no mere wishful thinking.

Our Korean friends, in a manifesto just published on their memorial day, March 1, state that had the democratic nations been far-sighted enough, after the Russo-Japanese War, to take concerted

action with China in upholding Korea's independence, the world
to-day might not have had to fight this World War II. There is much
truth in what they say. The friendly Powers were then incapable
of looking into the distant future and perceiving the faintest sign
of the enemy's inordinate ambitions, so that the cause for the
present world disaster was implanted in the soil of Korea.

Concerning the criminal responsibility for letting loose this
cruel war upon the world, the European victims have invariably
pointed their fingers at Germany and Italy. This is not the whole
truth. It is, as our Chinese saying goes, "Knowing the one, not
knowing the two." The real, and not so remote, cause of this
world war was Japan's invasion and seizure of Manchuria in 1931,
and the failure of the League of Nations to apply sanctions, in
accordance with the League Covenant, to stop her. Germany and
Italy in Europe, knowing the League to be too feeble and impotent to
do anything, were encouraged to follow Japan's example, each embarking on an aggressive career of her own. The war in Asia and
the war in Europe coalesced and became World War II. Japan is
therefore the original culprit responsible for starting this world war.
But the remoter cause was the Sino-Japanese War of 1894-5, which
brought Japan into Korea as her overlord, culminating in the
complete suppression of Korean independence. In this historical
aspect, the survival or extinction of Korean independence has,
directly and indirectly, affected the relations of nations. Let us
hope that after this war world statesmanship will have learned a
lasting lesson, and acquired a keener vision, so that it will be able
to devise a better future for mankind under a more durable and
equitable peace.

2

But the realization of a durable peace is conditional, I am convinced, upon the recovery of national freedom for all peoples.
This point is generally conceded by enlightened statesmen of the
world to-day. President Roosevelt and Prime Minister Churchill,
when they issued jointly, in the name of their Governments, the
declaration now known as the Atlantic Charter, both recognized
the importance of restoring national freedom to peoples who have
lost it. The third point in their joint declaration says :

" They respect the right of all peoples to choose the form of
   government under which they will live ; and they wish to see
   sovereign rights and self-government restored to those who
   have been forcibly deprived of them."

There are people, however, who think and say that this principle of national freedom is confined in its application only to those European nations recently conquered and enslaved by Nazi Germany and Fascist Italy. This is tantamount to saying that the Atlantic Charter is a charter for European freedom, that it applies solely to Europe, and has nothing to do with the freedom of all non-European peoples. This, I think, is a perverse distortion of the real meaning. The two statesmen cannot have been so near-sighted as not to have envisaged the plight and the sufferings of peoples under subjugation and tyranny in parts of the world outside Europe, when they met to draw up this joint declaration.

In September 1941 Prime Minister Churchill, when addressing Parliament shortly after his return from the Atlantic meeting with President Roosevelt, did say that

" At the Atlantic meeting, we had in mind, primarily, the restoration of sovereignty, self-government, and national life of the states and nations of Europe now under the Nazi yoke."

But a few months later there was a radical change in the world situation. Twenty-six countries had signed the declaration of the United Nations at Washington on New Year's Day, 1942, subscribing " to a common programme of purposes and principles embodied in the joint declaration . . . dated August 14, 1941, known as the Atlantic Charter. . . ." The Atlantic Charter might have been regarded as a charter for European freedom when it was first announced in the summer of 1941. It has undoubtedly now become a charter for world freedom, embracing the destinies of peoples and states in all parts of the world besides those of Europe.

When victory is won, the United Nations will have to found a new world order, more equitable and more durable than the old one. Freedom and sovereignty will have to be restored to all conquered and enslaved nations and states. It is not enough to restore Czechoslovakia, Poland, France, Belgium, the Netherlands, Norway and the countries in South-eastern Europe. Nations and states in Asia, who have been deprived of their freedom and sovereignty during the past century or so, are equally entitled to reclaim and resume their rights to nationhood. Korea, for one, must recover her independence from Japanese repression. India, that great country to the south-west of us, must also sooner or later win its freedom from British domination. Other Asiatic countries, such as Burma, Annam and the East Indies, must ultimately be emancipated from alien bondage, whether white or yellow.

11

In the present war in the South-West Pacific, the only place where there has been protracted native resistance to the enemy invasion is the Philippines, where guerrilla fighting was resorted to by the native population in support of white American troops. This is practically a unique instance. Why is it so ? It is because America's policy toward the native Filipinos has been an enlightened and liberal one. Complete independence to the Philippines was pledged by the American Government to be enacted by law in 1946. In the meantime, and by way of transition, the Philippine Commonwealth, with its own President and Legislature, elected by popular suffrage, was inaugurated in 1935. The United States, almost from the beginning, when the sovereignty over the islands was taken over from Spain in 1898, have never treated the Filipinos as a conquered colonial people, but have regarded them as " the little brown brothers " to be protected and educated and trained for self-government and ultimate free nationhood. Such an enlightened and high-minded policy has undoubtedly endeared the American Government and people to the native population of the islands. The epic defence of Luzon proves this.

As an instructive contrast, let us consider the situation of the British colonies in South-East Asia. Malaya and South Burma, Hongkong and Singapore, were all lost in rapid succession, almost as soon as the enemy landed. In all these places there were no native armies to participate in their home defence. No native armed bands took part in repelling the invaders or gave help to save their old masters. Plainly speaking, this exposes the short-sightedness of Britain's past colonial policy in Asia. British colonial administrations did nothing during the long years to train and equip the native populations for home defence, or prepare them for autonomy and independence. British colonial officials have often been stupid people, who were wont to treat their native wards with an attitude of contemptuous superiority. Witness the beating and kicking of burden-bearers and ricksha-pullers by European police inspectors in Singapore or Hongkong ; and can anyone blame the native peoples under British rule for harbouring hatred of their white rulers ? With a native population both hostile and un-organized for home defence, the colonial garrisons were under a handicap from the outset. They capitulated quickly and completely the moment they thought the situation had become untenable. The utter failure of their colonial policy should prove both a bitter and helpful lesson to the British, who are in many ways, we must admit, a great and wise people.

The liberation of enslaved peoples, both in Europe and Asia, is not just a vain hope or a castle in the air. We of the United Nations must champion and promote the cause of all oppressed peoples, the weak and the small, to make their freedom and independence the chief objects of our anti-aggression crusade. Enlightened public opinion in America and Britain is already agreed on this point.

It is unthinkable that world statesmanship is so bankrupt that a just and rational solution of this problem of freedom for the small and weak nations cannot be found when victory comes. If pre-war imperialism should resume its evil work, and if national freedom for all enslaved peoples cannot be realized in the post-war world, then the end of this war will simply mean the beginning of preparations for a third and greater war. No man in his senses would want that to happen. It is my conviction that mankind is yet capable of living in peace and goodwill under the guidance of a highly practical though lofty ideal—that of freedom and equality for the weak and small nations.

3

Yesterday (March 21, 1942) I read an article in the daily Press in which there was a statement to the effect that colonial and backward nations attempting to form new independent states by means of nationalist struggles fail of their aims, for the opportune time is past. This is a flagrant misstatement. The War of Resistance in our country is a war for national liberation ; therefore it is a nationalist struggle in the strictest sense of the word. The fact that we have been fighting for five years must be attributed to the inherent strength of our nationalism. Our victory will be a victory for Chinese nationalism, the victory of our aspiration to be a free and independent nation-state. Soviet Russia's heroic struggle against the invasion of Hitlerite Germany is not merely a struggle between Socialism and Capitalism. It is also a patriotic war for national liberation and the survival of the Russian fighter's fatherland. It is therefore also a nationalist struggle for freedom. When this present world war is fought to its logical conclusion, and victory is secured, it will result in the survival of China and the U.S.S.R. as free and independent States. It will also result in the restoration of the conquered nations to freedom. How can we say that the opportune time for colonial and backward peoples to recover their freedom and form independent states by means of nationalist struggles is over ?

It is true that this great war was first started by the newly-risen forces of Japanese imperialism, greedy for colonies on the continent of Asia. This movement for imperialist expansion was later taken up by the Axis partners in Europe, with the aim of forcing a redistribution of natural resources at the expense of the great colonial empires of Britain and France. This World War II, like its predecessor, had its origin in imperialism and imperialist rivalry. But the present situation is quite different from that of the last great war. The present war is influenced by two great factors, China and the U.S.S.R. : both are fighting to establish a new order under which their national freedom and existence shall be secured against lawless aggression on the part of their neighbours. Securing their own freedom will necessarily mean guarding the freedom of all nations in the post-war world. With these two mighty forces on the side of human justice and world freedom, mankind stands a chance of avoiding its past mistakes and escaping from the blind alley into which humanity had stumbled in the pre-war world. I am sure that with the conclusion of this war, we shall see all the conquered, enslaved, crushed and oppressed nations of the world resurrected, one after another, as independent sovereign States. How, then, can we say that the time for the erection of new States by nationalist struggles is over ?

In the post-war world there will still, of course, be great and small nations and states of various sizes. China, U.S.S.R., the U.S.A. and India, for example, will continue to be countries of continental dimensions. Britain, together with her overseas dominions in Canada, Australia, New Zealand and South Africa, will remain a great, world-wide commonwealth. These will be the Great Powers in the post-war world, and must take the leading rôles in the conduct of world affairs. Some of the resurrected and newly risen States will perforce be smaller entities. But between all nations, irrespective of their size and strength, there should be equality and mutual respect of each other's national sovereignty and territorial integrity. Then equality and freedom among the nations will be realized. It is by no means necessary that all should be great Powers before equality can be established.

Next in importance, new international organs must be set up to handle economic as well as political matters of common interest and concern. New ways and means will be needed to resolve new problems and difficulties as they arise from time to time in the course of the development of international relations. It will then be possible to realize the common ideals of freedom from fear and freedom from want, as stated in the Atlantic Charter. I hold that these ideals, freedom and equality among nations, and security and abundance for all peoples, are the universal demands of mankind, which must be secured and safeguarded once for all as the great prizes of this war against aggression and tyranny.

4

Finally, let us consider the present and future position of Korea and the war against aggression in the Far East.

In the Pacific, the common enemy of the United Nations is Japan. In our joint effort to defeat Japanese imperialism, the 25 million people of Korea should be given a great part to play as they occupy a highly strategic position in the enemy's rear. The Koreans have lost their independence now for almost thirty-five years, yet the pain and sorrow of their national extinction as a free State are still fresh in the memory of the older generation of Koreans, who must still cherish " enmity and hatred deep as a sea of blood " against their oppressor ; while the younger patriots, inspired by the struggle for world freedom in this great age, and urged on to continue the fight for national revival by their elders, should be ripe for organized risings to overthrow the enemy. At this juncture, helping the Korean patriots in their mission will mean a great contribution to the winning of the war. The enemy's collapse may be hastened, and the duration of the war may be shortened. We should therefore render aid to the Korean people, helping them to rise in armed revolt by all means at our disposal.

To give aid to Korean independence, one thing we can do immediately is to declare our recognition of the Korean Provisional Government, which was first formed in 1919 at Shanghai, simultaneously with the declaration of independence by Korean patriots. This Korean Patriot-refugee Government was, in fact, recognized by Dr. Sun Yat-sen in the spring of 1921, when he assumed the presidency of the Southern Revolutionary Government in Canton. After this, and up to the time of our national resistance, we did not give much aid to the Koreans, apart from our sympathy, because the time was inopportune, and we were powerless to help them. Now the moment has come to help them, and we are in a position to do so. With the outbreak of the Pacific War we are no longer fighting the enemy alone, but side by side with twenty-five other united nations. The ultimate defeat and complete expulsion of the enemy are no longer in doubt.

China's last attempt to support Korea was frustrated by our defeat in the war of 1894-5. In another two years, it will be the fiftieth anniversary of this war. I think we shall commemorate our old defeat with a great victory, when Imperial Japan will be so thoroughly and decisively beaten that it will pass out of existence for ever, nevermore to menace us again. That day of victory will see the restoration of Korean independence with the retrocession of Taiwan, the return of Talien and Lushun, and the whole of the North-East to China. This is no longer an empty dream. But we must be resolutely determined not merely to rest satisfied with the recovery of all our own lost territories, but further, to carry on the war until the hated enemy is driven out of Burma, Siam, Indo-China, the Malay Peninsula, and all other lands in South-East Asia. General Stillwell told Chinese journalists in the war-time capital the other day that the final war aim of the United States is to have the U.S. Army march into Tokyo side by side with the Chinese Army. The defeat of the enemy and the " march to Tokyo " is now the common objective of the United Nations. Let us therefore no longer doubt the possibility of Korean independence after the war. We must help them to achieve it by first according recognition to their Provisional Government.

The Korean Provisional Government has been leading the revolutionary struggles of its people for the past twenty-three years. It has represented the Korean nation ever since its formation. There are, of course, different parties among the Korean patriots at home and abroad, but there is no other Provisional Government claiming to speak for the nation. Thousands of Korean *émigrés* in America, in their recent mass meetings, have pledged their support to this Government. Korean residents in the Soviet Far East and in our North-Eastern Provinces also uphold this Provisional Government. All this indicates the united attitude of the Koreans. It is therefore up to China to take the lead in giving recognition to this Korean Provisional Government, so that other friendly Powers may do the same later. This move will tend to strengthen the hands of the Korean patriots in their struggle for liberation.

I want to say a few words more to our Korean friends present. Let them rest assured that China will never turn imperialistic. This is borne out by our past relations. When the common enemy is driven out, our two countries must act in close collaboration to safeguard peace and security on the continent of East Asia. We are bound by ties of race and culture, as well as by geographical propinquity. These ties must be cemented closer after the war, when an independent Korea will take her rightful place in the building of a better and happier world.

Final Victory and Peace Terms *

I

FROM the outbreak of war at Lukouchiao on July 7, 1937, to the outbreak of war in the Pacific on December 8, 1941, was a period in which we fought the Japanese alone. During this period, our strategy was to draw the enemy further inland, so as to waste his man-power and material ; that is, in other words, a strategy of trading space for time. In the political field we had been following a two-fold policy : internally, to make use of the opportunity offered by the War of Resistance to speed up the work of State construction, that is, to establish a firm basis politically, economically and socially, for a San-Min-Chu-I republic, so as to reinforce our military strength for the winning of foreign sympathy and help to a state of active co-operation for the annihilation of the common foe.

Strategically, we accomplished our task during the first period in which we fought alone. The Japanese thought that China could be crushed within three months of the outbreak of war. Not only had the enemy failed utterly to crush us, but further, because of his inability to settle the so-called " China Incident," he had to undertake further suicidal commitments. Thus, he declared war on the United States and the British Empire.

Politically, we have also achieved much in internal reconstruction. In the field of political reforms, the nation-wide adoption of measures for the speeding up of local self-government and the participation of people in local and central government are indications that the principle of People's Rights is being put into effect. Administrative efficiency has been gradually increased as the Government takes in more trained men for various posts. In the field of economic and social reconstruction, similar accomplishments have likewise been achieved, such as the development of State-owned enterprises, the establishment of Government organs for national economic control, and the increase of production in the rear. In the field of foreign relations what we have achieved is clear to all and hardly needs recalling.

Yet, in spite of all these achievements, much remains to be done. We are still far from the full realization of the principle of People's

* An article commemorating the fifth anniversary of the outbreak of war at Marco Polo Bridge, published on July 7, 1942.

Rights. Official corruption has not been completely stamped out, and the rule of law has still to be firmly established. In the field of national economy there has been a tremendous increase in our national expenditure for the prosecution of the war, and yet the tax burden of our people is still far from being equally shared by the rich and poor alike. While peasants and consumers generally have been taxed almost to the limit, large landowners, property-holders, and particularly war profiteers, have not as yet contributed their fair share to the national treasury. With these people, much still remains to be done by the efficient enforcement of the various measures of direct taxation. As to the acute price problem, and the maintaining of some kind of an equilibrium between supply and demand of commodities, much also remains to be done.

2

Since last December 8 our War of Resistance has become a part of the global war, and China has become one of the four main pillars of the United Nations, which consist of some twenty-eight nations, as a result of the Japanese attack on the United States, the British Empire, the Netherlands East Indies and Australia, with the outbreak of war in the Pacific. With the changed international situation, we should look forward to the changed future which lies ahead with new hopes and understanding.

In the period during which we fought the Japanese alone, our greatest hope had been to immobilize the millions of Japanese soldiers sent to China by our poorly equipped fighting forces, at a sacrifice several times greater than the losses which we could inflict on the enemy. When the enemy had come to realize the difficulties he had to encounter, and the man-power and material which he was wasting in his war against China, he would then either voluntarily or involuntarily withdraw his troops from China, and restore to us the territories once under his occupation. Should we be able to carry on our single-handed resistance to a finish, and should the enemy be willing to withdraw his troops from China, and ready to negotiate peace with us, the most advantageous terms we could have obtained under the circumstances would have been the restoration of the *status quo ante* July 7, 1937, or, at most, the restoration of the *status quo ante* September 18, 1931. We should have been quite happy and willing to conclude peace with Japan if she had restored to us the four North-Eastern Provinces and had withdrawn her troops from our coastal areas and various points inland.

We should then have imagined ourselves as having won the final victory. But there is one point to consider. Although the enemy would by then have suffered severely as regards his Land and Air Forces, his Navy would still have been intact. He would still have been able to maintain his naval supremacy on the Yellow Sea, the East China Sea, and the South China Sea. If the enemy had insisted on only one condition at the peace parley, that of Sino-Japanese economic co-operation, and had been willing to make other concessions, what should we have done should we have accepted his terms or not? If we had rejected them, although his troops would by then have been withdrawn from China, he could have sent them back in a day or two, and our coastal ports would again have been under enemy blockade. If we had accepted them, even though the enemy might have suffered military defeat, he could still conquer us politically and economically. What we might have regarded as final victory would in the end have been nothing but defeat. So, fighting alone in our War of Resistance against Japan, we might have achieved all kinds of successes, save only the destruction of the enemy's Fleet. And as long as the Japanese Navy remained intact we could not possibly have won a secure victory ; and what peace we might have concluded would not have been worth the paper on which it was written.

But since December 8, 1941, our formerly single-handed resistance has become part of the common struggle of the United Nations against Japan. What we could not possibly achieve when fighting alone can now be achieved by the common efforts of the United Nations. Although the enemy succeeded in capturing one strategic point after another in the early months of the war, his weakness lies in his inability to replace his tremendous losses in warships and merchantmen. According to a London report dated June 18, 1942, 2 enemy battleships, 6 aircraft carriers, 19 cruisers, 28 destroyers, and 15 submarines have already been sunk ; while the figures for other damaged ships were not included.

In the first half year of the war the enemy has already sustained a loss of 20 per cent. of his Navy and Merchant Marine. Continuing at this rate, the precious possessions on which the enemy relies, i.e. the Imperial Japanese Navy and his Merchant Fleet, would be completely wiped out in a short time. When that day comes, the enemy troops on our soil would look eastward across the sea to the land of the Rising Sun with a sigh, and face complete annihilation.

3

That Japan is bound to go down in defeat in this war goes without saying. When victory comes, China wishes to recover not only all the territories under enemy occupation since September 18, 1931, but also those which were taken from us by the enemy after the first Sino-Japanese War of 1894-5. That is to say, China should recover such territories as Taiwan (Formosa), and the Penghu Islands (Pescadores), which Japan took from us as a result of the first Sino-Japanese War ; Talien (Dairen), Lushan (Port Arthur), and the South Manchurian Railway, which the enemy seized at the end of the Russo-Japanese War in 1905 ; the four North-Eastern Provinces of Manchuria and Jehol, which have been under enemy occupation since September 18, 1931 ; and all the territories held by the enemy since July 7, 1937.

Besides the recovery of those parts of our domain which have been under enemy occupation, we might, in our desire to maintain peace and security in the Far East, state our peace terms as follows :

(1) Japan to surrender to China all her remnant of warships still afloat ; completely to demilitarize and dismantle all fortified zones and naval bases ; to close down all training schools for the Navy and, during a period of fifty years, to be prohibited from building any naval vessel.

(2) The Japanese Air Force to be completely liquidated ; all remaining military aircraft to be dismantled ; all aircraft factories to be demolished ; all aviation schools to be closed down, and during a period of fifty years, Japan is not to be allowed to produce any kind of aeronautical equipment.

(3) The Japanese Army to be completely disarmed ; all arsenals to be dismantled ; all schools of military training, from staff college down to infantry school, to be discontinued ; and during a period of fifty years Japan is not to be allowed to have any organized army, except for the maintenance of domestic peace and order ; she may have a police force.

(4) While withdrawing her troops from China, Japan to be held responsible for keeping all properties, public and private, Chinese as well as foreign, intact and in good condition, to be taken over by Chinese authorities.

(5) Japanese emigrants who have come to China since September 18, 1931, all to be repatriated.

(6) Japan to withdraw from Korea and recognize and respect Korean independence.

(7) Japan to surrender to China half of the remnant of her Merchant Fleet.

(8) Half the Japanese metallurgical and steel works, shipyards, machine-tool factories, cotton and paper mills, cement works, chemical fertilizer plants, etc., to be dismantled and their machinery and equipment shipped to China for re-erection.

(9) Half the collections of Chinese and Japanese books, and all those in other foreign languages in the Japanese universities and libraries, to be sent to China. Half the laboratory equipments in Japanese universities and research institutes should also be sent to China.

(10) All Chinese antiques and works of art which have a bearing on Chinese history and culture, and Chinese arms, equipments and utensils captured by Japan since the first Sino-Japanese War, in the collections of Japanese museums or in private collections, to be restored to China.

(11) The Japanese Press is not to be permitted to publish anything which may incite anti-Chinese feeling among the Japanese, and the Japanese Government is to be held responsible for destroying all such anti-Chinese literature published and in circulation before the peace settlement.

(12) In order to ensure the faithful execution of articles 1, 2, and 3, the United Nations are to despatch an Allied Army of Occupation to Japan, to be stationed at Tokyo, Yokohama, Kyoto, Osaka, Kobe, Nagoya, and other important places. The expenses for the maintenance of such an Allied force to be borne by the Japanese Government.

The above terms may appear to be too idealistic. To-day, however, they are feasible. All depends, of course, on our war effort and that of the United Nations. Victory lies ahead of us.

New Strategy to Destroy the Japanese Pirates *

I

CHINA has been fighting for six long years. Our people have endured unbelievable hardships and sufferings in their struggle. But through all this their faith in ultimate victory has not waned, and remains unshaken. During the last year the armed forces of the United Nations have turned the tide of battle. The immortal victories of Stalingrad and North Africa have been recorded. Our own troops have defeated the Japanese in Western Hupeh. These are all proofs that the final victory of the United Nations will be sure and certain.

Axis propaganda used to deride the inability of the Democracies to conduct a total war. This propaganda has been given the lie by events. The peoples of the Democracies are performing deeds of heroism at the front and in the factories in defence of their liberties and their national existence as free men. The history of the present century will be written in letters of gold as a record of the complete victory of Freedom and Democracy over Fascism and Tyranny.

Victory will be ours. But we still have much to do, and it is impossible to predict when and how victory will come. However, the main task of each and every one is to hasten the coming of victory by redoubling our efforts in the prosecution of the war. In war the human factor is most important, and any unnecessary prolongation of the war may bring about unexpected difficulties. It is true that to the Chinese people the demands of war seem unending, but they are still ready to gird up their loins and endure privation and suffering, so long as these are necessary for the final and speedy victory. Time, up to now, has been our friend, but there might be a moment when it would come to the assistance of our enemies.

2

The recovery of Burma may not by itself appreciably shorten the war in Asia and the Pacific. This can readily be understood because of the climatic limitations of that theatre. In Burma campaigning is handicapped by the monsoon. Operations can

* Commemorative message on the sixth anniversary of the War of Resistance against the Japanese aggressor, July 7, 1943.

only proceed between October and May, during the dry season of the tropics. Under the most favourable auspices Allied preparations for a campaign in Burma cannot be completed before October of this year (1943), and a full-scale offensive may begin during the last months of 1943.

Burma has already become a powerful base for the Japanese, and they are in a position to draw large supplies and reinforcements from Malaya, Thailand and Indo-China. The recent experiences in North Africa have shown that for the reconquest of Burma equally large forces will be needed, and the fighting will be both long and hard. The next monsoon may be upon us before the enemy is liquidated and Burma cleared.

The purpose of the reconquest of Burma is to reopen the Burma Road for the flow of supplies to China, in order that the Chinese armies, who have again shown their effectiveness in the victory of Western Hupeh, can take the offensive to drive the Japanese into the sea. Thus, the first task will be the repair of the railways and roads in reconquered Burma, and the concentration of motor and water transport in large quantities. This alone can hardly be completed until the winter of 1944.

In the past the transport capacity of the Burma Road was limited. To equip the Chinese main armies sufficiently to assume the offensive we shall require at least a million tons of war materials. On the basis of what has been done in the matter of transport it would take five years to bring these supplies over the road, so that the offensive campaign could not reach its climax before 1949.

If we aimed at a less ambitious programme, and brought in 500,000 tons before starting our offensive, three years would be required ; it would still be 1947 before our troops would be able to take the offensive. If these premises are correct, the supplies coming up the Burma Road may be too slow and too scanty.

I want now, urgently, and at the same time cautiously, as becomes a layman, to suggest certain points concerning the best strategy for the defeat of Japan.

At the Casablanca Conference it was decided that Hitler should be defeated before Japan. This strategy caused uneasiness among the Chinese people. We felt that this was tantamount to saying that the defeat of Japan would have to wait a long time. Among thinking people in Great Britain and the United States there was also uneasiness, as it was rightly considered that the delay would give Japan time to dig in and consolidate her gains. The recent Washington Conference between Mr. Churchill and President

Roosevelt seemed to have brought the required modification in the previous line of strategy, although at the conclusion of the Conference the statement by the White House spokesman consisted of only one sentence.

Mr. Churchill, in his speech before Congress, gave an indication of a real global strategy, which was an improvement upon the Casablanca decisions. He said that the greater part of the United States armed forces is being concentrated in the Pacific. This, with the recapture of Attu and the preparations for the Burma campaign, gives us a more encouraging picture of the future. It goes to show that the leaders in conference have realized that to leave Japan even temporarily alone would be to present the Japanese with " time " in return for nothing, not even " space." Also, it shows that the island-to-island strategy, coupled with an assault on Burma, would not be strong enough to force the unconditional surrender of the Jap pirates.

If our strategy is not able to bring about the defeat of the main strength of the Japanese Army and Navy, and also to cut the long lines of communications between the home base and her newly acquired possessions in the South and South-West Pacific, we shall not be able to smash the Japanese war machine and blast it out of the war. To continue the past strategy would mean a long war of attrition. It cannot bring us to the heart of Japan, and cannot bring the Japanese main Fleet to battle. This means that the initiative is still in the hands of the enemy, and while we are nibbling at the outer defences the Japanese behind these defences will be strengthening themselves against the time when they will be ready to resume the offensive, either against India or Australia, or even against the American mainland. Such strategy is contrary to the accepted principles of military science.

There are indications at present which give us a less pessimistic picture. If our Allies are ready to employ their increasing might, both military and productive, more effectively and with greater boldness and decision, we can employ an entirely new strategy, which will result in gaining our three main objectives in the Pacific War : namely, to force the main Japanese Fleet to give battle, to cut the lines of communications between Japan and the outer possessions, and to open the front door of China to an adequate flow of materials for the final offensive against the Japanese on the Asiatic mainland. Only by this can we bring the enemy pirate empire to total destruction.

This new strategy, which is here presented for consideration, depends very largely on the United States, which possess the greatest strength in the Pacific, and which are shouldering as heavy a responsibility for the operations in the Pacific as we are for the operations on the Asiatic mainland. The tactical plan for carrying out this strategy is at once to concentrate large sea, land and air forces in the Central Pacific, with Hawaii as a base. This expedition can proceed due West across the Pacific and cut a sea lane by force right to the front door of China.

The objectives of the task force would be : (1) To sweep the Jap pirates off the outer ring of defences in the Central Pacific : from the Marshalls, Carolines, and Marianas. This aims at the recapture of Wake, Guam, and Luzon, which were lost after Pearl Harbour, and the assault upon and capture of Formosa. (2) To entice the Japanese main Fleet—on which depends the piratical destiny of Japan—to give battle. Its defeat and sinking would leave the garrisons in the South and South-West Pacific unprotected and unsupplied, since the lines of communications would be cut. (3) To act in co-ordination with Chinese forces for the recapture of Canton and Hongkong. Supplies could then be brought direct to the Chinese mainland in greater quantities by merchant ship convoys.

If the strategy is adopted it may result in the war against Japan being over within two years. President Roosevelt has stated that Tokyo can be reached by many roads. This road from Hawaii, due west, seems to be the straightest road to Tokyo.

The main feature of the war in Asia and the Pacific against the Japanese is an exact and minute discernment of the proper economy of forces, and the co-ordination of assault, from Attu through Paramushiru, from New Guinea in the direction of Luzon, from Burma and from China, with the main, overwhelming striking force from Hawaii.

Assuming that the European War will last two years, the concurrent conduct of the war against Japan would mean the simultaneous conclusion of the global war.

3

While we extend ourselves for victory, we must pay attention to the future peace more carefully than at the conclusion of the last great war. The main purpose of this war is the defeat of the enemy and the laying of the foundations of a lasting peace. Victory alone does not necessarily bring peace. In the last war Germany was completely defeated, but that did not prevent her from recovering, to become the strongest aggressor nation in this war.

It is not true that at the Peace Conference in Paris the victorious States did not foresee the recovery of Germany. The Versailles Treaty imposed great limitations upon Germany. Still, under Hitler, she was able to let loose upon a peaceful world a new and more terrible war. What were the reasons for this? Firstly, the Allies did not destroy the German military machine; secondly, the Allies did not disarm Germany industrially.

To reconstruct peace in the Far East we must remember these lessons; we must smash the Japanese military machine and disarm Japan industrially. To do the first, it is necessary fundamentally to eradicate militaristic education in Japan. The Japanese people have given the world the impression that they are a war-like and war-loving people. But the love of war is not necessarily an inborn characteristic of the Japanese. It is the result of education. Mr. Grew, in his book, *Report from Tokyo*, states : " . . . it was a common sight in Japan . . . and a startling one to recently arrived Americans . . . to see little fellows scarcely big enough to walk togged out in military caps and playing military games. Anyone who passed a school yard would be even more startled to hear the blood-curdling yells coming from the throats of twelve-year-old-boys as they charged across a field with real guns and bayonets, and in a manner so realistic as to be chilling . . . from early childhood Japanese children were being reared for war, and reared with the thought that their greatest good fortune would be to die on the field of battle." It is through such an education that Japan has become a menace to the world.

To carry out this destruction of the Japanese military machine it is necessary that the Japanese officer cadre and the military caste be relentlessly destroyed. Granted that the Japanese are a warlike people, they would then have no military leaders to guide them. The officers of the Japanese Army have shown themselves brutal and cruel arch-criminals, and as a body they should be tried and dealt with. Above the rank of major-generals they should be shot ; above the rank of lieutenants, they should be interned or imprisoned for life ; the non-commissioned officers should be dispersed to other countries and condemned to hard labour. In this way the military caste and cadre will be separated from the people at home. There may be persons who will object to so drastic a punishment for these war criminals, but we have to remember what the Japanese have done to millions of innocent men, women and children in the devastated and conquered areas. We should grieve for these victims and also for the helpless war prisoners, including the United States Army airmen who heroically bombed Tokyo, whom the Japanese have murdered in cold blood. This treatment of war criminals is both rational and just. As the Chinese saying goes, " Magnanimity to the enemy is cruelty to your friends."

To carry out the industrial disarmament of Japan it is necessary to demolish whatever is left of the Japanese war industries, the heavy industries, and the machine-tool industry. If these plants are not destroyed they should be sent to areas devastated by the Japanese pirates as part of the reparations. There should also be a limitation of Japanese light industries. By this I do not mean that Japan should be forced to return to an agricultural economy ; but her light industries must be limited to the production of articles for daily civilian use. This will prevent the Japs from recovering too quickly in order to rearm and revive their war industries.

Some of our friends think that we should not impose poverty upon Japan. Such friends generously propose that the greater part of the Chinese market shall be reserved for Japan. Such ideas are dangerous for peace. It is true that we should not reduce our neighbours to poverty and engender hatred in the hearts of the masses of the Japanese. But we must make Japan taste the bitter fruit of defeat and poverty. This may reduce the standard of living, but we must know that so long as the traditional policy of expansion is not dead, a prosperous Japan will hasten the revival of an aggressive Japan, and recurrence of war in the Pacific. These acts of just retribution may engender hate and revenge in the people for a time, but let them practise the arts of peace for thirty to fifty years, and they will come to realize that the sanctions imposed are justified and in their own interests.

When Japanese militarism is destroyed root and branch, and the Japanese people can effectively control the actions of their Government through democratic institutions, then shall we have peace, friendship, goodwill and prosperity among the nations living on the shores of the Pacific.

12

The Mikado Must Go *

I

THE abiding significance of the " Double Tenth," the anniversary of the Chinese Revolution—our own October Revolution—which gave birth to the Republic of China, must be noted by the world to-day.   It is this : on this very day thirty-two years ago, October 10, 1911, a long epoch in Chinese history was ended and an entirely new era ushered in.   It ended the immemorial institution of absolute monarchy in China and, in its place, introduced the republican, democratic form of government, which Dr. Sun Yat-sen, Father of the Republic, took from the West and gave to the Chinese people.

Oriental despotism and imperial rule were the original and traditional forms of polity in which the Chinese people had been reared, and under which they had suffered generation after genera- tion for countless ages.   Our forefathers were taught, long before the ancestors of the present-day Japanese had ever heard of such dogma, that the Emperor was divine, in fact he was the very " Son of Heaven," anointed and appointed by Heaven to rule over his myriad subjects, the " pai-shing," or hundred names scattered throughout the land.   " All under Heaven was the King's land, all living within the seaboards are the King's ministers," so said the Shu-ching, the History Classic, written 3000 years ago.

After the Manchu Conquest in 1644, the alien rulers fastened upon the country a system of despotism more absolute and hateful than any of its predecessors.   The Manchus, like the Japanese before them, had their history rewritten to show that their first ancestor was directly descended from a supernatural being ; thereby justifying their seizure of supreme power, and, in their own eyes, legitimized their claim to Chinese submission and loyalty.

The October 10 Revolution not only toppled the Manchu throne after almost three centuries of hated rule, but shattered for all time in China the idol and myth of divine kingship and imperial despotism.

Yuan Shih-kai, while President of the Republic in 1915, dared to ignore the spontaneous verdict of the Chinese nation, and con- spired to subvert the Republic and set himself up as Emperor

* Special article written for American and Chinese Press, published on October 10, 1943.

174

Hung-Hsien of the new Empire. He failed miserably, and died a
disillusioned man. Chang Hsün, war lord and an illiterate, likewise missed this lesson of history, for in the summer of 1917 he was
foolish enough to attempt the restoration of the Manchu Emperor.
The little boy Emperor again sat on the Dragon Throne in the
Peking Palace, but only for eleven days, and he was deposed a
second time.

The lesson we draw from the " Double Tenth " is that aggressive
militarism against which we are all fighting to-day, as in the case
of absolute monarchism in China, can and must be decisively destroyed for all time, so that there shall be no recurrence of the
scourge of German Nazism or Japanese Militarism for at least the
next hundred years.

2

Among our Allies in this war, and in particular our American
friends, there is current a mistaken sentiment concerning the institu-
tional position of the Japanese Emperor. This has been derived
from a wrong notion which attributes to the Mikado the position of
spiritual and moral leadership, to which all Japanese would pay
unquestioned respect and blind reverence. The Tenno, being god
in human form, must remain sacred to the Japanese people, no
matter what happens. There is also a conception that the Japanese
Emperor is all powerful, and therefore able to control all elements
and tendencies within his domain, or that he will fulfil the rôle as
a modifying and liberal influence on his hot-headed and Fascist
officers, all of which is simply bunkum.

The present-day " divine " position of the Japanese ruler is just
the recent creation of the militarist caste, who having mislearned
their lesson from ancient Chinese history, imitated the Duke of Tsi
by " taking the son of heaven by the arm in order to command
obedience from his numerous vassal lords." In order to command
absolute submission on the part of the people so as to carry out
their nefarious designs for aggrandisement and glorification, the
militarist caste simply makes use of the Tenno as their willing
puppet, who submits himself to be deified before his death.

It may be interesting to recall that when the first Japanese
history was fabricated in the eighth century of the Christian Era,
in the time of our T'ang Dynasty, it had to be written in the Chinese
literary language, after the ruling caste had learned to use it, since
there was no Japanese literature in those days. The author of

this History of Japan was hard put to it to invent proper-sounding Chinese names for the unbroken line of non-existent heavenly rulers. For a period extending more than a thousand years, all their emperors lived extraordinarily lengthy lives and must have enjoyed superhuman vitality, for most of them were said to be centenarians, and every one of them begot his heir only after his eightieth birthday.

One of the more authentic latter-day Japanese emperors, who died about A.D. 1500, was so poverty-stricken that he had to set up shop outside his palace gate in old Yedo, to sell scrolls of calligraphy and water-ink painting in the Chinese manner, done by his imperial hand and chopped with the imperial seal, all for the purpose of collecting a few paltry coppers to pay his keep. After his death, the corpse had to lie unencoffined and rotting for more than forty days before the imperial household could gather sufficient means for his proper burial. This shows how much respect and reverence were shown the emperor by the ruling *Shogun* and his *samurai* in those good old days, when Japan was still a hermit kingdom, isolated from the world, but perhaps already laying plans for its conquest.

My point in the foregoing is simply this : there is no reason why the Japanese Emperor and the cult of emperor-worship should not be overthrown after the Jap pirates are defeated in this war.

To fight this war to a decision means that the common victory must be so decisive as to preclude any resurrection of a militarist and aggressive Japan, or the probability of any recurrence of war in the Pacific. Japan must be so beaten and crushed, and so pulped and pulverised, that she will not dare to entertain an aggressive thought for at least a hundred years. This can be done only by a fundamental revolution in the constitutional make-up of present-day Japan. Sweep away the military caste and its officer cadre, yes, but along with it, sweep away also the Emperor and the cult of emperor worship. Only then will the self-deluded Japanese people realize that the reign of Imperial Japan is ended, never to return. Only then will the grandeur-dazed Japanese people make up their minds that from then on, after their last defeat in battle, they will have to begin life anew as a nation. They will have to learn how to rebuild the political institutions of their country from the examples and experiences of their former enemies. They will have to learn the intricacies of democratic self-government without the hypnotic spells of a " divine " ruler.

3

The Japanese Empire must be overthrown and the Japanese Republic set up in its place. It is only by this means that real democracy can be introduced and instituted in Japan, and the peace of the world safeguarded. In these modern days, and especially after what we shall have gone through in this global conflict, no democratically governed nation will want war. Aggressive wars are invariably forced upon peace-loving peoples by the dictators who rule them. The Japanese people, once they are rid of their present rulers, who are bringing ruin and suffering and despair to countless homes in their own land, will never want to undergo another war, if they can exercise their will freely. But they will not be able to go their way so long as the Emperor remains a divine institution and the cult of Emperor worship a State religion.

Whereas the Chinese Revolution started as a spontaneous movement of the Chinese people, led by the revolutionary party as their vanguard, the proposed Japanese Revolution will have to be initiated and introduced by the victorious United Nations after defeating the Japanese military power. In China, our people were fortunate in having our leading party, the Kuomintang, first under the guidance of Dr. Sun Yat-sen, and later, since his death, led by Generalissimo Chiang Kai-shek, as the agency by which the transitional period of political tutelage could be directed in order to transform the country from despotism to democracy. No such revolutionary party has yet appeared in Japan. It is conceivable that before final disaster overtakes her, an indigenous movement comparable to our own may emerge in Japan. But we must not count on it ; hence necessary measures should be devised in anticipation of the day when United Nations forces will land and occupy the country, to compel the Japanese militarists to accept our condition of unconditional surrender.

When Japan is finally occupied, and the Emperor deposed and banished, it will devolve upon the United Nations, and principally upon the United Nations and China, to set up organs of control and advice whereby democratic institutions will be introduced and developed in a country which has suffered so long from the distorted precepts of militarism, " Tennoism," and Fascism. The task will be enormous and difficult. But unless it is done, the victory would not be decisive and durable.

It may be objected on the ground of the Atlantic Charter that to impose a republican-democratic form of government on Japan would be interference in the domestic affairs of the vanquished. Meddling with the domestic politics of a foreign state with whom we are at peace would be highly objectionable, and could find no justification. But destroying the root and branch of jingoism and militarism in an enemy state in order to ensure peace and prevent future war is, on the contrary, highly desirable. We owe it not to our own peoples alone, but to the enemy peoples as well, that adequate steps be devised and taken to forestall any possible future conflict by uprooting its very cause. Both high-minded wisdom and national self-interest dictate such a course. We must not, therefore, let irrelevant considerations cheat us of our forthcoming victory.

Let not our American friends misunderstand us. We do not want anything of the Japanese enemy when he surrenders unconditionally save what he has wrongfully and illegally taken from us. He has stolen our lands, which he must restore. He has dismantled and taken away machinery and equipment from our mills and factories. These he must be made to replace. But there are losses which he cannot indemnify. Millions of our defenceless men, women, and innocent children he has already slaughtered. These lives he cannot restore to us. We are determined that never again shall the Japanese enemy invade our country and burn, kill and lay waste as he has done in these last twelve years since September 18, 1931. To ensure that such a catastrophe shall not happen again to our country, and that the blood which has been spilt shall not have been shed in vain, the " Mikadoship " must be abolished when the militarist cancer is cut from the body of Japan. Of a democratic republican Japan we need have no fear ; on the contrary, we shall be ready and willing to re-establish normal relations with a new Japan, revolutionized after her defeat, whose Government will be democratically constituted and responsible to the Japanese people as a whole. Such a new Japan must and will take her rightful place among the world community of law-abiding and peaceful nations.

PART FIVE

To Peace

The Future of China *

I

THIS War of Resistance has been going on now for some years. On July 7, 1941, we shall mark its fourth anniversary. What stage have we reached? It seems to me the final one will be upon us ere long. We may divide the war into three phases. The first is that of the enemy's advance and our retreat; the second is a stalemate, in the midst of which we are just now; and the third, that of our counter-attack and the enemy's rout. At present, he is at the end of his tether, being unable to advance farther, in spite of his superior equipment, and having to wait for us to knock him out. We can do that soon by shortening the phase of stalemate, if we rely on our indomitable will and marshal all our resources for the final struggle.

Meanwhile, the world situation and its probable developments are beginning to turn in our favour. For three bitter years and more we have fought alone; although there was some material aid and no lack of moral support, they were of little avail to us, for there was too little of the former and the latter was merely in the shape of airy words. While the world looked on but sat tight, mouthing praises and sometimes cheering us, the enemy was given free access to whatever supplies he wanted. In the last half year, however, things have decidedly changed for the better. There is prospect that we shall begin to receive some real and substantial help, while the enemy's source of arms and materials will be cut off.

2

Of all the countries in the world, the first one to sympathize with our resistance, and that in a material way, was Soviet Russia. Twice I went on missions to Moscow, so perhaps I can speak on the subject with some authority.

* A speech delivered before the Students' Assembly at the National Fu-Tan University, Peipei, February 13, 1941.

In the past, however, the Soviet Union was not free to aid us unreservedly, for she had, and still has, her own difficulties and her own standpoint.   Three years ago Japan signed an anti-Comintern Pact with Germany and Italy ; if unrestricted help were extended to us by her, the U.S.S.R. feared that she would be attacked in Europe by Germany, and then a world war might follow.

At the same time, countries friendly with China, i.e. Britain and the United States, if they saw any unusual connections between the Soviet Union and ourselves, could easily misunderstand the matter. Those two have long been suspicious and apprehensive of her, as they are capitalistic, while she is socialistic in structure.   If she rendered assistance to us on a large scale, so as to enable us to thrash the enemy thoroughly, those other two Powers might be drawn to the side of Japan against the U.S.S.R.   Then we should both be in an awkward position.

She had, therefore, to be cautious, not too free, not too open, in lending aid, which is, however, not a little under the circumstances. There is no report in the daily papers that Soviet Russia has ever given us any loans of money or arms, but the thing has been done none the less.   Up to the present, among all the friendly countries who have helped us with aircraft, arms, and loans, the U.S.S.R. stands foremost.

Next, let us consider America's attitude toward us.   With a mighty Navy in the East Pacific she has found, of course, her natural rival and potential enemy in Japan, the greatest naval power on this side of the ocean.   If we can weaken that rival and enemy for her, so much the better.   Hence, since we exchanged our first shots with Japan, her sympathy for us has been growing daily. Unfortunately, during these three years and more, help to us and disservice to the enemy have not yet been effectually expressed in positive actions.

The American Navy, if concentrated in the Pacific, could well take care of our enemy.   But there are the Atlantic sea-lanes and coast for her to guard and protect.   After we had accepted the enemy's challenge, the American Government was uncertain whether Europe would burst into flames, and if it did, whether she herself would be imperilled.   Thus, wavering, she did not dare to aid us, fearing lest there might be a conflict with Japan ; and then, if the European magazine were to blow up after all, she would have too much on her hands.   Two years later, all Europe was ablaze.

Another cause of the American reluctance to help us is her own isolationism.   After 1918, American public opinion was for closing the doors and shutting out all troubles, whether they originated in Europe or in Asia—as if that were possible ! Since that mistaken and, to the world, irresponsible view permeated the nation, all diplomatic measures taken by the President or his Government were strictly under public surveillance, and if they smacked of minding other countries' business, were immediately frowned on or censured.

In October 1937, President Roosevelt delivered a speech at Chicago, calling on the world's peaceful nations to come together and quarantine the aggressive forces, in order to prevent aggression from spreading further abroad. We were then holding the Japanese at Shanghai with all our might, and so were greatly heartened by the far-sighted President's words, but American opinion was sorely annoyed. The reasons for this annoyance was, that as America's power was considered inadequate to police the world, she was under no obligation to undertake any such quixotic adventure for others. These sentiments were fully expressed in Congress, in heated debates and pointed criticisms. Consequently, the President had to desist from doing anything, and kept quiet.

About two years later, in July 1939, when the enemy's sinister plot to absorb Asia had become plain as daylight, the United States notified Japan of their intention to terminate the commercial treaty between them. Six months later the annulment became a fact. With that event, we had hoped, would come real economic sanctions against our enemy. But actually, only after much further waiting, the export of aviation gasoline was subject to special permit, which was meant as a hindrance to the enemy. After yet another period, certain kinds of scrap iron and steel were forbidden to be shipped to Asia. But the embargo did not bring the desired results, except that of displeasing the Japanese, for they could buy any amount of crude oil and pig iron and steel ingots in the American market and bring them home. Even scrap iron could still be purchased by them through many channels, to be shipped first to Central or South American ports, and then reshipped to Japan, to feed the Japanese war industries. To be brief, the main anxiety of the United States for the first three years or so had been to avoid conflict with our enemy.

As regards Britain, her policy, guided by Mr. Neville Chamberlain, had been directed toward the appeasement of Japan no less than of Germany. After we had fought for a year, the silver bullion deposited in the Bank of China vaults, as well as our beloved patriots incarcerated in the British Concession at Tientsin, were both handed over by the British authorities to the enemy. There was little excuse for such acts.

Last summer, after Chamberlain had resigned, and the British Government was led by Mr. Winston Churchill, the Burma Road was closed for a vital three months under Japanese pressure. At the same time Britain announced that it was hoped that the Sino-Japanese dispute would be settled within that period. Did the British Government believe that a nation of four hundred and fifty millions, after fighting for four years, would lay down its arms before the invader had been completely defeated and driven in head-long flight from the fatherland? The feeling of our people against Britain was very bitter indeed. But on reflecting what we should do if we were in her shoes, we might feel that Britain, too, had her point of view. Last August and September the Battle of Britain was raging, and the Nazis were hurling down, by day and by night, death and destruction from the skies to subdue her. While engaged in that life-and-death struggle, the British were naturally unable to risk the threat of war with Japan in the Far East. Therefore, we should not blame her too much for her failure to assume a stronger attitude toward the Japanese.

3

According to international practice, a country's behaviour in international dealings is dictated by her current interests. But Soviet Russia and the United States, having contributed something in greater or lesser measure to our national resistance, can be said to have been motivated to a greater extent by the sense of Justice. The fundamental truth is that we have been fighting for the democratic countries against a common foe. Without despatching a soldier or firing a shot, they are hitting him full in the face with our hands, so, very naturally, they are glad to help us. This help, while based on enlightened self-interest on their part, is, however, a valuable thing to us, and one to be appreciated. In other words, victory is not yet ours ; friendly help should be sought ; any assistance given us is therefore welcome.

There are, strangely, people who view such friendly help with misgivings. They think that since we have fought for the past three and a half years all alone, we have already won immortal glory ; and moreover, our ultimate victory would crown our efforts. If capitalistic Britain and America come to help us to win the war, it is argued, this would amount to our fighting all these years for their sake, which would mean that the blood of our heroes would have been shed for other than the national cause. This is a mis-apprehension. It should be made clear to us that though our faith is as unshakable as ever, and, that though, by resisting to the bitter end, victory is sure to be attained, yet if we could not alter the world situation in our favour, but had to bear the staggering burden alone throughout the whole war, not only must the duration of the war be unnecessarily prolonged, but its world-wide significance would also be lost. The historic lesson should not be lost on us. In war-time, a country, whatever its political credo, should never refuse outside help. It is true that we are fighting for our own existence, but at the same time we are also fighting for the very life of world peace and justice, with which our friends are deeply concerned. Therefore, we should welcome Soviet Russia, America and Britain if they join in a common effort to safeguard world freedom against the common enemy.

The enemy's international position to-day is radically different from that of more than three years ago. He was then cocksure that he could easily dominate the Far East. But this interminable war with us taught him that there was no hope of his conquering us by his own might alone. He had of necessity to conclude a triple alliance with Germany and Italy last September. The international implication of our national resistance has also undergone a great change. Just as the dark forces of Europe and Asia have joined hands, the champions of freedom and democracy in these two continents are perforce linked up into a united front. The standpoints of Chinese, British, and Greek resistance may be various and distinct from one another, but the fortunes of these Promethean struggles are now common to all.

If in Europe, Britain could not withstand the relentless onslaught of the German military machine, she might be struck down like a second France. In that case, America would be menaced by invasion from the Atlantic, and her Pacific naval forces would have to be rushed to the East coast. The Japanese would at once be given a freer hand by the American withdrawal from the Far East, and would become emboldened by the success of their European partner. If this really came about, we should have to continue our lonesome fight under even greater difficulties. This clearly demonstrates the indivisibility of our cause with that of the other democratic countries.

4

We have been fighting the enemy's land forces for three and a half years. The Japanese war machine is not invincible. We shall defeat it when adequate equipment is available for our use. Nor is his Air Force so terrible. It is most effective when used against our open and defenceless cities. But against his piratical Navy, prowling along our seaboard and blockading our ports, we are powerless. We have no Navy. It can be asserted that final victory will be ours only when the enemy's Navy is sent to the bottom of the sea.

For example, if he follows his bent to advance southwards, he will have to be sparing in distributing his land forces on our various battle-fronts. It is not impossible that some day he may withdraw his troops in stages from our hinterland. Suppose, in doing so, he still keeps his clutches on Tientsin, Tsingtao, Shanghai, Canton, Amoy and Swatow. Then, his threat to us would be considerably lessened, and we could put more spirit into our counter-attacks. But if he could use his Navy to protect his troops of occupation in those ports, not letting them out of his grip, we should still be unable to throw him out.

Let me illustrate my point with another supposition. The enemy, feeling that 20,000 million yen of war expenses and 1·7 million casualties are too much for him, and that the war was likely to drag on indefinitely, might decide on complete withdrawal. It might then seem that we had won our victory and recovered all our invaded territories. But would this seeming be a reality? No. He could sail southwards to occupy Singapore and the East Indies, and chase Britain and America out of Asia by a series of amphibian expeditions. When that was done, he could return to us and begin the same old story over again.

Our mortal weakness lies in our having no Navy. The best kind of friendly assistance to be obtained is, first of all, the combination of British and American naval strength in destroying the sea power of the enemy. But we cannot hope that America will undertake this commitment so long as events in other parts of the globe make greater demands on her attention. Of course, if the Japanese are bent upon advancing southwards at all costs, a full-scale naval conflict between the two countries is inevitable. But even that must largely depend on whether Britain could stand up against the assaults of the Nazis.

There is a school of American opinion which regards Germany as the main enemy. When Nazi Germany has been defeated, it is thought, the combined forces of Britain and America could then turn round to deal with our enemy. They believe that even though by that time Japan may have spread her tentacles over large areas of our soil, and grabbed the natural riches of British Malaya and the

Dutch East Indies, she will nevertheless have to let go.   This reasoning is not without its grounds.   But it presupposes that Britain
would be more than able to beat off the attacks of Germany, and
would have enough energy left after the latter's defeat, so that her
Navy would then be available for active service in the Pacific.

5

How is the war going to end?   To my mind, there are three
possibilities.   First, if Germany were overcome by Britain and
America, the Japanese Navy would be crushed by their combined
sea forces.   The main burden for this would, perhaps, be borne by
America, as Britain may not have the requisite strength left.   Then
we should have at least some thirty years free from the danger of
future invasion, within which to construct a modern State.   The
enemy has a Navy of nearly two million tons.   If it were destroyed,
it would not be possible to restore it within two decades.   This is an
ideal outcome of our resistance.

Next, if the European contest should end in a negotiated peace,
Britain and America could still settle scores with the Japanese, as
their navies would be intact.   At present, the European struggle is
in a stalemate.   When spring comes, Germany will attack again.
We hope that Britain will be able to stand her ground.   In the case
of a draw in Europe, we should, of course, continue our resistance,
and with the combined Anglo-American Navy released from the
Atlantic the Japanese might be forced to give up Occupied China.
They would not be satisfied with this result.   Thus, we could only
have five or ten years' respite before we should be attacked again.
And we should have to speed up the building of our State against
that emergency.

The last and worst possibility is Germany's large-scale invasion
of Britain and Britain's surrender sometime between the coming
spring and summer.   America would then withdraw from the Far
East, and Japan's power would be supreme in this area.   That
would not mean the cessation of our resistance, but then our difficulties would multiply a hundredfold.   It would remain for the
world to see whether we had enough backbone in us to go through
the ordeal and come safely out of it.

6

Whatever the relation between our war and the European,
however ours is going to be wound up, the one thing we can do
now is to prosecute the war with all we have until victory is achieved.

That alone can give us any future, and a glorious one at that; without it, extinction.

Economic construction, especially the building up of heavy industries, can have victory as its sole basis. America's annual output of steel has recently been reported to be 83 million tons; Germany's—including the output in the Occupied countries—42; Soviet Russia's, 30; Britain's, 20. Our pre-war production stood at the paltry figure of 0·3 million tons. If we could not forge ahead and catch up with them, increasing the output of our basic minerals, metals, fibres, chemicals, oil, etc., by the hundredfold, there could be no construction to speak of.

Plant for smelting iron and making steel must be imported. According to reliable sources, the maximum transportation capacity of the Burma Road and the North-western Highway cannot reach 200,000 tons a year. This means that the equipment indispensable for setting up blast furnaces and rolling mills simply cannot be imported, for these two highways must be used to-day for supplying us with arms, which are more urgently needed. When victory is ours, and the sea lanes and our ports are wide open, the equipment for economic construction can be obtained from abroad. Great strides should be taken by us then, for before long we may be compelled to face another treacherous assault of enormous dimensions. If the enemy's Navy were left afloat, the establishment of our heavy industries would have to be speeded up to reach completion within the first five years.

More than ten years ago, when the Government was in Nanking, we might have been far-sighted enough to have set up heavy industries in the interior, instead of doing nothing about it. What industries we had were all on a small scale. They were scattered along the coast, and our retreat from Shanghai and westward along the Yangtze stripped us bare of even the pitiful mite of industry we did possess. The provincial authorities of Kwangtung, before this war, built up arsenals, ordnance foundries, cement factories, sugar refineries and paper mills in the suburbs of Canton; when that city fell, all those were lost. Our past lack of planning and foresight should be a hard-earned warning to us in the future. Time passes, never to return. When, luckily, the chance comes again, we ought to make the most of it.

7

Post-war large-scale economic construction should, and could, be carried out only by the State. Private enterprise can never hope to accomplish such a huge job within a short period. Under free competition and the private initiative of capitalism, it took Britain more than a century, the United States eighty years, Germany seventy years, and Japan sixty, to industrialize themselves. We shall not be allowed to muddle through the process in a leisurely and haphazard manner over half a century or more. The enemy set out on his career of brutal conquest over three and a half years ago at Lukouchiao because he wanted to prevent our development. He intended that, before we had time to make a beginning, China should be turned into a colony for good and all. If our reconstruction were not carried to a successful conclusion within five years or so after victory, the enemy would be likely to come again. We must decidedly do whatever we can now, and as soon as the time is ripe it must begin on a grand scale, and push on for the fulfilment of our plan with break-neck speed. Only so can we get things done in time to anticipate and forestall any future energency which may beset us.

8

Nation-wide economic construction, especially the founding of heavy industries, cannot be carried out to-day owing to obstacles in transportation. But the building up of political systems could and should be greatly accelerated. The San-Min-Chu-I aims at the building up of a State and the establishing of a Government of, by, and for the people. For fully thirty years, since the downfall of the Manchu Empire, there has been little real progress toward making the Republic worthy of its name. It is high time that we paid our long overdue debt to the nation, particularly now, as we have come to appreciate in this war how precious and desirable is the way of life which we call democracy.

The fundamental system of our future political make-up is the institution of local self-government, by which local affairs will be managed directly by the people themselves. At present we have only bureaucratic administration. The governors of provinces are appointed by the Central Government ; the administrators of the *hsien*, as well as the mayors of cities, are sent out by the Provincial Governments. Everything proceeds from the top downward, since the people are incapable of organizing themselves to care for their own well-being. As if bound hand and foot, they are powerless ; incohesive as a stretch of loose sand, they cannot initiate and participate in important public acts.

In instituting local self-government, there should, of course, be definite stages, but we should move forward in a practical manner rather than strive to attain the ideal right away. It is not necessary, although highly desirable, to have the people all literate in order to exercise their popular rights, since even though we had enough schools, there would be a lack of teachers to educate them all at once. In the case of election, for instance, the " official " promoters of local self-government should give the people a chance to try their hand, and thus make the thing really popular. Such constructive steps in the political development of the country can be taken immediately without any further waiting for the end of the war.

Besides elementary political tutelage, the development of co-operatives, and mass education to wipe out illiteracy, should be speeded up. Anything that can be done without the use of unobtainable industrial equipment and machinery should be undertaken instantly, so as to make a flying start for an orderly political and economic life when victory comes.

9

To-morrow's economic construction, with basic heavy industries for national defence at the head, might be carried out by means of two Five-Year Plans. As I have said elsewhere, our post-war economy should not be exclusively agricultural, for a purely agricultural economy such as we have now will never make us a rich country. We must intensify our industrialization. To cite the Russian example : in 1913, the ratio of the Empire's production in agriculture and in industries respectively was 6 to 4 ; at present, after the two Five-Year Plans, the Soviet agricultural-industrial production ratio has become 2 to 8. Only industries can develop a country's latent power. Farming alone can barely supply the people with subsistence. This has been our experience for centuries.

On the other hand, in a well-industrialized country, with twenty people out of every hundred in the population working on the farms, the other eighty can be amply supplied with food and clothing. They are thus free to raise the cultural level, to increase the power and add to the wealth of the nation. In our case, 80 per cent. of our population are farmers, yet they cannot produce enough to feed the nation, least of all themselves.

But to industrialize a country does not imply the neglect of farming ; quite the reverse. It should be improved and made more efficient, though the relative value and importance which it occupies in the total production of the nation may be considerably reduced. The population of the entire world—of 2000 millions—is now, we are told, sustained by the products of only 12 per cent. of the world's total land surface. Recently, America and Soviet Russia, especially the former, have been employing scientific methods to increase crops. With the systematic and widespread improvement of farming processes, the world's population can be doubled without having to increase the acreage of the world's arable lands. In that case, by a similar modernization of our farming, with the general use of chemical fertilizers, as well as through mechanization, we could sustain a population of 900 millions in China.

Our young people should not be led astray by the mistaken notion that since China's poverty is due to over-population, it is their duty to promote and practise birth control. The premise is utterly unfounded, as the conclusion is fallacious. As a result of encouraging births, Soviet Russia has in recent years increased her population to 193 millions, her annual increase being 3 millions and more. This means that after three generations, or in less than one hundred years, they will have 600 millions. The Germans also are intensifying procreation. Hitler plans to have Germany's Nordic population increase to 250 millions after seventy or eighty years so as to enable Nazidom to maintain numerical supremacy in Europe. If our numbers remain stationary, we shall be liable to fall back and take a third, or even fourth place in the world by the end of the present century.

10

In the first post-war decade, the productive power created by our industrialization should at least catch up with Japan's peak during the war. The output of steel must be increased to at least four to five million tons a year ; other metals and materials should be produced in quantities called for by the level of production. Mass production with the best machinery and by the latest technical processes could yield results ten times greater than our present efforts. Only then shall we be able to increase the wealth and defensive power of the nation against the recurrence of any emergency which we may have to meet.

It would be sheer folly to think that there is going to be perpetual peace when the guns cease to roar and the echoes of the bomb crashes die away. We have learned enough during these two

13

decades to warn us against such sophistry. After the first Great War, America made up her mind never to take part in any fighting in other parts of the world ; but when the present orgy of force was begun in Europe the Americans began to look to their arms production. From Hitler's rise to power in 1933 up to the opening of hostilities in 1939, Germany worked day and night preparing for revenge. France, curling up to sleep in her air-conditioned Maginot caverns, was only half ready for waging a war of the type of the last war ; she was quickly beaten. Britain had not prepared for war at all. When war seemed unavoidable, Chamberlain had to " bring along goblets, asking for enlightenment " from Hitler. And we ourselves—what did we do between Mukden and Lukouchiao ?

II

For our post-war national defence, first of all, we should have a first-class Army. It is true that the enemy has learned a lesson from us. But, pig-headed as the Japanese are, they will in all likelihood come back to be taught again. Next time, our Army should be much stronger than theirs, not merely in numbers, but also in training and physique. By carrying out the Conscription Law to the strict letter, it should not be difficult to have a million men a year under military training, as our supply of man-power is almost inexhaustible. In the past, because we had a poor recruiting system and our local administrative machinery was sadly inefficient, we could not have millions of soldiers ready at hand as soon as the call to the colours was given.

If we became a first-class land Power five years after victory, there might be no necessity for us to fight again. By that time, Japan would have to think twice before embarking on such a venture. Japan attacked us light-heartedly over three and a half years ago simply because she held us in utter contempt, seeing that we had virtually no national defence.

The experience of Soviet Russia may be taken as a further illustration. For twenty years no country has dared to do her injury. Our enemy is now asking for a non-aggression pact with the Soviet Union ; as yet without success. A few years ago, however, it was the U.S.S.R. that made the proposal, and Japan turned it down. Now it is Soviet Russia's turn to do the snubbing. Moreover, America also is trying to make friends with the Soviet Union. France and Soviet Russia were originally bound by a mutual-help pact, but the document was thrown into the waste-paper basket by

Daladier, then in power, and France has had cause to regret this short-sighted policy. Soviet Russia has become a weighty factor in power politics ; many are trying to win her good graces. Why ? Because her national defence is well organized. If we want to maintain peace in the future, we must have arms to guard that peace.

Between 1919 and 1928 the greatest Air Power was France. Wallowing in luxury and ease, and paralysed by petty internal politics, the French slowed down their efforts, and thereby gave up their position as the dominant Power in Europe. In 1939 Germany produced 3000 aircraft a month, against France's 80 and Britain's 200. The United States has now begun to turn out 1000 and Britain can probably manage 1500. Their total production is still below Germany's. That is one of the chief reasons why Hitler has been so bold.

We cannot hope to be a first-class Air Power within a few years after the war, for this presupposes a highly-developed industrial basis, plus meticulous technical and designing skill. But we definitely should strive for the second rank ; and we should be capable of producing 500 to 1000 planes a month. Japan's Air Force is only third or fourth class, being surpassed by all the Great Powers with the single exception of Italy. And lacking a sufficient supply of oil and important metals, she cannot go much higher. If we could achieve our aim, we need no longer fear her in the air.

Neither can we build up a formidable Navy in five or ten years. However, when a country can take first place in any one of the three arms—i.e. land, sea or air forces—it can be counted a strong Power.

To-day, Japan's Army and Navy are both more or less of the first order, while her Air Force is definitely inferior. Britain's and America's Navies are both first class. Not very long ago, before the phenomenal rise of his imitator, Hitler, who soon overshadowed him, Mussolini strutted and ranted with pomp and grandiloquence on the international stage ; recent events have shown that Italy's three arms are all second rate. The land, sea and air forces of France were respectively first, second, and third class. Both Germany and Soviet Russia have first-rate armies and air forces. China must have an army of the very first rank, supported by an air force of some weight, in order to safeguard the nation's independence.

12

Our heroic resistance in the last four years has improved our international standing. If Britain and America want to maintain their position in the Far East, they will have to give us positive, unstinted help. But foreign aid can come only in the form of military armaments and aircraft. For competent men to man these arms and, what is more important, to undertake the burden of the post-war political and economic reconstruction, guiding our people's work into ordered channels, we have to depend upon ourselves. Consequently, a properly trained personnel and efficient organization are vital.

Here, education and technical training must play their essential parts. Our present system of higher education weeds out eight students for every one it accepts. It is a pity that these eight are denied the chance to increase their ability to serve the country. Taking our whole population of 450 millions into consideration, we should have one out of every five persons a pupil, from the kindergartens up to the university graduate schools. College students should number about a million at all times. Our present enrolment in the universities, colleges and technical schools together, is only about 50,000 ; this would have to be multiplied by ten or twenty in order to meet post-war needs.

There ought to be no fear of unemployment after graduation. Certainly, if there were to be no future for our country, it would be a different matter. But in the promising dawn of revival and progress such a fear is groundless. Our present college graduates should each do the work of twenty. If every average family of five throughout the nation sent a child to the grade school, there would be 90 million grade school children, and if one-tenth of these were afterwards to enter the middle schools, there would be 9 million middle school boys and girls ; thus grade and middle schools would need well over a million college graduates to be their schoolmasters and teachers. Moreover, when national reconstruction is in full swing, communications, transportation, industry and agriculture will also require millions of trained men and women.

When Soviet Russia inaugurated her third Five-Year Plan, she intended to have, besides other things, 250,000 physicians, surgeons and dentists. Her goal was to supply, on the average, 750 people with one general practitioner. Suppose in China there was one to every 1000 of our population, we should need 450,000 physicians to take care of our health. Again, the Soviets' collective and co-operative farms, being located on the great plain, are all cultivated by machinery, using some 600 thousand tractors. A year ago, when I paid my visit, I saw they were training 200,000 women tractor drivers. The U.S.S.R.'s population is less than the half of ours ; our urgent need of workers in the future must be more than double that of Soviet Russia.

Above all, we shall require skilled and highly intelligent workers. These can be trained and educated in the higher seats of learning only. Our national funds for education must be multiplied four-fold, twentyfold. We are going to build schools, more schools, and a great many more.

Youths in our colleges and universities—the country is looking forward to your serving her to-morrow ! You are going to be the pillars of the new China ! It is up to you to set her on a par with America and Soviet Russia in ten or twenty years from now ; then she, too, will be powerful enough to speak a decisive word for world peace, whenever the occasion arises. I hope to live long enough to be a witness of your success, for this will mean the successful out-come of the nation's efforts to transform our country into a modern State. You must all have read the history of our 1911 Revolution, when the Manchu Dynasty was terminated. The events which took place then may seem remote to you, but to those of our old comrades, who participated in the Revolution, they seem only yesterday. Time passes, waiting for nobody. Ten years, or twenty, for the construc-tion of a full-fledged modern State, out of the ruins of the past and the ashes of this war—how inadequate, how short they are ! All the more reason why you young people must, therefore, strive resolutely to catch up with time, and do your part toward the creation and safeguarding of a great future for China !

State Construction in Time of War *

I

THE Herculean tasks of national resistance and State construction which we set out to perform three and a half years ago may be taken in two different senses. They may be regarded either as two separate tasks, to be carried out simultaneously and in conjunction with each other, or as one integral whole, with the former playing the part of the means and the latter that of the end. In our great hinterland, up to the very fringes of the war front, people have been busy discussing these alternative interpretations. Not infrequently new constructive measures have been initiated in different places. After a close scrutiny of these we have come to the conclusion that a good deal of the labour has been misspent, for many people have failed properly to understand what reconstruction should be undertaken in the midst of resistance. The limitations imposed by time and space have not been duly taken into consideration. Many an undertaking that is impossible of accomplishment in war-time has been rashly begun, or one which is unnecessary at this juncture has been pushed on with blind ardour, while what can and should be done is altogether forgotten or ignored, and thus left untouched.

It seems to me that what is of fundamental importance, and within our power to carry out, is the establishment of political and economic systems based upon the people's direct interests. To be explicit, politically, local self-government must be introduced and completely established throughout the land ; and economically, an all-embracing system of people's co-operatives ought to be set up. These two institutions form the foundation of State construction, which may be regarded as the two elemental forces of the nation. We need not depend on outside help to realize them ; they demand no material support or physical force for their realizations ; our own concerted and concentrated efforts are all they require.

According to the guiding principles of Dr. Sun Yat-sen, in order to achieve democracy for the nation, local self-government as laid down by him should be the basic condition of all other political activities. When all internal obstacles are overcome, and the

* A speech delivered before the Central Executive Committee of the Kuomintang at the Sun Yat-sen Memorial Service, held in Chungking, February 24, 1941.

military phase of the Revolution draws to an end, the Government should immediately put that into execution, as it is our chief task in the period of Political Tutelage. Unfortunately, since we set up our Government in Nanking, circumstances have arisen to interfere with the progesss of the plan. Actually, however, it is because we did not strive hard enough that we have not methodically brought forward the graduated scheme left us by the late leader, and carried it through in the stipulated time. In fact, democratic government has been given no impetus to start with, and the political network of the nation is left incomplete and unfinished. Local self-government promises to rid the various grades of territorial administration of their present evil—government by bureaucrats. Our local political machines are now inefficient, and measures vital to the nation are left in a muddle, simply because the local populace is not actively participating in public affairs.

2

A few years ago, Chairman Kalinin of the Russian Supreme Soviet drew up an apt distinction, in his address to local Soviet administrators, between a bureaucratic and a revolutionary government. The former, he said, is merely order-giving politics : the official bureaux, regardless of whether the people understand the new political and administrative measures, or whether they are able to do what is asked of them, simply give orders and issue proclamations. As the people know nothing of the matters in question, they play a purely passive rôle ; they either do not pay any heed, or they present an appearance of complying. Finally, the police force may have to be called in, causing much trouble and yielding little result. Revolutionary government adopts a different method. Before the governmental organs give orders, the people's own political bodies are first charged to acquaint the public of the proposals ; all and sundry have the opportunity to study and discuss them, and in the end, when it is quite clear to everybody that the measures presently to be introduced are closely bound up with the common weal, the relevant orders are given. As the people have no further doubts and misunderstandings, there is naturally no obstruction or indifference.

Democratic government is revolutionary in nature. It requires the people actively to manage their own affairs. If the local populace of the township or village feel any need to initiate something good and new, or to terminate certain old practices which are contrary to the local interests, their institution or abolition can be summarily effected on the spot. Whenever the will of the whole nation tends in certain directions, as expressed in the orders of the Central Government, which is guided and checked by the People's Assembly, the public of the various localities, fortified by previous understanding and consequent willingness, will help to back up those orders with justice and firmness. We want without further delay to speed up to fruition such a basic system of popular rights. This organization of local self-government will not only be an effective tool for mobilizing nation-wide man-power to carry out a grand material reconstruction after victory, but will also form, while this war is going on, a smooth channel for the successful administration of conscription, the levying of direct taxes, rationing, and the public sale of food and similar public measures.

Our political efficiency is low when compared with that of the more advanced nations. The chief cause of this is to be attributed to the deficiency mentioned above. The nation's public life to-day may be likened to a power plant fitted with a high-voltaged dynamo but no suitable transformer and transmission line. Though we have good laws and new rulings in plenty, they are not widely applicable because something vital is missing.

The duty of guiding the people to attain self-government rests with the Kuomintang. We, as its members, should, with resolute will and clear knowledge of the method, lead them forward in sure, quick steps. Much invaluable time has been wasted by us; it is high time that we should seriously take up our long-postponed missions.

The detailed process of *hsien* self-government has been well formulated after long legislative discussions. We must see to it that it is enforced all over the country before the end of the war in order that our peace-time reconstruction will have a handy instrument to use. Otherwise, State power, instead of being based upon the whole people, will have to rely on the armed forces, the Government, and some few party members for its support; in other words, the State would be based on a small minority, a dangerous thing for the future of the nation.

I have another point to add. In helping the people to develop local self-government, expedient methods may be resorted to, for these are not normal, peaceful times. With the country in great peril, there is no more time for us to waste. We ought not to proceed perfunctorily and indiscriminately by requiring all the people to liquidate illiteracy. They should be given a chance to learn by practice. It has been well said by the present Party Leader, Generalissimo Chiang Kai-shek, that the final stage of Constitutional Government may begin before the intermediate period of Political Tutelage comes to a close. Local self-government is precisely what we ought to expedite, so that the people may learn to exercise their popular rights by trial and error, during this transition between the two stages.

3

Next, the establishment of the economic system of the co-operatives : In his lectures on the Principles of the People's Livelihood, the Father of the Republic emphasized the co-operative movement with a view to improving the system of consumption and to introduce socialized distribution. What we advocate now is to build up a new national economic system by an extensive application of the principles and methods of co-operation.

This elemental economic engine, like its political counterpart, should be set up by the people themselves and for their own interests. The common folk should make use of it to satisfy their daily demands fully and liberally, while the State does the same to develop its own or the nation's collective wealth. With these two mighty engines, the State can work miracles ; its resources and power will be infinitely expanded.

The country where the co-operative movement flourishes best and is employed for Socialist construction is Soviet Russia. Since 1921 the institution has been extensively applied throughout the length and breadth of the country, to develop national production and improve the people's standard of living. At present it forms, together with the State-owned enterprises, the warp and woof of the Russian economic texture. On the production side, there are the village co-operative collective farms and the minor industry and handicraft co-operatives. In consumption, virtually all daily needs of the people are supplied, and even the workers' residences in towns and cities are built by the co-operatives. The Soviet people have two kinds of common properties, national and public, respectively under State and co-operative management.

If the party wishes to install during war-time this new economic system in conformity with the Min-Seng-Chu-I, bold determination, swift methods and positive action should make it a success. We regard this as one of the two main tasks for which the party should be responsible at this moment. All party members, irrespective of whether or not they are directly taking charge of party affairs, will have to work as one to realize it. Before the coming of victory and peace, co-operatives ought to be duly distributed in cities, towns and rural districts. Both production and distribution types should be equally stressed.

In the case of production, farm co-operatives will, for instance, help the tillers to improve their implements, seeds and fertilizers. Small landholders and tenant farmers, being unable to buy new implements, should be supplied with these by the co-operatives for common use. Transport-and-sales co-operatives are also urgently necessary at present, on account of the difficulties in moving the farm products to cities and towns ; besides, they yield more profits to the farmers, since the middlemen class, consisting of a chain of merchants, is eliminated, while the city and town consumers can get their goods cheaper. Produce-and-sales co-operatives possess the merit, among others, of improving and standardizing farm products ; as these are sent to the market by the farmers themselves, better and uniform qualities have to be maintained in their own interests.

Rural produce co-operatives should also handle the products of the farmers' home industries and handicrafts. Our countryside is now gripped by the evils of financial stringency and usurious rates of interest. Rural credit co-operatives are thus indispensable for giving low-interest loans to the farmers and to help in driving out the money-lender sharks. Furthermore, welfare co-operatives like health and life insurance co-operatives, and those for mutual aid in obtaining medical services and supplies—all these, for the special protection of the poorer people, the farmers as well as the city workers, should be promptly attended to, so as to make up whatever omissions the Government measures leave, for the time being, in their wake.

Finally, the thorough application of the co-operative system to the nation's economy has an additional advantage, beyond those of enriching the people's material life and offering the State a mighty engine for increasing the national wealth. Habits formed by continual contacts will tend to heighten the people's public spirit, draw together their divergent interests, banish narrow egoism and selfish individualism, and foster in the people collective habits making for a healthy communal life.

4

If we want to set up these two kinds of popular organs of the people, masses of workers having faith in the San-Min-Chu-I and of high executive abilities will have to be mobilized. Myriads of executives cannot be trained at short notice ; personnel turned out from the short-term training centres are insufficient to serve the purpose. The co-operatives in one province alone would amount to several thousand units ; for nation-wide service, some 200,000 to 300,000 men would be required. For meeting this emergency, all local party members should tackle these two jobs seriously and with revolutionary ardour, finishing them within three years. By thus doing their duty to the San-Min-Chu-I they would not only lay a concrete base for post-war reconstruction, but would also revive the progressive spirit of the party, and thus restore the people's confidence in them.

Among party members who are not participating in party activities, there is the mistaken idea that they are not closely concerned with it. Party workers receiving maintenance pay for their work are often unable to get into touch with the non-worker members, and therefore fail notoriously in the performance of their tasks. Party headquarters thus become the *yamen* of idlers. This is a sign of decadence ; if it were to continue unchanged, the party would fulfil no useful function at all.

How does the danger come into being ? It is because the party members are not assigned definite, well-planned work to perform, so that they forget their heavy responsibilities to the nation. Whatever party activities have been pursued during these last few years are miscellaneous and trite ; there are no annual plans with centres of gravity. If the establishment of the two aforesaid systems is to be taken up by the party Central Committee in earnest, party members will then have a definite plan of action to keep them busy for the next few years. This would solve the problems of the party crisis mentioned above. Anticipating the great work of State construction awaiting us in the post-war era of our country, we must consistently forge ahead with the aim of catching up with, if not surpassing, the more advanced States in the world to-day. Only thus shall we be able to safeguard the victory that will be ours.

The North-East (Manchuria) After the War *

WE have been at war for five years (September 1942), and final victory is not yet in sight. To discuss post-war problems now may seem premature. But however remote the end of the war may be, it is necessary that we should plan out beforehand the steps to take when the day comes for the restoration of our North-East. We shall then be able not only to carry out measures for the rehabilitation of these four provinces, but at the same time to lay down definite plans for the building up of a new land of prosperity and happiness. This point we should emphasize now, while marking this 18th of September, eleven years after 1931.

I

Before we discuss the problem of rehabilitation, we are first of all confronted with the question of the possible ways to effect the redemption and deliverance of the North-East. Let us start with an assumption. If we were to wage the war alone, as we have done during the first four and a half years, and to terminate it prior to the emergence of the United Nations war-front, how would this Sino-Japanese conflict end? There could be only two possibilities.

First, direct negotiation for peace. This implies that both belligerents, being exhausted, and no longer desirous of continuing the war, would agree to an armistice and start negotiations. Under the circumstances, since we should have won no conclusive victory, the results of such negotiations would not include the recovery of the North-East.

Secondly, mediation by a third Power. This means that the two parties, utterly worn out in fighting, accept the intervention of a friendly Power to cease hostilities and enter into a negotiated peace. This event also would have been attended by our failure to redeem the lost provinces.

The lesson to be drawn from the above assumption is : since by our own strength alone we cannot bring the enemy to total

* A speech delivered on the eleventh anniversary of the Mukden outrage, when Japan attacked and seized Manchuria, before a meeting of the Patriotic Association of the Four North-Eastern Provinces, Chungking, September 17, 1942.

defeat, to end the war alone by an inconclusive peace with him would mean for us losing the war, and the loss of everything we have been fighting for these many years.

But since the 8th of last December the enemy has run amuck and attacked Britain, America, and other countries, and has thus brought on himself the great war in the Pacific. Since that day we are no longer fighting alone. The Sino-Japanese conflict has merged into the World War of the United Nations against the Axis aggressors. Thus the objective conditions for the hypothesis mentioned no longer exist. No longer is there the possibility that this war will end in a negotiated peace between China alone and Japan. It can and will end only in the utter defeat of the common enemy. I am therefore more sanguine than ever of our ultimate complete recovery of the lost North-East Provinces.

There is, however, one point which needs our constant vigilance and persistent emphasis. It is that the United Nations will have to make up their minds never to accept a compromise in the midst of the war. This resolution must become stronger as the war is intensified and victory still eludes us. However long the war may last, whatever its cost to us in blood and treasure, the travail must be borne ungrudgingly until final victory. If there were the least wavering, or should there be no clear recognition of the situation on the part of the United Nations, the enemy, when he had reached a certain point in the war, and saw no further advantage in its continuance, would most likely start a peace offensive to lure our Allies and even ourselves into the trap of a negotiated peace. Such a probability is no mere chimera. War in Europe has gone on for just three years, and Germany has already made several attempts at peace. We, too, have had many such experiences in the last five years; we therefore know better than others what the cunning enemy may achieve with his treacherous intrigues and artful strategems. Our watchword must be constant vigilance.

What can we do to strengthen the resolution of the Allies to fight Japan until she surrenders? We can, I think, contribute much toward victory by hardening ourselves to the tasks before us, bearing greater and heavier sacrifices in the war effort than we have borne up to now. We must by deed and example show our Allies that we are absolutely determined to go through with it to the end, that we shall never be weary of the war until the common enemy is finally crushed and complete and total victory is ours.

That only fighting this war to a finish with the greatest determination will enable us to recover our lost provinces is now obvious to all of us. But this will involve still heavier sacrifices and further difficulties. Already not a few of our people living in the rear of the battle-fronts are showing signs of war-weariness. We must tell them that while it is true that conditions are becoming more difficult, this is to be expected in time of war in any country. Sacrifice and suffering are the price we have to pay for national freedom. What we in the rear are going through is nothing when compared to what our heroic fighters are daily undergoing on the front lines of battle. They have given, and are still giving, their own lives so that the nation may survive. Yet we have not heard of any complaints, any whinings from them. Beside the valour and gallantry of those millions of soldiers, our very kith and kin, what are our trifling discomforts and petty sufferings worth? If we only remember this, no sacrifice, however painful, and no calamity, however terrible, can chill our courage or damp our spirit. With such moral strength we can carry on as long as it is necessary, without ever admitting defeat or accepting a compromise. Who in the world, then, can force us to lay down our arms? With such indomitable resolution on our part, our Allies of the United Nations cannot but be likewise resolved. As a consequence, ultimate victory will be assured us, and along with it, the recovery of the lost North-East will come as a matter of course.

2

Now let us consider our war situation, and see how this objective may be attained. Take the case of continental China first. Suppose we want to liberate the Occupied areas in Central, South and North China, and the important cities and ports on the Yangtze and along the coast, extending through more than ten provinces. We shall have to employ adequate military forces because, in this new situation, unlike that obtaining during the past five years, when we could only keep the enemy bogged in a quagmire, large-scale offensive operations will be called for, so as to throw him out once for all. Flank attacks, with which we succeeded in driving back the enemy a month ago in the battle of Chekiang and Kiangsi, will not serve our present purpose. We shall have to use plenty of heavy arms and equipment to launch serious frontal assaults on the enemy. For only with such attacks will it be possible to destroy his troops and win decisive victories. The strategy and tactics which we have been employing are aimed at gaining time to get large supplies of modern arms and munitions with which to equip our armies for the final offensive. We must demand from our Allies an adequate supply of such means, to enable us to deal with the enemy on the mainland of Asia.

We know that during these past five years, the first friendly State to extend material aid to us has been Soviet Russia. Later, both Britain and America have given us some help, for which we are not ungrateful. But it must be emphasized again that all the assistance we have been getting from them is far short of the amount needed for our great purpose.

Last year (1941) the United States Congress passed the Lend-Lease Bill, empowering the President to render material aid to other United Nations unconditionally and without cash payment. A few days ago, President Roosevelt reported publicly, for the sixth time, the distribution of American war material among the Allied countries during the last three months. He said that during this last quarter U.S. $2000 million in arms and stores were sent to other United Nations. Of the total shipments, 35 per cent. went to Soviet Russia, another 35 per cent. to Britain, and the remaining 30 per cent. to India, Australia and the Near East. We in China, however, got very little, on account of the difficult transport situation. If this unsatisfactory situation is not changed for the better soon, our armed resistance will have to assume an entirely passive rôle, and the war will drag on interminably.

Even since the cutting of the Burma Road, land transport has been an unsolved problem. To ameliorate our difficulties we have been daily expecting America to speed up her air-transport link with us. The enemy's air power is relatively weak ; hence it cannot hope to dominate our air entirely. If one hundred large transport planes were employed daily, our supply problem could be reasonably solved. If each of these planes can carry ten tons per flight, this would mean 1000 tons of war supplies per day. In one year's time we should have some 360,000 tons, enough for us to start a large-scale offensive on at least one front, to drive the hated enemy to the sea. This is not really asking too much of America, and with help forthcoming, the Chinese Army alone would be able to deal a great blow at the enemy forces of occupation. Should things develop in such fashion as to bring our friend, Soviet Russia, also into the conflict, it would be all the more certain that the Japanese forces in China would be totally exterminated before the war is over. America and Britain between them would be quite capable of taking care of the enemy's Sea and Air Forces. That day, I believe, will not be far away.

We should not think that, because of his early successes in the South Pacific last year, the enemy is invincible. His deliberate and treacherous attacks succeeded because all his Navy was concentrated in this region, while American sea power was scattered over the two oceans, and Britain's over the North Sea, the Mediterranean, and the Indian Ocean. The enemy therefore had complete control of the region which he selected for his operations. At the same time the enemy was supreme in the air over Malaya, Singapore, and Hongkong, and in Burma and the Netherlands East Indies, since he threw in all the air force he could muster there, while our Allies' air power was practically absent from the Far East. His success and superiority on the sea and in the air are only temporary, and will prove to be short-lived.

Since the bombing of Tokyo by a carrier-based American air squadron in the middle of last April, the enemy has twice sent out task forces aimed at Australia and the Hawaiian Islands. But in the Coral Sea action early last May, and the Midway encounter in June, he suffered smashing defeats. Three months have elapsed, and he is still shy of attempting a third venture on the sea. His sea-borne Air Force is probably two-thirds eliminated, for no less than seven of his carriers were sunk and more than two hundred airplanes lost. Modern naval warfare cannot be waged except with a strong air cover. Our conclusion is that he will not dare to risk a third offensive on the sea before he can make good his crippling losses. The Japanese Navy is now licking its wounds and assuming a defensive rôle not too far from its home shores.

The enemy's air power is in the least favourable position when compared with that of our Allies. From what the American Air Force in China has experienced during these last few months, the ratio of the enemy's air losses as against America's is about five to one. His aircraft production is estimated at not more than 500 planes a month, while American production, which is only half way to its peak, is already about 5000 a month. In other words, the enemy's naval and aerial power is declining, while that of the United Nations is growing mightier every day.

In the matter of sea transport and communications, the enemy is also in a precarious position. Before the outbreak of the Pacific War, his ocean-going tonnage was approximately 5·5 million ; of the total, some 4·5 million tons were made up of vessels in excess of 1000 tons each, and capable of being used as war transports. The Japanese themselves recently announced that they would need some 20 million tons of shipping to meet their present and future needs.

For the establishment of their so-called " Greater East Asia Co-prosperity Sphere," they must have at least 15 million tons.   Such is their day-dream.   But where can they find this mass of shipping, which means three to four times their total original tonnage ?   War in the Pacific has gone on for less than a year, but already a quarter of the enemy's merchant shipping is lost.   As a result, he is meeting with increasing difficulty in moving troops, arms and supplies for his overseas forces to the newly conquered areas, and in bringing back the rich natural products to his home islands.   If the United Nations' forces in the South-West Pacific can destroy another quarter of his shrinking tonnage within, say, a year, he should be on the verge of cracking up.   His food production at home has been insufficient to meet his peace-time consumption.   Since his attack on us in 1937, what with the depletion of able-bodied man-power for farm work, and the steady cutting down of chemical fertilizers to revitalize his fields, his food crop output has shown a further progressive decline.   It is estimated that the annual shortage of rice in Japan now is in excess of 10 million piculs, which has to be made good by imports from Indo-China and Siam.   When one-half of their merchant shipping is destroyed, starvation will stare the Japanese in the face.   What will then be uppermost in their minds would be no lasting victory, which has so far consistently eluded them, but how to keep out the wolf from their doors.

The enemy may crack up within the next two years.   His Navy will be destroyed by America.   When his sea lanes are cut, he will have practically lost the war.   His occupation troops on our mainland will then have to pack up and clear out as best they can.   The order of his prospective retreat and ultimate flight will be something of the following order : first, evacuation of the Dutch East Indies, the Philippines, Burma, Malaya, Thailand and Indo-China ; next, withdrawal from South China, from the Yangtze Valley, beginning with Ichang in the West, Yochow, the Wuhan cities, Kiukiang and Nanchang, down to Nanking and Shanghai on the East coast, and then from the North China areas ; finally, he will have to give up even our North-Eastern Provinces.   If he declines to surrender the last we shall throw him out, bag and baggage.   Our own North-East, lost to us now for eleven years, will then have been finally and unconditionally recovered.

3

After Manchuria is liberated and recovered, some urgent work of rehabilitation will be needed immediately.   For the past eleven

14

years hundreds of thousands of the enemy's troops have occupied and ravaged the land, and a gang of detestable traitors have aided the hated enemy in the merciless but systematic exploitation and oppression of the inhabitants.   To rehabilitate the land and to revive the political, economic, social and cultural life of the people, as well as to re-incorporate that vast area as a part of our re-united country, it is most important to lay down a clear and definite policy.   I therefore propose the following ten points for your consideration :—

(1) Re-institution of the provincial, *hsien*, and other local administrative organs, as well as the whole order of law courts.   The underlying principle for the resumption of Chinese national rule over the four provinces is to consolidate their structural unity with that of the Republic, in order to prevent a recrudescence of the old habit of separation and regionalism.   The re-instituted national and local authorities must assume responsibility for the administration of all national laws and the execution of the decrees of the Central Government.   The North-East is part and parcel of the Republic ; it is not the private preserve of certain powerful individuals of a feudalistic frame of mind.   Only with the eradication of separatism and regionalism can a strong, unified country be built up.

(2) Enforcement of a system of national education and culture. This should be made to grow up and bear its fruit in the common, free clime of the mother-country.   The Nipponification of education that has been forced upon the country for the past twelve years must be completely liquidated.   The people, especially the younger generation, should be taught to realize that they are not subjects in a Japanese colony, but free citizens of our great Republic.   The slave-consciousness inculcated in their minds by the school text-books of the enemy must be thoroughly eradicated.

(3) Speedy preparation and early inauguration of local self-government.   This by no means conflicts with my first point. National legislation has already provided a complete system of local self-government for the country.   It calls for the institution of *pao* and village assemblies, town and *hsien* councils, as local self-government bodies responsible for the administration of local affairs. When this system is in full function the *pao* and village headman, the town mayor and the *hsien* administrator will be elective public officials directly answerable to the local constituencies.   This democratic system of popular self-government must be introduced the moment all enemy occupied areas are liberated and recovered.

It is true that having been long under the tyrannical yoke of the enemy, the people in the North-East will require time and much preparation before they can operate such local institutions with the necessary aptitude and experience to make them function properly.

(4) The railway and communication services taken over from the enemy and puppet administrations must be restored to national control and operation, in conformity with national policy and national interest. Since the erection of the puppet state, " Manchukuo," by the enemy, all State services have been arbitrarily severed from the national system and have become regionalized. These publicly managed services must be restored to the national system. This is positively required for reasons of political unity, national security, and cultural integrity, as well as in the interests of post-war reconstruction. The enemy-owned South Manchuria Railway will have to be taken over by us as State property and duly reorganized.

(5) State ownership and management of industries and mines. All enemy and puppet-owned and operated industries and mines, whether they be in the hands of enemy private interests or the enemy Government, must be resumed and declared State enterprises. Natural resources in the North-East are abundant beyond estimation. Its coal and iron, soya beans and lumber, have long been leading items among the country's products. The South Manchuria Railway alone has developed and exploited a number of mines. Since the seizure of Mukden in 1931, many enterprises have been built up by the enemy. Radio Tokyo announced recently that total enemy investments in the four provinces have reached 17,000 million yen. All these must be taken over and nationalized. Preparatory measures must be initiated now to carry this out when the time comes for us to take control.

(6) Unification of banking and currency. All enemy and puppet banks will be liquidated. Currency notes issued by them will have to be recalled and exchanged for national legal tender notes. Enemy and puppet properties confiscated can be set aside to form a reserve fund for the redemption of their illegal currency. Such a measure will ensure the people against heavy personal losses, which they would suffer should the puppet currency be declared illegal and repudiated outright. The thousands of millions of puppet currency represent nothing but the tangible wealth and purchasing power of the 35 millions of our countrymen scattered throughout the four provinces. Confiscation and repudiation without compensation would mean penalizing our own people, robbing them of their

possessions and the fruits of their labour. Should the assessed value of national currency of enemy and puppet properties prove insufficient to cover the full face value of the aggregate puppet note issue, the Central Bank of China will devise ways and means to deal with the situation.

(7) When the enemy begins to withdraw, he must be served notice holding him strictly responsible for handing over intact all private enemy properties and installations, together with those of the puppet officialdom, to the proper military and civil authorities charged with their taking over. For every part thereof damaged, destroyed or removed by him, he must be held accountable and made to indemnify the owners, or return it or restore it to its original condition.

(8) All enemy subjects who have immigrated into the four provinces, with the exception of those who sincerely wish to become Chinese citizens through naturalization, are to be repatriated to their homeland. In 1937 the enemy population in the North-East totalled 1,349,900. At present this number must have swollen to beyond 2 millions. Repatriation of enemy subjects is a sound policy, for it will anticipate future friction by preventing the occurrence of any national minority problem. The case of the Koreans may be treated differently, for Korea will have by then recovered her independence, and Koreans living in Manchuria will no longer be willing to remain Japanese subjects.

(9) All naturalized aliens, especially former enemy subjects, shall be required to learn the Chinese language and speech within a reasonable time ; their young folks must be regularly educated in public schools. Thus, they can be made into useful and loyal citizens of the Republic.

(10) The import and export trade of the North-East, forming a large part of the nation's total, should conform with the national foreign trade policy. Although our future policy regarding international trade has not yet been finally determined, the prevalent war-time tendency is toward State control and State management, especially with reference to certain chief items of export. Already the export of rare metals like tin, antimony and wolfram, and certain farm products such as raw silk, tung-oil and hog bristles, is a State monopoly. When this line of policy is followed after the war, the chief exports of Manchuria, such as soya beans and coal, for instance, may be declared a State monopoly. Whatever the future policy may be, the North-East will have to operate within the national orbit.

4

We now come to the discussion of questions relating to the construction of a new North-East. This subject may be divided into four topics.

First, the Min-Seng-Chu-I policy of land nationalization should be carried out. This implies that the State will resume title to all land by appropriate legal procedure. While the State owns all land, the people may enjoy the rights of use and cultivation, just as they are doing now, only they cannot buy and sell land as private property. Private parties wishing to put up factories, build houses, or engage in farming and cattle-raising, can apply to the State land bureau for the desired allotment. The tax-rents on farm lands could be fixed quite low to encourage self-cultivators. Yet the State revenues collected from this source may be many times the current revenue from the present land-tax. Unearned increment and rent as income from private land-owning will be eliminated. Since users of land will not pay rent any longer to private landlords, their burden will be considerably lightened. Both as a State revenue measure and as a beneficial social policy, nationalization of land is therefore a desirable thing.

There is still another point. In China, from time immemorial, land has been regarded by the monied class as a form of investment and guarantee of security. As a result of this traditional practice, people who have become rich, by hook or by crook, have all invested a great part of their money in buying up land in order to create family estates. Money thus invested is practically wasted from both the national and social standpoints, because no new wealth is created by the landlord's act of putting his money into the land, while the ex-owner, who has sold his holdings, may use the money thus acquired for foolish and wholly unproductive purposes. With land nationalized, no longer an object of private trading and speculation, money formerly invested in land may be diverted to better uses, such as the development of new industries, or it may be deposited in savings banks, or paid into the national treasury in exchange for Government bonds, etc. This will have the effect of hastening the industrialization of the country as well as preventing or retarding inflation.

Secondly, collective and co-operative farming should be introduced generally and organized in large-scale units where local conditions are favourable. Not only the traditional system of land tenure, which still smacks of the relics of feudalism, but also the antiquated and inefficient method of small-farm individual tilling should be abandoned, and replaced by the State or common ownership of land and collective and co-operative cultivation. Small-scale individual family farming no doubt served its useful purpose in pre-industrial days, when there was practically no other productive employment for surplus man-power. But in an era of rapid industrial growth, calling for more and more workers from their villages to enter the factories, modern labour-saving methods must be introduced in our agriculture in order to release the man-power required by industry. At the same time, farm production, especially of commercial and industrial crops, must be increased to feed the new demands created by national industrialization. To respond to this twofold requirement in an adequate and even rapidly expanding measure, the best expedient is the introduction of the successfully proven system of large-scale collective farming after the Russian model. Only when innumerable small farms are joined into larger units can mechanization be successfully employed. Expensive agricultural machines like tractors and harvester-combines are beyond the reach of our small, peasant farmers, to say nothing of their absolute uselessness in tiny, checkerboard patches. An agrarian reformation has become necessary. Hence my insistence on the adoption of the collective and co-operative system of agriculture for the North-East, as well as for other regions where local conditions permit.

A study of Soviet Russia's experience will confirm the soundness of this view. Before the Revolution, the Russian peasants were in a worse plight even than ours. In fifteen years, thanks to collectivization and the mechanization of agriculture, small peasant farms have entirely disappeared, modern methods of cultivation with the aid of machines has become general, crops have improved, and their yield has enormously increased. As a result of this success, industrialization has been achieved, and the Russian peasants have attained higher living standards.

In America, though there is no collectivization, modern farming with tractors and machines is widely practised. Measured by the volume of crop production, American agriculture is outstandingly successful. Of her total population of some 130 millions, only 7 per cent., or about 9 million people, are engaged in agricultural pursuits. In China, out of an estimated population of 450 millions, probably 350 millions are dependent on farming for a livelihood. Whereas in America it takes only seven farm workers to produce food for one hundred people, we should require seventy-five to eighty farmers to grow enough food for a like number of people. And yet the American Department of Agriculture thinks that the number of American farmers is still too large, and should be reduced to about 5 millions within the next ten years. How clearly this shows that by using labour-saving machines to carry on the work of man and beast, a tremendous reserve of man-power can be released from the farms for producing national wealth elsewhere !

Thirdly, industrialization should be planned and nationally controlled. Of the various regions of China, the North-East is most favoured by nature to become a great industrial base, and also in the matter of railway mileage, which is more extensive than in any comparable area. Heavy industry has advanced farther than in other provinces. Further development in industrialization will be a matter of course. But such development should follow a well-considered plan. As for heavy and key industries, large-scale enterprises should be undertaken by the State. These will include iron and steel, chemicals, electric power, and such major manufacturing industries as will require large capital investment which cannot be provided by private interests. Certain light industries, using abundant local raw materials, may be undertaken by private enterprise, such as artificial textiles, paper and plastics, cement and building materials, and the processed food industry. There is plenty room for everyone. State ownership and operation of some industries need not be so exclusive as to preclude the rapid development of similar lines by private initiative and competition.

Lastly, a well-thought-out and long-term policy of transfer of surplus population from the metropolitan provinces to the North-East should be established. The four provinces comprise an area of some 1·3 million square kilometres, supporting at the present time a population of 35 millions. The density is under 30 per sq. km. ; far below the average density in the metropolitan area. By a system of planned migration under State aid and direction, the present population may be doubled or even trebled in the next thirty to fifty years. A population of something like 100 millions in the four provinces outside the Great Wall is by no means impossible. Such a population, developing and building up the country, will guarantee us lasting possession of the great territory to be recovered, against any danger of renewed invasion and conquest by the enemy.

To sum up, I say the future of the North-East is quite rosy. In space it occupies approximately one-seventh of the country's total area. In population it contains one-twelfth of the nation's aggregate. But as regards foreign trade, in 1931, the year when the enemy started this world-wide conflagration, it already accounted for a full quarter of China's total. If only the export trade is considered, as much as a third of our entire contribution to the world market came from these four provinces. With thorough and effective measures along the lines I have just suggested, as soon as the enemy is finally expelled and the territory recovered, the North-East, known to the world at large as Manchuria, will surely become an inexhaustible reservoir of national wealth and prosperity. It may well develop into a new centre for the renaissance of Chinese culture and civilization.

Dangerous Thought on Post-War Problems *

TWENTY-FIVE years after the conclusion of the first World War, we now find ourselves again in the midst of another war, more deadly and widespread than the previous one. When the present war comes to an end, the people of all countries, whether of the United Nations or of the enemy states, will have learnt a bitter lesson. They should think of ways and means to establish a permanent peace. While the war is still going on, and final victory is yet to come, intellectual leaders in the United Nations have already realized the importance of studying post-war problems. We may recall that at the end of 1918, when the first World War so suddenly came to a close, the victorious Powers were caught unprepared for the peace. Such a dilemma must not occur again.

It must be admitted that although the last World War was won by the Allied nations, they, nevertheless, failed to make a lasting peace. The reason for this is not difficult to find. The responsible statesmen who directed national policy and the intellectual leaders committed a grave mistake ; so that the causes of another war were inherent in the peace settlement also. And what was the mistake which they committed ? It was that their proposals for post-war settlement were contrary to the fundamental principles of equality and justice. If we should fail to reach a just settlement again after this war, then the causes of a third world war will not have been eliminated. If we are not firmly resolved to rectify the mistakes committed in the past, then the future of the world will be very, very dark indeed. Another war more deadly than the present one would become inevitable twenty or thirty years from hence.

2

Some months ago, a friend who came to Chungking from America told me this story : He said that a certain professor in one of the American universities had written an article on post-war Chinese problems, which was published in a leading American magazine. In this article, the professor advocated that the four

* An article published in the Chinese Press, Chungking, January 1, 1943.

North-Eastern Provinces which are now under Japanese occupation should be given to the Soviet Union after the war. Although I myself have not read that article, nor did my friend tell me on what grounds the author bases his opinion, yet it is safe to say that this kind of proposal is utterly against the principles of fairplay and justice. This is what I call dangerous thought. If it should be carried into effect, therein would lie the causes of another world war.

China is the first great Power which took up arms to fight against Fascist aggression. The North-Eastern Provinces are Chinese, just as the North-Western Pacific States are American. Since the Japanese occupation of our North-Eastern Provinces, they have made them a base for further threats and aggressions against the people and Government of China. In order to maintain our national integrity and existence, we had to resort to armed resistance against Japanese aggression. If the anti-aggression nations should succeed in defeating Japan, thereby achieving final victory, and if China were not given back those of her territories which were once under enemy occupation, then what meaning would there be in the heroic sacrifices which the Chinese people have been making? Such proposals as the one mentioned above are utterly regardless of the national interest of China, and run counter to the patriotic aspirations and just demands of the Chinese people.

It can be reasonably assumed that such unreasonable proposals would not be approved by thoughtful leaders in the United Nations, nor would our great friend, the Soviet Union, care to give them the slightest attention. Yet the fact remains that such a proposal should see the light at all at a time like this is a clear indication that confusion of thought on post-war problems still exists.

3

In August 1942 a supplement was issued by the American magazine *Fortune* in which there was published a Memorandum on the post-war peace settlement under the joint auspices of *Time*, *Life*, and *Fortune*. The second part of the Memorandum deals with Pacific problems, and particularly with the problems of American policy towards the Far East. There are two points included in the Memorandum which are quite interesting, but which, from the point of view of justice and fairplay, are unacceptable. The first of these two points is that a new State be created in South-Eastern Asia, to be known as " Indonesia," which is to include Thailand, British Malaya, the Netherlands East Indies, and Portuguese Timor.

My feeling is that if a new State should be created at all, it would be more logical to include only British Malaya, the Netherlands East Indies, and Portuguese Timor. For the majority of people in this area are Malayan by blood, and according to the principles of nationalism they should form a national State. But the case of Thailand is altogether different. Thailand is historically, culturally, and racially different from the Malayan countries. She has long been an independent State. Although she has now given way to Japanese aggression, she did so primarily because she was not in a position to resist. In our discussions of post-war world reconstruction, we should never propose to destroy those States which have already enjoyed independent existence, and try to incorporate them arbitrarily into some new formation. If this proposal to incorporate Thailand in this new " Indonesia " should be put into effect, then on the day when this new State was born there would also be sown the seeds of internal conflict. Civil strife in the new State would disturb and endanger the tranquillity and security of South-Eastern Asia. To incorporate Thailand in this new " Indonesia " would therefore be against reason, justice, and the interests of future peace.

Another point worth noting is the proposal, in Section IV of the Memorandum, to establish a trans-Pacific defence belt, which would be under the administration of an international body. The belt would extend south-westwards from Hawaii, through Midway, Wake, and Guam, to include the Marshall, Caroline and Mariana groups of islands (which are now under Japanese rule, by virtue of the League of Nations' mandate, and which should be under the control of the United Nations after the war), the Bonin and Ryukyu groups, and Formosa. It further proposes that Formosa should be the terminus of the United Nations' air fleet, and the island should be placed under international administration. The proposal also suggests that Formosa should not be restored to China, nor should the Formosans be given the right to vote themselves into the Republic of China, though in tariff and monetary matters Formosa should be included in the Chinese system.

That the proposal is against the principle of justice and international fairplay goes without saying. Formosa was originally a part of China. It was only after the conclusion of the Sino-Japanese War in 1895 that Japan took possession of the island. When final victory comes, China should recover from Japan all that Japan has forcibly taken from us in the past fifty years ; and Formosa, being of such importance to China, should naturally be given back to her.

Moreover, the people of Formosa are predominantly Chinese by blood. They would naturally hope to be re-united with the motherland.

Those who propose this scheme of an international defence belt have in mind the objective of keeping a strict watch over Japan in the future. If this should be the case, I do not see any reason why Formosa should not be restored to China instead of being under international control. Formosa can fulfil that mission quite as well without being detached from China. If in the minds of those who propose this scheme there is any suspicion of China, any thought that post-war China would constitute a threat to the South Pacific, and if, in order to forestall that event, they wish to make Formosa an air-base from which it would be possible to dominate China and the China Coast, then the lack of confidence in China as a peaceful nation is in itself a clear sign of danger.

I have pointed at random to two or three examples of the so-called dangerous thought on post-war world reconstruction now current abroad. It is to be hoped that the intellectual leaders of the United States will take note of these utterances, and rectify the impressions created by such proposals. It is further to be hoped that erroneous views of this kind will not find further utterances lest they should be the cause of friction and ultimate war.

I wish also to point out to our friends in the United States that China, being a San-Min-Chu-I Republic, will never entertain any ideas of aggression ; but that she insists on recovering Formosa and the North-Eastern Provinces, which were and should be hers. China strives only for the full realization of her revolutionary aims, which are none other than national liberation and independence. China only hopes that there will be an equitable and just peace, and when once that settlement is reached, causes of future wars may be eliminated, and mankind may live at peace and in the pursuit of happiness.

A New Chapter in Chinese-American Relations *

I HAVE been requested by the Chinese-American Institute of Cultural Relations to speak on the new relations between China and the United States created by the recent abrogation of the unequal treaties. In this talk, I am aiming at a forecast of the future rather that a retrospect of the past.

I

The conclusion of the new treaty between China and the United States opens up a new chapter in the history of diplomatic relations between the two nations, in which the dominant note will be one of equality and mutual respect for each other's sovereignty. In fact, ever since the outbreak of the Pacific War, the United States and China, both being great democratic countries, have become Allies in a common cause, fighting side by side against a common enemy. Of course, we have yet to go through many bitter struggles before ultimate victory will be ours. It is for this reason that the peoples of these two nations are unanimously hoping for closer contacts and a more lasting co-operation, so that they may the better assume their joint responsibility to the world. Just as mutual trust and reciprocal understanding are necessary to the cementing of friendship between individuals, so they are necessary to the furtherance of friendship between nations. It is only when the American and Chinese people seek to understand each other that they can hope to proceed from their present equality in principle to equality in practice.

But there is no denying the fact that some of our American friends are not yet quite clear about the real conditions in China, and their lack of adequate knowledge has resulted in many mistaken views with regard to the Chinese situation. For instance, the problem of post-war world reconstruction has been discussed by a number of American scholars in various periodicals. A perusal of these articles shows us that quite a few of them seem to lack a real understanding of China. It does not necessarily follow, however, that any particular section of American society represents the views of the majority, for in America everyone is given perfect freedom to voice his own opinion, even though such opinion may prove to be contrary to the Government policy, or even their national interest.

* An address delivered before the Chinese-American Institute of Cultural Relations, Chungking, January 21, 1943.

We should on no account entertain any doubts or misunderstandings in respect of our Allies when they give utterance to their personal opinions. But the publication of unsound opinions is likely to arouse misgivings among us, and for this reason it may not be out of place for me here to cite one or two particular instances.

2

During the past year, the study of post-war world problems has been vigorously pursued by certain American thinkers, and, as a result of their studies, opinions have been expressed to the effect that Japan, after her defeat, should not be allowed to collapse, but, on the contrary, should be assisted to re-establish and maintain her military power as a check upon China, so that the latter may not become too strong and constitute a new menace to America. What is aimed at is nothing less than the creation of a new system of balance of power. It is also their fond hope that after her defeat, post-war Germany will have sufficient vitality and military prowess left to serve as counterweight against the Soviet Union. In their unfortunately mistaken view, American safety lies only in the balance of power between China and Japan in the Orient and between Russia and Germany in Eastern Europe. This is precisely what Professor Spykman, of Yale University, has proposed in his recent book, *American Strategy in World Politics*.

On the other hand, views diametrically opposite to this have been set forth by Professor Nathaniel Peffer, of Columbia University, in his new book, *The Basis of Peace in the Far East*. The more liberal school of American opinion is altogether opposed to any attempt at the revival of the discredited system of the balance of power. It is rightly argued that the balance of power system is obsolete, since it has repeatedly proved its failure as a means of maintaining world peace, before both the last war and this.

It was the desire to keep the balance of power between the Anglo-French-Russian Entente and the Central Powers that started the first World War, and the attempted restoration of this system in Europe brought about the second war in that continent. If at the end of this war we should again harp upon the same string, and try to give support to Japan and Germany, what would this mean but sowing new seeds of dissension for the future ? The idea of the balance of power as a means of maintaining world peace is untenable, and should be given up once for all. In the opinion of Professor Peffer, who has based his statement upon a genuine understanding of China, America should stand opposed to any balance of power in the Far East, and should help China to become strong and prosperous so as to be a stabilizing force in Asia.

There may not be many people who share Professor Spykman's opinions, but the question is, how did Professor Spykman come to hold these views? I presume it is owing to the fact that he did not have a clear understanding of the Chinese situation both in the past and in the present. His inadequate understanding has led him to place no real confidence in China, and to doubt whether she is a peace-loving nation, thus harbouring unwarranted misgivings lest China should prove to constitute a threat to America, once she attains to a state of abundance and prosperity. Unfortunately Professor Spykman does not see that for China to become an imperialistic power would be expressly contrary to the very nature of the San-Min-Chu-I and the policy of the Kuomintang. Nor would it be in line with our national tradition.

3

To remove similar misunderstanding among our Allies, there is, of course, much to be done in the way of publicity, but—what is more important—we should also let our deeds speak for us. With our deeds clearly visible to the eyes of the world, Professor Spykman, who is a learned and diligent student of world affairs, will not fail to perceive that a new China dedicated to the San-Min-Chu-I cannot be imperialistic.

But, so far, the San-Min-Chu-I has not been carried out in its entirety, and we have not yet been able to substantiate our words by concrete examples. Under conditions like these, naturally, foreign observers cannot be expected to judge of our future merely by our utterances. All our foreign friends are anxious to see if we are really sincere and determined to realize our national destiny in accordance with the pattern outlined by Dr. Sun Yat-sen. Their immediate attention is fixed on China's attitude toward her neighbours. For example, the problem of Korea's independence after the war is considered by many as the touchstone of China's real intentions. In their investigations of the situation in the Far East, foreign observers are watching with great concern China's attitude towards British Burma and French Indo-China, in case these two should demand their independence at the end of the war. They are also interested as to how the Chinese National Government is going to work out its domestic policy with regard to Tibet and Outer Mongolia. When the time comes for the Chinese Government to readjust its relations with Tibet and Outer Mongolia, what course will it take ?   If we are going to adopt high-handed measures, our foreign friends will certainly regard us as imperialistic and be on their guard against us.   In their opinion, a China imperialistically inclined is something to be feared even more than Japanese militarism reasserting itself after defeat.   The only way to remove suspicions and misunderstandings of this kind is to reconstruct our country in strict accordance with the San-Min-Chu-I.   With these principles fully carried out, there would be no possibility of China becoming an imperialistic power, and by that time there would be no more reason for any such misgivings and suspicions as our Allies may have concerning China to-day.

Misgivings are likely also to arise among foreigners who lack an adequate understanding of China's present political programme and reconstructional work.   They fear that China may imitate the methods of the Fascist nations.   But how do these fears arise ? They arise mainly because of the fact that our foreign friends are not well informed about the real situation of present-day China. The political experience of the English and American people accustoms them to think of multi-party rule as the only possible basis of democracy.   To them a government run by a single party is entirely out of keeping with democracy, for democracy under the tutelage of one party is unknown in Western political history.   They do not know that China has developed her political structure in a way peculiar to herself.   The task of reconstructing China has devolved on the shoulders of the Kuomintang through the whole-hearted support of the entire nation, not excepting even the opposition factions.

The Kuomintang is a revolutionary party of long standing which brought about the overthrow of the Manchu Empire, to whose impotence must be attributed the unequal treaties of the past hundred years.   Following the overthrow of the Manchu regime the Kuomintang, in its desire to achieve national unity, surrendered power to Yuan Shih-kai, and worked hard for the inauguration of a parliamentary system ; but this merely served as a stimulant to Yuan's ambition to assume imperial power, which finally led to the restoration of the monarchy with himself as emperor.   Yuan's death was followed by more than a decade of war-lordism, which almost drained China of her national vitality.

The lesson learned by the Chinese people during this period is too bitter to be forgotten.   To relieve the people of their sufferings, the Kuomintang, whose duty it was to fulfil the historic mission of national reconstruction, carried out a second revolution in 1927. However, no sooner was China united under the rule of the

Kuomintang, and ready to put her house in order, than Japan started her undeclared war against China. Were it not for the leadership of the Kuomintang in her heroic resistance against the aggressor, China, under the onslaught of Japanese mechanized power, might already have ceased to exist as a nation.

Thus, we see, the Kuomintang and the reconstruction of China as a modern nation are inseparably linked together. The Kuomintang is destined to shoulder the responsibility of tutoring the people of China for democracy. According to the programme of our national reconstruction, political rights would be restored to the people of the whole nation—all of whom would become supporters and adherents of the San-Min-Chu-I—by the time the period of tutelage ends. From thence onward constitutional government will begin.

There is another historic fact which our foreign friends would do well to understand. The Kuomintang is one of the foremost among the declared enemies of Fascism. When the Revolutionary Government of the Kuomintang still had its seat in Canton, a group of reactionary merchants and compradores conspired to set up against it a " Government by the Merchant Milita," which was Fascist in its very nature. Its prompt suppression by Dr. Sun Yat-sen must be considered the first blow aimed at the Chinese Fascist movement. This incident may not be quite familiar to our friends abroad. Let me cite a parallel instance in American history to make clear what I mean.

During the War of Independence, the American Government was also under a one-party rule. The party headed by Washington was a republican party, with the royalists in opposition, but the latter were soon suppressed. China now finds herself in a similar position. In its rôle as the tutor of the Chinese people, the Kuomintang is really paving the way for true democracy. Even in the present war, reconstructional work such as the new system of *hsien* administration, local self-government, and the organizing and strengthening of public opinion has been carried on with redoubled energy in order to lay a sound basis for the future constitutional government of the country. The bureaucratic system should be done away with as soon as possible, for a bureaucratic government, as a rule, always fears lest the people should organize themselves. The lukewarm attitude of the local authorities toward the decree for democratization issued by the Central Government, and their hesitation to put these decrees into effect, have in the past caused foreign observers to doubt our sincerity and capacity for self-government. Such a situation should no longer be allowed to exist.

15

4

Post-war international economic policy is also a question that is engaging the attention of various circles in England and America, from the Government authorities down to the man-in-the-street. Brains are being racked to find ways and means for the realization of permanent peace on earth. Our painful experience in the past has ingrained in our minds the truth that, failing a rational solution of the world economic problem, there will be no safeguarding of world peace.

It is generally believed in America that the guiding post-war policy should be a return to free trade, the demolition of the tariff-wall, and the removal of all obstacles to economic co-operation. Since the First World War, economic nationalism has come into vogue, resulting in the shrinking and almost the killing of world trade. It was with a view to preventing the recurrence of such an unhealthy situation that the United Nations signed, on New Year's Day 1943, a common declaration urging free trade as one of their post-war policies. As China is one of the signatories to the document, we have nothing to say against it as a matter of principle. But this does not mean that we are willing to give unconditional support to such a policy. The reason is, that we are an economically backward nation. If immediately after this war free trade is to be adopted in China, as it will be in economically advanced nations like England and America, then a new economic inequality will be likely to set in. Although, in respect of treaties, we are now on an equal footing with England and America, yet so far as economic life and productive power are concerned, we lag far behind them. They are both highly industrialized nations. Once we adopt free trade and abandon the protective tariff policy, all the agricultural raw material will be purchased by the industrial nations and sold back to China at a cheap price in the form of manufactured goods. China will naturally suffer under such a situation, and her programme of industrialization will be indefinitely postponed. China will remain an agricultural country, supplying other nations with raw materials, while all the goods she needs for consumption will have to be imported. In that case America, as well as China, will have everything to lose but nothing to gain from the economic point of view, for no matter how much America dumps her goods, she will not be in a position to compete with Japan in the Chinese market, and the Chinese would be economically dependent upon Japan. This is something which we cannot tolerate. Being a signatory to the said document, we do not ask for a repeal of the proposed policy. What we suggest is a new programme to deal with the peculiar situation in China.

In our opinion, free trade should be adopted in industrially advanced nations, such as England, America, Germany, and Japan, as soon as the war is ended ; but in China, the time element should be taken into account. It is only after ten, twenty, or thirty years, when China has completed her industrialization, that we can be expected to join an international regime of free trade.

We wish to make known to our American friends our hope that America will do her best to help China's industrialization in the first ten years after the war, just as at present she is doing her best to help us to win the war. Of all the United Nations we find that America is the only one equal to the task, for all the other nations, being exhausted after their war efforts, will have their own recon-structional problems to solve, while America, owning abundant resources and great productive power, will not be so adversely affected by the war. She will still have things to spare for helping the reconstruction of China.

It may be questioned whether ten years is a long enough period for the process of industrialization in China. As revolutionists we answer the question definitely in the affirmative. The successful completion of the first and second Five-Year Plans in Soviet Russia is an example. In her reconstructional work Russia made no use of foreign capital, though foreign technicians were employed. All that the Soviets spent in their reconstruction was saved from what they could spare from their food and clothing. The Soviet people at that time wore rags and had black bread for food, but they were not heard to complain. They tightened their belts and saved their butter for the purchase of German machines. Not infrequently the following words were inscribed on the machines in the factories : " Comrade workers ! This machine has cost us so many poods of butter. We must make the best use of it ! " Soviet industrial products, such as linen cloth and furs, were exported to Europe and America in large quantities. It is because the Soviet people could endure such hardships that they were able to complete their in-dustrialization in a period of ten years and prove themselves such a formidable power. They have shown their strength in the present war, and their recent victories on various fronts bespeak the result of their tenacious efforts in the past. We should regard them as our example, nay, our teachers. When I first interviewed Stalin in Moscow, he told me that old as she was, China would soon be able to stand on her own feet and make herself young again in the face of foreign aggressors. He further expressed the hope that China's reconstruction after the war would even surpass Soviet achievements in speed. In this connection I am glad to say that five and a half years of resistance against the aggressors have seen China making much progress along various lines, thus greatly strengthening her national confidence. We expect our post-war progress to be still greater when foreign capital becomes available to meet our needs.

5

For the completion of our reconstructional work in the first stage of industrialization let us assume that a sum of ten U.S. billion dollars, amounting to two hundred billions in Chinese currency, would be loaned to us by America for industrial equipment. In addition to this, we need another ten billion U.S. dollars for the building of factory plants and the payment of wages. Such a figure is by no means as astronomical as it may seem to us at first sight. It is generally known that America's war budget for the fiscal year July 1943 to June 1944 has been fixed at one hundred billion U.S. dollars, amounting to two thousand billions in Chinese currency. About two-thirds of this sum is ear-marked for war production. Thus, as we see, China's proposed loan of American money to the amount of ten billion dollars, for her first stage of industrialization, is equal to only one-seventh of America's war production budget for the coming year, while an annual expenditure of one billion means only 1 per cent. of America's entire war budget for the fiscal year 1943-4.

Now, what can we hope to achieve with such a sum in our industrial development? It is not an extravagant hope if we put our annual production of iron and steel after ten years at five million tons. That is about 5 per cent. of the American production for one year. The annual production of iron and steel for Japan, England and Germany is put at seven millions and a half, fifteen million, and twenty-five million tons respectively, while in America it almost reaches the figure of one hundred million tons.

As has been said before, a small number of Americans are watching with suspicious eyes the development of China lest she should become a menace to America. Such gloomy views of China can be easily dispelled by our own endeavours. Once misunderstanding is cleared up as regards these Americans, the American Government, as well as the American people, will only be too willing to see a strong and rich China emerge from this war, and to co-operate with us in safeguarding the peace on both sides of the Pacific. If it is sincerely believed by the whole world that a strong China is necessary to the peace of the Pacific, and that an industrialized China is a stabilizing force in maintaining the free trade of the world, then no effort ought to be spared to speed up China's industrialization.

6

If at the end of the last war world statesmen had had enough courage and foresight to accept Dr. Sun Yat-sen's plea for international aid to China's programme of industrial development, the present war might have been averted. Unfortunately the Governments of the Powers were too preoccupied with their own immediate problems to think in terms of the world as a whole. Hence the agony of this war. We cannot afford to commit a second error. We must learn by experience. We let a golden opportunity slip twenty years ago, but we must lay firm hold of it this time. In Dr. Sun Yat-sen's programme of national development, we find plans to build 100,000 miles of railways and 1,000,000 miles of highways to solve our communication and transportation difficulties. We should now lose no time in working for their early realization. What is of paramount importance is to convince our foreign friends of our worthy intentions, and to win their willing help.

We believe that the development of Sino-American relations will affect the future of the Far East and the whole world, and we also believe that America alone, with her far-sighted leaders, will be in a position to help us. We will frankly inform the American Government and the American people that China's industrialization is indeed intended to solve the problem of her internal reconstruction, to raise the living standard of her masses, and to increase her national strength ; but there is another side to the question. It is not out of mere self-interest that we aspire to be a modernized nation ; we have also the future of the world in mind. Among every five men in the world, there is one Chinese. When four hundred and fifty million people can live a decent life and find themselves able to contribute to world prosperity, the face of the world will certainly be tremendously changed. Whether this will remain a mere dream or will become a fact hinges upon the development of Sino-American relations. Both the American and Chinese people are therefore called upon to shoulder their joint responsibility, and to make timely efforts to achieve their common goal toward world peace and prosperity.

Reconstruction of the Post-War World *

I

It has often been said that what the United Nations lacked was a plan for war. Be that as it may, we cannot afford to be unprepared for the peace to come. It is for this reason that people in Britain and America, whether the holders of responsible positions in their respective Governments, or just the common man in the street, are now seriously interested in post-war world problems. Not only are the publicists and experts expressing their views on post-war problems in technical journals or newspapers, but Government machinery and civic organizations have been set up for the study of post-war problems. How are we going to restore stability and prosperity after the war? How are we going to lay the foundations of a lasting peace? These are some of the problems now engaging the attention of students and statesmen alike.

It is hardly necessary to emphasize the fact here that the Chinese people are a peace-loving nation. Tradition, philosophy and history all point to that. We have been endeavouring to maintain peaceful relations with our neighbouring peoples for thousands of years. We have an ingrained traditional love for peace. And what is more, for the past fifty years or so, we have been having the beneficial influence of the teachings of Dr. Sun Yat-sen, and the experiences of our National Revolution. All these go to make China one of the main pillars for the maintenance of permanent world peace. As a matter of fact, we have already been defending that peace. The War of Resistance against Japanese aggression, which we have been fighting for the past five years, is but a part of the world struggle for preserving peace and order.

Before the outbreak of Sino-Japanese hostilities, many foreign friends had told us that, from the point of view of national self-interest, it would be better for China to be patient and to play for time. Not that we were not fully aware of the fact that once war should break out between ourselves and Japan, China would have to undergo tremendous sufferings and make great sacrifices. But in order to extinguish the flames of aggression so as to maintain permanent peace, we finally had to go to war.

* A speech delivered at the inaugural meeting of the Committee on Post-war World Reconstruction, Sun Yat-sen Institute for the Advancement of Culture and Education, Peipei, January 31, 1943.

It is needless for me to reiterate that the Chinese people have a strong love for peace and justice. We, as a nation, refuse to be dominated by ideas of self-interest. We value our national existence, but at the same time we are intimately concerned with the existence of the entire human race. In order to save the whole of humanity from further sufferings, we would rather undergo all these sufferings ourselves. We are not unaware of our strength, yet we would be neglecting ourselves if we should not fulfil the mission which, we think, the Chinese people have towards mankind. Keeping constantly in mind such sayings of our sages as, " Drops of water go to make the river," we have at least succeeded in immobilizing a huge part of the Japanese forces which would otherwise be used against our Allies.

The global war is now at its turning-point. The victory is in sight. But how, from painful experience of the past, are we going to make a new world in which we can enjoy permanent peace ? This has again become a problem for all far-sighted, thinking, and peace-loving peoples. If we should succeed only in stopping aggression, without laying the foundations for permanent world peace, then this war would have been fought in vain. The Chinese people have sacrificed millions of lives and untold treasure in this war : we shall naturally contribute all that we possibly can towards the establishment of permanent world peace.

2

Owing to difficulties of communication we have not been able to get all the current literature concerning post-war world reconstruction which has lately been published in Britain and America. From what I myself have been able to get, I have noticed that although there are articles and treatises which have been written in a spirit of justice, there are, nevertheless, others which were prompted by narrow considerations of self-interest and were in line with traditional prejudice. Not long ago an article of mine was published in the Press, entitled " Dangerous Thought on Post-war Problems." * In that article, I pointed out some of the biased opinions which are now current abroad. Since then I have come across a recent book, *American Strategy in World Politics*, by Professor Nicholas John Spykman of Yale University.

The author advocates the establishment of a new balance of power for the post-war world. His main thesis is this : The formation of the united bloc of nations, comprising chiefly Soviet Russia,

* Chap. 19 of this book.

Britain, America and China, is at the moment prompted mainly by considerations of self-interest. Each member of this bloc of nations has his own designs and aims in this present struggle. At the conclusion of the present war, each will go his own way. From the point of view of political realism, America should now consider its own case ; for a strong Japan, or a strong China, would equally be a threat to America. The author is therefore of the opinion that after defeating Japan in this war, America should help Japan to restore its military power. A powerful Japan will serve as a check on China, and only by check and balance can peace in the Far East be maintained. As regards Europe, the author thinks that peace in Europe can best be maintained by the establishment of a new balance of power between Soviet Russia and Germany. Assuming the rôle of a prophet, Professor Spykman warns the American people that " The ally of to-day is the enemy of to-morrow."

It need hardly be said that the so-called new balance of power is nothing really new. It amounts to a re-affirmation of the doctrines entertained by the Haushofer school of geo-politicians which find so much favour among the Nazis. But we must not ignore the significance of Professor Spykman's pronouncement. Professor Spykman has been Director of the Yale Institute of International Studies, and is Professor of International Relations at Yale University. This University, together with Harvard University, occupies an important place in American politics. What seems only to be academic discussion may sometimes exert considerable weight in shaping the national policy of America.

Naturally there are many others in America whose views are directly opposed to those of Professor Spykman. Such, for example, are those of Professor Nathaniel Peffer of Columbia University. In his book, *Basis for Peace in the Far East*, Professor Peffer strongly advocates the theory of " imbalance of power." The author thinks that a powerful China is the only safeguard to peace in the Far East. As peace in the new hemisphere is maintained by the existence of a powerful United States, so peace in the Far East is to be maintained by a powerful China.

The East-West Association, which is under the chairmanship of Pearl Buck, has also produced several articles criticising such reactionary views. From England, I have come across another recent book, Professor Carr's *Conditions of Peace*. The book contains some very well-reasoned views regarding post-war reconstruction, most of which are quite in harmony with the fundamental spirit of the Three People's Principles.

3

In our study of post-war world reconstruction we must keep a close watch over the prevailing opinions abroad. We must give our support to those which are just and condemn those which are harmful to China. It is regrettable that, so far, not much interest has been shown in these matters by our academic circles. Our Government organizations whose duty it is to look after these matters have been quite negligent in this respect.

We all know that in a democratic country public opinion can influence national policy. If biased opinions should be widespread, it would be difficult even for clear-sighted statesmen to eradicate them. A case in point is the way in which America joined this war.

President Roosevelt is indeed a great statesman. As long ago as in October 1937 he made his famous Chicago speech, in which he denounced aggression and called for the quarantine of the aggressors. He knew very well that it is impossible for America to stand aloof in world politics. But public opinion, as then prevailing, was strongly isolationist in attitude, so that President Roosevelt's speech was violently attacked by the Press, and for a long time he had to remain quiescent. His appeal for the passing of the Neutrality Act was held up by Congress. When France collapsed, America had a standing army of only some 360,000 men. Not until September 1940 did the American Congress pass the Selective Draft Act, introducing compulsory military service while the United States was still at peace.

From the above we may see what a great and far-sighted statesman like President Roosevelt had to endure before his views were finally accepted by his fellow-countrymen. All this indicates how powerful is public opinion in America, and how it influences the shape of American national policy.

This has been so in the past, and will continue to be so in the future. I must therefore advise you not to ignore the views expressed in the Press concerning post-war world reconstruction in Britain and America. Imagine if such views as those of Professor Spykman's should gain the ascendancy and become so powerful as to be capable of influencing American national policy ! What a post-war world should we then have ?

4

If the so-called " realists " should succeed in influencing the national policies of the United Nations, then I think the world situation would be something like this : In Europe they would like to see the war between Soviet Russia and Germany go on as long as possible with neither side scoring big victories nor suffering disastrous defeats.   They would like to see both parties becoming exhausted so that they themselves may be able to take advantage of such a situation, and become what we Chinese called the " lucky fisherman." In the Pacific, the United States would, of course, come to the support of China, for otherwise there could be no balance of power.   The appeal which has been made by so many clear-sighted men to come to China's aid quickly, so as to strengthen her power of counter-offensive, has, however, to be weighed on the scales of the balance of power in the Far East.   As regards the post-war period, there will be intrigues and counter-intrigues just as in the old days.   When Power A is needed to check Power B, then the friendship of Power A will be courted ; and when Power B is needed to check Power A, then the friendship of Power B will be sought after.   This is what we mean by balance of power.

For self-interest, all this sounds very well indeed.   But can world peace be maintained under such a system ?   No, definitely no !   If by maintaining such a system world peace could be maintained, then we should not have had this present war at all.   Should the so-called new balance of power become a reality, then the blood of our soldiers and those of the United Nations would have been shed in vain, and the sacrifices which the whole of humanity had been suffering would have been rendered meaningless.

The aspirations of the Chinese people are simple.   We desire only that China may live in peace with the entire human race. We earnestly hope that the close relationship now existing between China and her great Allies, Soviet Russia, Britain and America, may be permanently maintained after the war, and that the spirit of the Atlantic Charter may be carried out without reserve in establishing peaceful relations between various countries in the Far East. As regards Japan, the ideal solution would be to transform militarist Japan into a democratic Japan by the concerted efforts of the four great Powers.   After she had become a democratic country, we might invite Japan, in a spirit of equality, to join the union of democratic nations.   The permanent peace of the Far East is to be maintained by collective strength.   If this should be deemed to be too ideal a solution, we might then follow the other alternative ; that is, to annihilate completely the military strength of Japan and never again to allow her to become a threat to Far Eastern peace.

Such are our ideals.   If, however, our ideals cannot be carried out, then we may resort to "realism." Here we have a twofold policy. Firstly, in consideration of the geographical and other factors, we must have closer relations with Soviet Russia so as to prevent Japan from becoming again a threat to Far Eastern peace. Secondly, at the same time, we may turn to defeated Japan after the war and establish closer relations with the Japanese people, who would by then have learnt a good deal in this war.

This " realist " policy of ours is again a simple one, because if we should adopt such a policy, we should do so for the sake of our own security. We cannot, however, be in favour of " realism," because we know that " realist " policies are no safeguard to permanent peace. They will only lead to further conflagrations.

The enthusiastic support and material aid given to China by our Allies in this war will never be forgotten by the Chinese people. But I must point out that in respect of the ideals of post-war world reconstruction, we are still friendless. On previous occasions I have indicated that people have viewed a powerful post-war China with apprehension. They imagine that a strong China after the war will be a threat to the world. All this suspicion is uncalled for. It reminds me of the Chinese saying, " Once bitten by a snake, one is even afraid of the sight of a rope." The rope will not bite anybody ; one is afraid of it only because one is nervous.

After World War I, many Western thinkers, such as H. G. Wells, Bertrand Russell, and Harold Laski, dissatisfied with the chaos and confusion to which Western philosophy had led them, became interested in Chinese political philosophy. Although their views may not be always correct, they have, nevertheless, shown their interest in the study of Chinese traditions. Unfortunately, interest in the Chinese thought was short-lived ; so to this day the spirit of the Chinese people is still something mysterious to the minds of the West. We have ourselves to blame, for we ourselves have not accepted the responsibility of letting the West know what we really are.

5

I wish also to say a word to our Allies. If in the peace settlement after the war, the views of a country which represents one-fifth of the total population of the world, such as China, were not respected, and if such a country were not given an equal opportunity in the peace settlement, then whatever settlement might be reached would not be lasting. It is not the question whether traditional Chinese political philosophy should have world-wide acceptance or not ; it is merely a simple mathematical problem. One-fifth of humanity cannot be lightly ignored.

Finally, I would like to give you in a few words my own personal opinion concerning the fundamental principles to be followed in post-war world reconstruction. The most important of these principles, I think, is the principle of the equality of the nations. If in the post-war world the division between ruling peoples and subject peoples should continue to exist, then national hatred and ill-feeling would also continue and intensify. Under such circumstances there could be no guarantee whatever for permanent world peace. If a new world should be created after this war, we must thoroughly abolish all racial theories entertained by the Nazis, and put into effect the principles of national freedom and national equality as enunciated in the Atlantic Charter. As regards the so-called backward peoples, the advanced peoples should help them to raise their cultural level, as elder brothers helping the younger. Christ commands people to love their neighbours, and this rule should be followed in international intercourse.

Secondly, the post-war world should be so reconstructed as to increase the general well-being and happiness of mankind. To this end, we must first of all raise the standard of living among the various peoples. There should be not only rationalization of production, but also rationalization of distribution and consumption. For if we should concentrate on rationalizing production alone, this would involve us in all kinds of troubles. What is needed is some kind of co-ordination between production, distribution and consumption. The post-war China will undoubtedly follow closely the principle of People's Livelihood. The standard of living of our people will have to be raised. We shall have closer economic relations with other nations.

As we examine the causes of the failure of the peace established after the First World War, we cannot but feel that in order to maintain permanent world peace, the above two principles must be strictly adhered to in the peace settlement following this present war. It is the avoidance of past mistakes that marks human progress. It is sincerely to be hoped that past mistakes will not be repeated after this war.

I do not know whether after this war there will still be room for military activities ; but to prevent such activities is undoubtedly our responsibility. Also I do not know whether our proposals for post-war world reconstruction will be acceptable to all ; but regardless of this we must do our part.

For a Just and Enduring Peace *

It is my duty and privilege this aftertoon (August 29, 1943) to preside at this meeting to commemorate the 298th anniversary of the death of Hugo Grotius.

We are gathered here not only to do honour to the memory of a distinguished scholar of the seventeenth century, one whose genius initiated and stimulated the development of the modern system of law between nations ; but also to look forward to the dawning of a new era for mankind—an era of which Grotius must have dreamed when he wrote his famous work, *De Jure Belli et Pacis,* " The Law of War and Peace."

The teachings and theories of Hugo Grotius find a ready response among intellectual circles in China, since they coincide with the Chinese philosophy of the supremacy of the moral law, the law of the right and just, as opposed to the theory that international law can be founded on compacts which may negative the righteous cause, and that the Sovereign State is its own judge of right or wrong.

According to Grotius, the conduct of a state should be judged by the same moral law as that which exists between individuals in any civilized state. This concept of international conduct was held by the Chinese for wellnigh two thousand years before the birth of Grotius. And this view still prevails in the consciousness of the Chinese people to-day.

For two hundred years the West drifted away from Grotius's concept of international law, and positivist views prevailed down to the end of the last World War. Since then the tide has turned, and the catastrophes of 1914, 1937, and 1939 have brought back into prominence the ideal which Grotius put forward in a world which at that time was torn with dissension and ridden with strife.

This World War, the second of the twentieth century, is a relic of the centuries just past, when wars paid dividends. The wars of the last years of the eighteenth and the whole of the nineteenth century were wars which gave the victors easy loot, glory, and aggrandizement. Indemnities obtained from China served as the financial base upon which Japan's economic structure and military machine were both built up. But it has now been shown that

* Opening speech at a meeting held under the auspices of the China Society of International Law, Chungking, August 29, 1943.

233

world economy is so balanced and interwoven that wars do not any longer pay. However, the Japanese militarists, and Hitler and his satellites, still believe that by aggressive wars sufficient loot and territory can be obtained, not only to pay for the war, but also to provide profits for the aggressor State.

The Japanese invasion of China was undertaken for loot and conquest. Hitler even to-day is stripping Europe of much of its wealth for the enrichment of his Nazi Reich. For a time these aggressors were resisted only by their unfortunate victims, while the rest of the world stood aside in what was considered the right attitude of the neutral. Only too late was it finally realized that no country was safe from aggression ; none could stand aside unmolested as a neutral when aggressors were on the rampage.

Grotius laid emphasis on the " just war." He laid down the rule that a neutral should " do nothing which may strengthen the side which has the worse cause, or which may impede the motions of him who is waging a just war."

The teachings of Grotius point to the recognition by the nations of the world of the moral law in their mutual relations, and the fact that they should make their conduct conform to the fundamental principles derived from that law. The same principles of law that hold good for individuals must be upheld for nations. Then, and then only, shall we have a moral and ethical basis on which to build up a better world.

The aim of students of international affairs, jurists, and publicists to-day, on the anniversary of the death of Hugo Grotius, is to revitalize and strengthen international law, so as to lay the foundation for a just and enduring world peace, securing order under law to all nations. The weak must be able to live without fear of the strong in a world which will be a realization of the United Nations Charter.

The establishment of a body of law governing international conduct which will make this practicable and effective must no longer be regarded as Utopian. The savageries of Hitler's Fascists and the Japanese militarists have shown that no laws governing the conduct of war are worth anything when aggressive Governments seek aggrandizement through world domination. It is only the establishment of a central world authority which can bring peace and security to this world of ours, and raise the dignity of the human race to a higher plane—the rule of law throughout the world.

Noted publicists have formulated postulates for the organization of a better world. In general they call for the outlawing of war and its repudiation as a legalized procedure for the settlement of disputes :

the acts which shall be regarded as aggression must be specifically defined, as well as the conditions calling into effect the right of legitimate self-defence. An act of aggression committed against one nation must be regarded as an act of aggression against all the other members of the international community.

Each nation must consider that it has a vital national interest in the maintenance of international law and order, and that every threat or act of violence against one member of the community constitutes a direct threat to each and all. The primary objective of the new international organization must be the protection of each and all of its members against acts of violence, so that every nation may rely for its security upon the collective action of the community.

These are some of the concepts which will carry into effect the teachings of Hugo Grotius and the great sages of China. It is only when the society of nations is built up on the basis of these concepts, in whatever form the architects of the central world authority may deem best, that we shall have peace on earth, and that man will be free to develop to his full stature as a human being.

Appendix A

GENERAL PRINCIPLES FOR NATIONAL RECONSTRUCTION *

(1) The National Government shall reconstruct the Republic of China on the basis of the revolutionary San-Min-Chu-I and the Five-Power Constitution.

(2) The prerequisite for national reconstruction is to promote the economic well-being of the people by providing for their four fundamental necessities of life : i.e. food, clothing, housing, and means of transportation. The Government shall co-operate with the people in the development of agriculture, so that the food supply for the people may be sufficient ; shall co-operate in the development of the textile industry, so that the people may have adequate clothing ; shall construct houses of all kinds in accordance with great housing schemes, so that the people may be provided with decent living quarters ; and shall build railways, roads, and canals, so that the people may travel conveniently.

(3) The second in importance is democracy. The Government shall instruct and guide the people in respect of their political knowledge and powers, so that they may be able to exercise the powers of election, recall, initiative and referendum.

(4) The third in importance is nationalism. In regard to the racial minorities within the nation, the Government shall help them, so that they may acquire the capacity of self-determination and self-government. The Government shall resist foreign aggression. The treaties with other nations shall be revised, so that our position of equality among the family of nations and our national independence will be restored.

(5) The order of national reconstruction shall be divided into three periods : first, the period of military government ; second, the period of political tutelage ; and third, the period of constitutional government.

(6) During the period of military government, all institutions shall be subject to military rule. The Government, on the one hand, shall use military force to remove all obstacles within the nation ; and on the other hand, it shall preach the principles of the Revolution to the people of the whole nation, in order to enlighten them and guide them toward national unity.

(7) As soon as the order within a province is completely restored, the period of political tutelage in the province shall begin ; and the period of military government shall cease.

(8) In the period of political tutelage, the government shall send out properly trained and qualified officials to every *hsien*, to help the people to prepare for local self-government. A *hsien* is considered to be up to the standard of local self-government when a census of its population is accurately taken, its land entirely surveyed, its police force well organized, and its roads constructed. The people of the *hsien* shall be trained to exercise the four political powers. After they have discharged the duties

* Drafted and proposed by Dr. Sun Yat-sen, and adopted by the First Kuomintang National Congress, Canton, January 20, 1924.

of citizenship and have determined to put into practice the revolutionary principles, the people of the *hsien* may elect the *hsien* magistrate to administer the *hsien* affairs ; and they may elect representatives to make laws and draw up regulations for the *hsien*. When the *hsien* has done the above, it is regarded as a complete, self-governing *hsien*.

(9) In a completely self-governing *hsien*, the people shall have the powers of direct election, direct recall, direct initiative, and direct referendum.

(10) When self-government is instituted in a *hsien*, the value of the private land in the entire *hsien* shall be first assessed and determined. The procedure is that the landowners shall declare the value of their land. The local government may tax the land on the basis of this declaration of value, with the option that the *hsien* may purchase the land at any time for its declared value. After the declaration of value of the land, if there is any increment in its value on account of political or social improvement, such unearned increment shall belong to the people of the entire *hsien* and not to the private landowners.

(11) The tax on land, the increment of value on land, the products of public land, the proceeds from forestry and waterways, and the profit from mines and hydraulic power shall belong entirely to the local government, to be used for the care of the young, the aged, the poor, the distressed, and the sick, and other kinds of public necessity.

(12) The exploitation of the natural resources of a *hsien* and the industrial and commercial undertakings on a large scale, which are beyond its financial ability to develop and manage, and for the operation of which it must have outside capital, shall be carried on with the assistance of the Central Government. The profits shall be divided on a fifty-fifty basis between the Central and the Local Governments.

(13) Each *hsien* shall contribute a certain percentage of its annual receipts to the expenditure of the Central Government. The percentage shall be determined every year by the representatives of the people. It shall not be less than 10 per cent. nor more than 40 per cent.

(14) After the local self-government of a *hsien* has been established, it may elect one representative to the National Assembly to participate in the affairs of the Central Government.

(15) All candidates for office, and officers, whether in the Central or the Local Government, shall be persons qualified in public examinations held by the Central Government, and shall have had their qualifications certified.

(16) When all the *hsien* of a province have local self-government fully established, the period of constitutional government shall begin in that province. The representatives of the people shall elect the provincial governor, who shall supervise the self-government in the province. In regard to matters of national administration in the province, the governor shall be under the direction of the Central Government.

(17) During this period, the powers exercised by the Central and Provincial Governments shall follow the system of the functional distribution of powers. Affairs of national character shall be under the jurisdiction of the Central Government. Affairs particularly pertaining

to a province or a locality shall be under the jurisdiction of the local government. This division of powers shall emphasize neither centralization nor decentralization.

(18) The *hsien* shall be the unit of self-government. The province shall serve as a connecting link between the Central and the *hsien* Governments.

(19) In the period of constitutional government there shall be five *Yuan* which will endeavour to put into practice the system of the five governing powers. The order is as follows : the Executive Yuan, the Legislative Yuan, the Judicial Yuan, the Examination Yuan, and the Control Yuan.

(20) In the Executive Yuan there shall be provisionally the following Ministries : 1, Interior ; 2, Foreign Affairs ; 3, Military Affairs, 4, Finance ; 5, Industries and Commerce ; 7, Education ; 8, Communications.

(21) Before the promulgation of the Constitution, the Presidents of the five Yuan shall be appointed and removed by the President of the Republic, and be subject to his direction.

(22) The draft of the Constitution shall be prepared by the Legislative Yuan, based upon the General Principles for National Reconstruction, and the results of the periods of political tutelage and the constitutional government. The draft shall be publicized to the people from time to time, so that when the time arrives it may be adopted and put into practice.

(23) When more than one-half the provinces have reached the stage of constitutional government—that is, when more than one-half of the provinces have local self-government fully established in all their *hsien*— the National Assembly should be convened to decide on the adoption and promulgation of the Constitution.

(24) After the Constitution is promulgated the sovereign powers of the Central Government shall be exercised by the National Assembly ; that is, the National Assembly shall have the powers of election and recall of Central Government officers, and the powers of initiative and referendum of Central Government laws.

(25) When the Constitution is promulgated, constitutional government is considered fully established. The people of the whole nation shall hold a general election in accordance with the provisions of the Constitution. The National Government shall be dissolved three months after the general election. The governing powers shall be exercised by the Government so elected. Then the great task of national reconstruction is considered to have been accomplished.

SUN WEN,
April 12, 1924.

Appendix B

PROJECT FOR THE CONCENTRATION OF NATIONAL STRENGTH TO COMBAT THE MENACE THREATENING CHINA'S NATIONAL SURVIVAL *

CHINA's national crisis, due to external aggression on the part of a powerful and rapacious neighbour, has been aggravated since the Mukden seizure of September 18, 1931. Our North-Eastern Provinces have been lost, and their recovery is not yet within sight. Even though the recommendations made by the Lytton Commission of Inquiry despatched by the League of Nations was accepted by both parties to the conflict, the North-Eastern Provinces would be restored to China in name only, as they would be in fact placed under international control. Bewilderment and uncertainty beset us when we think of our future.

For over forty years the Kuomintang has immutably regarded China's Revolution as well as China's national salvation as its own historic mission. The supreme task resting upon its shoulders at this moment is to lead the Chinese people resolutely and without deviation in the struggle for national survival and the restoration of the lost territories. This is indeed the decisive hour for the Party to assume the great task of safeguarding, in its own hands, the destiny of the nation. This Third Plenary Session is therefore compelled to take up an arduous task, unprecedented in China's long history. The greatest problem confronting us to-day is determined resistance to Japanese aggression, with the supreme object of securing national survival.

But to resist the Japanese invader to the bitter end, we must first of all achieve internal unity. It is quite clear that only through resisting the aggressor can national unity be attained. These two conditions react upon one another as cause and effect, which cannot be isolated. When the one is achieved the other problem will be solved almost automatically. This is the greatest decision that this Plenary Session of the Kuomintang will have to make.

The underlying cause of China's non-resistance to Japanese aggression up to this moment is the Government's perplexity over the complicated conditions with which it is beset. The core of the problem is internal disunity, the causes of which are :

(1) The division of political parties and factions, which have been attacking one another as a result of their differences and dissension, in respect of political opinion, and the non-popularization of political power, as well as the absence of freedom of expression.

(2) The mutual distrust among military factions which tend to checkmate and oppose one another as a result of the failure to distribute administrative powers between the Central Government and the local authorities, and the failure on the part of the Central Government to produce an appropriate policy for the guidance of public opinion.

---

* Submitted by the author and adopted with minor revisions by the Third Plenary Session of the Fourth Central Executive Committee of the Kuomintang on December 15, 1932.

We must therefore endeavour to cure the disease with the right prescription.

Domestically, first of all, democratic government must be introduced so that the citizens shall enjoy the right to participate in political affairs and to exercise political power. The people must be given the chance to express their political views through peaceful and legal means, in order, step by step, to build up a constitutional and democratic State. Thus, the unjustifiable attacks on the Government by the opposition parties and factions such as they have been making, will be ended. Secondly, the military factions should be reconciled through the just disposition of the Central Government, thereby removing distrust and rivalry between them. It may be anticipated that national unity will be achieved in place of the present chaos if the Government will follow a resolute policy to oppose Japanese encroachments, and, at the same time, will adopt a liberal and tolerant attitude toward its political opponents.

Diplomatically, the necessary preparations and the right moves must be made in time. To cite an instance, action on the resumption of friendly relations with the Soviet Union was delayed for half a year, and almost side-tracked indefinitely. We have provided, through our own slackness and misjudgment of the international situation, almost every opportunity for the enemy to court the nations which should have stood on the same side with us. There is, of course, still time to retrieve the ground we have lost. But the international situation may change at any moment. If we commit further mistakes in formulating our foreign policy, this may lead to still worse disaster, too late for us to prevent it. In addition, we must make in good time all necessary preparations for strengthening our national defence and perfecting our military arrangements for any further emergency that may be likely to overtake us in the near future. To implement the foregoing statement, certain recommendations and proposals are hereby presented for the consideration and adoption by the present Plenary Session of the Central Executive Committee.

PROPOSED RESOLUTIONS

I. On Foreign Relations

Be it resolved :

(1) That our foreign policy be based, from now on, on the resolute determination to resist Japanese aggression, and, to implement this policy, on the closest possible collaboration with the Powers concerned ;

(2) That the policy of cementing our friendship with the United States of America, Great Britain, France, and other countries be actively promoted and, at the same time, all necessary steps be taken to meet the coming World War ; and

(3) That positive efforts be exerted for the restoration and improvement of friendly relations with the Soviet Union as our prospective ally in the Far East.

II. On Domestic Affairs

Be it resolved :

(1) That the Government issue definite and responsible assurances to the people to guarantee the freedom of assembly and organization, the freedom of speech and publication, the freedom of belief and the freedom of residence, in accordance with the political principles of the Party, and to prohibit all illegal acts of interference and high-handed arrests ;

(2) That regional political councils be established in certain locations to be designated to carry out effectively the functional distribution of powers between the Central Government and the provinces, and that members of the Central Executive Committee be directed to participate in these councils ;

(3) That the political councils in Peiping and Canton, already in existence, be formally reappointed and confirmed in their office by the Government ;

(4) That all local administrative functions be exercised by the respective competent local authorities in accordance with law, and that no administrative acts and orders be permitted and issued by unauthorized persons or self-appointed authorities in contravention of the established administrative system ; and

(5) That high political inspectors be appointed and despatched to the provinces to inspect the local administrations, to inquire into the sufferings and grievances of the people, and to report on their findings periodically to the Central Government, and that Central Government decisions and measures for reform and reconstruction be based on the findings and reports of such political inspections.

III. On Preparations for Constitutional Rule

Be it resolved :

(1) That the establishment of local self-government as envisaged in Dr. Sun Yat-sen's General Principles for National Reconstruction be vigorously enforced in order to enhance preparations for the inauguration of constitutional rule at the earliest possible moment ;

(2) That a Draft Constitution be prepared by the Legislative Yuan, which work is to be done during the period January to June 1933, and that the said Draft Constitution be made public on October 10, 1933, for nation-wide public discussion preparatory to its submission to the National Assembly ;

(3) That the First National Assembly be convened in April 1934, to pass and adopt the Constitution and determine a date for its promulgation and enforcement ;

(4) That after the promulgation of the Constitution, the Government be required to complete the establishment of local self-government throughout the country according to constitutional provisions, as well as to carry through all uncompleted tasks scheduled for the period of political tutelage ;

(5) That October 10, 1934, be tentatively fixed as the date upon which constitutional rule shall commence ; and

(6) That all the people have the freedom to organize political bodies to participate in political affairs, provided such actions do not endanger the Republic or violate the principles of the San-Min-Chu-I, and that all citizens, with the exception of those in active military service whose suffrage is temporarily suspended, have the right to elect, and to be elected, delegates to the National Assembly.

IV. On the National Assembly

(1) That the First National Assembly be composed of delegates elected by the people in the provinces, territories and municipalities in proportion to the population, and by professional bodies in the said areas, and that the ratio of representation and the methods of election be determined by law through enactment of the Legislative Yuan not later than June 1933 ;

(2) That the National Assembly be elected for a term of two years, that it be convened once a year for a one month session, that when considered necessary it may be convened in extraordinary session for a fortnight, and that during the period of its adjournment its functions be delegated and exercised by the Legislative Yuan and the Control Yuan, both to be elected by the National Assembly ;

(3) That the functions and powers of the National Assembly be the following :

    (a) To exercise sovereignty in the name of the entire people as the organ of supreme power ;

    (b) To make and amend the Constitution of the Republic ;

    (c) To pass laws and the budget, to declare war and conclude peace, and to decide on political, economic and military matters of great importance ;

    (d) To elect and constitute the Legislative Yuan and the Control Yuan ;

    (e) To supervise, censure and impeach the Government ; and

    (f) To supervise and promote the establishment of local self-government throughout the country ; and

(4) That the National Assembly be not subject to orders of dissolution or of interference of whatever nature, and that the delegates to the National Assembly be immune from arrest.

V. On the Provincial Assembly

Be it resolved :

(1) That prior to the convocation of the National Assembly the Government shall cause the convening of the Provincial Assemblies in the various provinces in accordance with laws enacted by the Legislative Yuan prior to June 1933 ;

(2) That the Provincial Assembly be elected annually to meet once a year for a session of fifteen days, and that the term and function of its delegates shall cease immediately upon conclusion of its session.

(3) That the functions and powers of the Provincial Assembly shall be the following :

   (a) To elect and constitute the Provincial Council, which shall participate in provincial affairs on behalf of the citizens of the province during the adjournment of the Provincial Assembly ;

   (b) To decide on ways and means to hasten the enforcement of local self-government, to pass the provincial budget and provincial regulations and by-laws ;

   (c) To act in the name of the people of the province in initiating impeachment proceedings against provincial administrative and judicial officers before the Control Yuan ; and

   (d) To present to the Executive Yuan on behalf of the people of the province recommendations for reform and reconstruction as regards provincial administrative matters ; and

(4) That no taxes shall be levied, no provincial debenture bonds be issued, and no additional burdens be imposed on the people of the province by the Provincial Government without the approval and concurrence of the Provincial Assembly or the Provincial Council.

VI. ON NATIONAL DEFENCE AND MILITARY MATTERS

Be it resolved :

(1) That a definite and practical plan for national defence be formulated with a certain neighbouring Power as the assumed enemy whom the nation will have to face, and that the minimum requirements for a defensive armament be provided for and secured ;

(2) That national defence shall be undertaken by the Central Government and peace preservation by local governments, that strategic zones be designated National Defence Areas, while other sections of the country be designated Rehabilitation Areas, that rehabilitation work in the latter be completed within a definite time-limit, and that both the defence and rehabilitation areas need not coincide with provincial boundaries ;

(3) That the peace-time strength of the National Army shall be fixed, that the division be made the largest peace-time unit of the Army, that a system of progressive conscription for military service be introduced, and that the peace-time military expenditures be limited to approximately one-third of the total national budget ;

(4) That Land, Sea and Air Forces be built up, and fortifications and sea and air bases be developed in consonance with the aim and requirements of national defence, and that the criterion shall be qualititative rather than quantitative ;

(5) That the present armed forces shall be reorganized systematically up to the desired strength, with a view to reducing superfluous and redundant personnel, that the demobilized soldiers be transferred to the local peace preservation corps and police force, or otherwise formed into labour battalions for work on land reclamation and river conservancy projects ;

(6) That a coastal defence fleet composed of submarines and fast motor-torpedo boats shall be built, and that construction of all

warships unsuitable for this purpose be stopped or that they shall be converted into merchantmen ;

(7) That an Air Force adequate for defence needs shall be built up and organized at the earliest possible date ;

(8) That military and air force training schools be established under unified control ;

(9) That war Industries be developed and operated under national administration, to be located in interior points safe from enemy attack ;

(10) That all military institutions of a private character be suppressed, reorganized or prohibited by law ; and

(11) That provincial military sub-councils be set up in localities to carry out military reforms and reorganizations under the direct orders of the Central Military Council.

Appendix C

FINAL DRAFT OF THE CONSTITUTION OF THE REPUBLIC OF CHINA *

PREAMBLE

By virtue of the mandate received from the whole body of citizens, and in accordance with the bequeathed teachings of Dr. Sun Yat-sen, Founder of the Republic of China, the National Assembly of the Republic of China hereby ordains and enacts this Constitution and causes it to be promulgated throughout the land for faithful and perpetual observance by all.

CHAPTER I

GENERAL PROVISIONS

Article 1.—The Republic of China is a SAN-MIN-CHU-I Republic.

Article 2.—The sovereignty of the Republic of China is vested in the whole body of its citizens.

Article 3.—Persons having acquired the nationality of the Republic of China are citizens of the Republic of China.

Article 4.—The territory of the Republic of China consists of areas originally constituting Kiangsu, Chekiang, Anhwei, Kiangsi, Hupeh, Hunan, Szechwan, Sikang, Hopei, Shantung, Shensi, Honan, Shensi, Kansu, Chinghai, Fukien, Kwangtung, Kwangsi, Yunnan, Kweichow, Lisoning, Kirin, Heilungkiang, Jehol, Chahar, Suiyuan, Ningsia, Sinkiang, Mongolia and Tibet.

The territory of the Republic of China shall not be altered except by resolution of the National Assembly.

Article 5.—All races of the Republic of China are component parts of the Chinese Nation and shall be equal.

* Drafted and revised by the Legislative Yuan, April 30, 1937, and released by the National Government on May 18, 1937.

Article 6.—The National Flag of the Republic of China shall have a red background with a blue sky and white sun in the upper left corner.

Article 7.—The National Capital of the Republic of China shall be at Nanking.

CHAPTER II

RIGHTS AND DUTIES OF THE CITIZENS

Article 8.—All citizens of the Republic of China shall be equal before the law.

Article 9.—Every citizen shall enjoy the liberty of the person. Except in accordance with law, no one may be arrested, detained, tried or punished.

When a citizen is arrested or detained on suspicion of having committed a criminal act, the authority responsible for such action shall immediately inform the citizen himself and his relatives of the cause for his arrest or detention and shall, within a period of twenty-four hours, send him to a competent court for trial. The citizen so arrested or detained, or any one else, may also petition the court to demand from the authority responsible for such action the surrender, within twenty-four hours, of his person to the court for trial.

The court shall not reject such a petition ; nor shall the responsible authority refuse to execute such a writ as mentioned in the preceding paragraph.

Article 10.—With the exception of those in active military service, no one may be subject to military jurisdiction.

Article 11.—Every citizen shall have the freedom of domicile ; no private abode may be forcibly entered, searched or sealed except in accordance with law.

Article 12.—Every citizen shall have the freedom to change his residence ; such freedom shall not be restricted except in accordance with law.

Article 13.—Every citizen shall have the freedom of speech, writing and publication ; such freedom shall not be restricted except in accordance with law.

Article 14.—Every citizen shall have the freedom of secrecy of correspondence ; such freedom shall not be restricted except in accordance with law.

Article 15.—Every citizen shall have the freedom of religious belief ; such freedom shall not be restricted except in accordance with law.

Article 16.—Every citizen shall have the freedom of assembly and of forming associations ; such freedom shall not be restricted except in accordance with law.

Article 17.—No private property shall be requisitioned, expropriated, sealed or confiscated except in accordance with law.

Article 18.—Every citizen shall have the right to present petitions, lodge complaints and institute legal proceedings in accordance with law.

Article 19.—Every citizen shall have the right to exercise, in accordance with law, the powers of election, recall, initiative and referendum.

Article 20.—Every citizen shall have the right to compete, in accordance with law, in State examinations.

Article 21.—Every citizen shall, in accordance with law, be amenable to the duty of paying taxes.

Article 22.—Every citizen shall, in accordance with law, be amenable to the duty of performing military service.

Article 23.—Every citizen shall, in accordance with law, be amenable to the duty of rendering public service.

Article 24.—All other liberties and rights of the citizens which are not detrimental to public peace and order or public welfare shall be guaranteed by the Constitution.

Article 25.—Only laws imperative for safeguarding national security, averting a national crisis, maintaining public peace and order or promoting public interest may restrict the citizens' liberties and rights.

Article 26.—Any public functionary who illegally infringes upon any private liberty or right, shall, besides being subject to disciplinary punishment, be responsible under criminal and civil law. The injured person may also, in accordance with law, claim indemnity from the State for damages sustained.

CHAPTER III

THE NATIONAL ASSEMBLY

Article 27.—The National Assembly shall be constituted of delegates elected as follows :

1. Each district, municipality or area of an equivalent status, shall elect one delegate, but in case its population exceeds 300,000, one additional delegate shall be elected for every additional 500,000 people. The status of areas to be equivalent to a district or municipality shall be defined by law.
2. The number of delegates to be elected from Mongolia and Tibet shall be determined by law.
3. The number of delegates to be elected by Chinese citizens residing abroad shall be determined by law.

Article 28.—Delegates to the National Assembly shall be elected by universal, equal, and direct suffrage, and by secret ballots.

Article 29.—Citizens of the Republic of China having attained the age of twenty years shall, in accordance with law, have the right to elect Delegates. Citizens having attained the age of twenty-five years shall, in accordance with law, have the right to be elected Delegates.

Article 30.—The term of office of Delegates of the National Assembly shall be six years.

When a Delegate is found guilty of violation of a law or neglect of his duty, his constituency shall recall him in accordance with law.

Article 31.—The National Assembly shall be convened by the President once every three years. Its session shall last one month, but may be extended another month when necessary.

Extraordinary sessions of the National Assembly may be convened at the instance of two-fifths or more of its members.

The President may convene extraordinary sessions of the National Assembly.

The National Assembly shall meet at the place where the Central Government is.

Article 32.—The powers and functions of the National Assembly shall be as follows :

1. To elect the President and Vice-President of the Republic, the President of the Legislative Yuan, the President of the Control Yuan, the Members of the Legislative Yuan, and the Members of the Control Yuan.
2. To recall the President and Vice-President of the Republic, the President of the Legislative Yuan, the President of the Judicial Yuan, the President of the Examination Yuan, the President of the Control Yuan, the Members of the Legislative Yuan and the Members of the Control Yuan.
3. To initiate laws.
4. To hold referenda on laws.
5. To amend the Constitution.
6. To exercise such other powers as are conferred by the Constitution.

Article 33.—Delegates to the National Assembly shall not be held responsible outside of Congress for opinions they may express and votes they may cast during the session of Assembly.

Article 34.—Without the permission of the National Assembly, no Delegate shall be arrested or detained during the session except when apprehended in *flagrante delicto*.

Article 35.—The organization of the National Assembly and the election as well as recall of its Delegates shall be determined by law.

CHAPTER IV

THE CENTRAL GOVERNMENT

Section 1. The President

Article 36.—The President is the Head of the State and represents the Republic of China in foreign relations.

Article 37.—The President commands the land, sea and air forces of the whole country.

Article 38.—The President shall, in accordance with law, promulgate laws and issue orders with the counter-signature of the President of the Yuan concerned.

Article 39.—The President shall, in accordance with law, exercise the power of declaring war, negotiating peace, and concluding treaties.

Article 40.—The President shall, in accordance with law, declare and terminate a state of emergency.

Article 41.—The President shall, in accordance with law, exercise the power of granting amnesties, special pardons, remission of sentences and restoration of civil rights.

Article 42.—The President shall, in accordance with law, appoint and remove civil and military officials.

Article 43.—The President shall, in accordance with law, confer honours and award decorations.

Article 44.—In case the State is confronted with an emergency, or the economic life of the State meets with a grave danger, which calls for immediate action, the President, following the resolution of the Executive Meeting, may issue orders of emergency and do whatever is necessary to cope with the situation, provided that he shall submit his action to the ratification of the Legislative Yuan within three months after the issuance of the orders.

Article 45.—The President may call meetings of the Presidents of the five Yuan to confer on matters relating to two or more Yuan, or on such matters as the President may bring out for consultation.

Article 46.—The President shall be responsible to the National Assembly.

Article 47.—Citizens of the Republic of China, having attained the age of forty years, may be elected President or Vice-President of the Republic.

Article 48.—The election of the President and Vice-President shall be provided for by law.

Article 49.—The President and Vice-President shall hold office for a term of six years, and may be re-elected for a second term.

Article 50.—The President shall, on the day of his inauguration, take the following oath :

" I do solemnly and sincerely swear before the people that I will observe the Constitution, faithfully perform my duties, promote the welfare of the people, safeguard the security of the State, and be loyal to the trust of the people. Should I break my oath, I will submit myself to the most severe punishment the law may provide."

Article 51.—When the Presidency is vacant, the Vice-President shall succeed to the office.

When the President is for some reason unable to attend to his duties, the Vice-President shall act for him. If both the President and Vice-President are incapacitated, the President of the Executive Yuan shall discharge the duties of the President's office.

Article 52.—The President shall retire from office on the day his term expires. If by that time a new President has not been inducted into office, the President of the Executive Yuan shall discharge the duties of the President's office.

Article 53.—The period for the President of the Executive Yuan to discharge the duties of the President's office shall not exceed six months.

Article 54.—Except in case of an offence against the internal or external security of the State, the President shall not be liable to criminal prosecution until he has been recalled or has retired from office.

Section 2. The Executive Yuan

Article 55.—The Executive Yuan is the highest organ through which the Central Government exercises its executive powers.

Article 56.—In the Executive Yuan, there shall be a President, a Vice-President, and a number of Executive Members, to be appointed and removed by the President.

The Executive Members mentioned in the preceding paragraph who do not take charge of Ministries or Commissions shall not exceed half of those who are in charge of Ministries or Commissions as provided in the first paragraph of Article 58.

Article 57.—In the Executive Yuan, there shall be various Ministries and Commissions which shall separately exercise their respeçtive executive powers.

Article 58.—The Ministers of the various Ministries and the Chairman of the various Commissions shall be appointed by the President from among the Executive Members.

The President and the Vice-President of the Executive Yuan may act concurrently as Minister or Chairman mentioned in the preceding paragraph.

Article 59.—The President of the Executive Yuan, the Executive Members, the Ministers of the various Ministries and the Chairmen of the various Commissions shall be individually responsible to the President.

Article 60.—In the Executive Yuan there shall be Executive Meetings composed of the President, the President of the Executive Yuan and the Executive Members to be presided over by the President. In case the President is unable to be present, the President of the Executive Yuan shall preside.

Article 61.—The following matters shall be decided at an Executive Meeting :

1. Statutory and budgetary bills to be submitted to the Legislative Yuan.
2. Bills concerning a state of emergency and special pardons to be submitted to the Legislative Yuan.
3. Bills concerning declaration of war, negotiation of peace, conclusion of treaties and other important international affairs to be submitted to the Legislative Yuan.
4. Matters of common concern to the various Ministries and Commissions.
5. Matters submitted by the President.
6. Matters submitted by the President of the Executive Yuan, the Executive Members, the various Ministries and Commissions.

Article 62.—The organization of the Executive Yuan shall be determined by law.

Section 3. The Legislative Yuan

Article 63.—The Legislative Yuan is the highest organ through which the Central Government exercises its legislative powers. It shall be responsible to the National Assembly.

Article 64.—The Legislative Yuan shall have the power to decide on measures concerning legislation, budgets, a state of emergency, special pardons, declaration of war, negotiation of peace, conclusion of treaties and other important international affairs.

Article 65.—In the discharge of its duties the Legislative Yuan may interrogate the various Yuan, Ministries and Commissions.

Article 66.—In the Legislative Yuan, there shall be a President and

Vice-President, who shall hold office for a term of three years, and may be eligible for re-election.

Article 67.—In regard to the election of Members of the Legislative Yuan, the Delegates of the various provinces, Mongolia, Tibet, and of citizens residing abroad, to the National Assembly shall separately hold a preliminary election to nominate their respective candidates and submit a list of their names to the Congress for election. The candidates are not confined to the Delegates to the National Assembly. The respective number of candidates shall be proportioned as follows :

1. A province with a population of less than 5,000,000 shall nominate four candidates. A province with a population of more than 5,000,000 but less than 10,000,000 shall nominate six candidates. A province with a population of more than 10,000,000 but less than 15,000,000 shall nominate eight candidates. A province with a population of more than 15,000,000 but less than 20,000,000 shall nominate ten candidates. A province with a population of more than 20,000,000 but less than 25,000,000 shall nominate twelve candidates. A province with a population of more than 25,000,000 but less than 30,000,000 shall nominate fourteen candidates. A province with a population of more than 30,000,000 shall nominate sixteen candidates.

2. Mongolia and Tibet shall each nominate eight candidates.

3. Citizens residing abroad shall nominate eight candidates.

Article 68.—Members of the Legislative Yuan shall hold office for a term of three years, and may be eligible for re-election.

Article 69.—The Executive Yuan, Judicial Yuan, Examination Yuan, and Control Yuan may submit to the Legislative Yuan measures concerning matters within their respective jurisdiction.

Article 70.—The President may, before the promulgation or execution of a legislative measure, request the Legislative Yuan to reconsider it.

If the Legislative Yuan, with regard to the request for consideration, should decide to maintain the original measure by a two-thirds vote of the Members present, the President shall promulgate or execute it without delay ; provided that in case of a bill of law or a treaty, the President may submit it to the National Assembly for a referendum.

Article 71.—The President shall promulgate a measure presented by the Legislative Yuan for promulgation within thirty days after its receipt.

Article 72.—Members of the Legislative Yuan shall not be held responsible outside of the said Yuan for opinions they may express and votes they may cast during its session.

Article 73.—Without the permission of the Legislative Yuan, no member may be arrested or detained except when apprehended in *flagrante delicto*.

Article 74.—No Member of the Legislative Yuan may concurrently hold any other public office or engage in any business or profession.

Article 75.—The election of Members of the Legislative Yuan and the organization of the Legislative Yuan shall be determined by law.

Section 4. The Judicial Yuan

Article 76.—The Judicial Yuan is the highest organ through which the Central Government exercises its judicial powers. It shall attend to the adjudication of civil, criminal and administrative suits, the discipline and punishment of public functionaries and judicial administration.

Article 77.—In the Judicial Yuan, there shall be a President and Vice-President who shall hold office for a term of three years, to be appointed by the President.

The President of the Judicial Yuan shall be responsible to the National Assembly.

Article 78.—Matters concerning special pardons, remission of sentences and restoration of civil rights shall be submitted to the President for action by the President of the Judicial Yuan in accordance with law.

Article 79.—The Judicial Yuan shall have the power to unify the interpretation of statutes and ordinances.

Article 80.—Judicial officials shall, in accordance with law, have perfect independence in the conduct of trials.

Article 81.—No judicial official may be removed from office unless he has been subject to criminal or disciplinary punishment or declared an interdicted person ; nor may a judicial official be suspended or transferred, or have his salary reduced except in accordance with law.

Article 82.—The organization of the Judicial Yuan and the various Courts of Justice shall be determined by law.

Section 5. The Examination Yuan

Article 83.—The Examination Yuan is the highest organ through which the Central Government exercises its examination powers. It shall attend to the selection of Civil Service candidates by examination and to the registration of persons qualified for public service.

Article 84.—In the Examination Yuan there shall be a President who shall hold office for a term of three years, to be appointed by the President.

The President of the Examination Yuan shall be responsible to the National Assembly.

Article 85.—The Examination Yuan shall, in accordance with law, by examination and registration determine the following qualifications :

1. For appointment as a public functionary.
2. For candidacy to public office.
3. For practice in specialized professions and as technical experts.

Article 86.—The organization of the Examination Yuan shall be determined by law.

Section 6. The Control Yuan

Article 87.—The Control Yuan is the highest organ through which the Central Government exercises its control powers. It shall attend to impeachment and auditing and be responsible to the National Assembly.

Article 88.—In the discharge of its control powers, the Control Yuan may, in accordance with law, interrogate the various Yuan, Ministries and Commissions.

Article 89.—In the Control Yuan, there shall be a President and a Vice-President who shall hold office for a term of three years and may be eligible for re-election.

Article 90.—Members of the Control Yuan shall be elected by the National Assembly from candidates separately nominated by the Delegates of the various provinces, Mongolia, Tibet, and Chinese citizens residing abroad. Each group of Delegates shall nominate two candidates. The candidates are not confined to Delegates to the Congress.

Article 91.—Members of the Control Yuan shall hold office for a term of four years and may be eligible for re-election.

Article 92.—When the Control Yuan finds a public functionary in the Central or Local Government guilty of violation of a law or neglect of his duty, an impeachment may be instituted upon the proposal of one or more Members and the indorsement, after due investigation, of five or more Members. Impeachment against the President or Vice-President, the President of the Executive Yuan, Legislative Yuan, Judicial Yuan, Examination Yuan or Control Yuan may be instituted only upon the proposal of ten or more members and the indorsements, after due investigation, of one-half or more ot the Members of the entire Yuan.

Article 93.—When an impeachment is instituted against the President or Vice-President or the President of the Executive Yuan, Legislative Yuan, Judicial Yuan, Examination Yuan or Control Yuan in accordance with the preceding Article, it shall be brought before the National Assembly. During the adjournment of the National Assembly, the Delegates shall be requested to convene, in accordance with law, an extraordinary session to decide whether the impeached shall be removed from office.

Article 94.—Members of the Control Yuan shall not be held responsible outside of the said Yuan for opinions they may express and votes they may cast while discharging their duties.

Article 95.—Without the permission of the Control Yuan, no Member of the Control Yuan may be arrested or detained except when apprehended in *flagrante delicto*.

Article 96.—No member of the Control Yuan may concurrently hold any other public office or engage in any business or profession.

Article 97.—The election of the Members of the Control Yuan and the organization of the Control Yuan shall be determined by law.

CHAPTER V

THE LOCAL INSTITUTIONS

Section 1. The Provinces

Article 98.—In the province, there shall be a Provincial Government which shall execute the laws and orders of the Central Government and supervise local self-government.

Article 99.—In the Provincial Government there shall be a Governor who shall hold office for a term of three years. He shall be appointed and removed by the Central Government.

Article 100.—In the province, there shall be a Provincial Assembly which shall be composed of one Member from each district or municipality to be elected by the district or municipal council. Members of the Provincial Assembly shall hold office for a term of three years, and may be eligible for re-election.

Article 101.—The organization of the Provincial Government and the Provincial Assembly, as well as the election and recall of the Members of the Provincial Assembly, shall be determined by law.

Article 102.—The government of areas not yet established as provinces shall be determined by law.

Section 2. The Districts

Article 103.—The district is a unit of local self-government.

Article 104.—All matters that are local in nature are within the scope of local self-government.

The scope of local self-government shall be determined by law.

Article 105.—Citizens of the district shall, in accordance with law, exercise the powers of initiative and referendum in matters concerning district self-government as well as the powers of election and recall of the District Magistrate and other elective officials in the service of self-government.

Article 106.—In the district, there shall be a District Council, the members of which shall be directly elected by the citizens in the District General Meeting. Members of the District Council shall hold office for a term of three years and may be eligible for re-election.

Article 107.—District ordinances and regulations which are in conflict with the laws and ordinances of the Central or Provincial Government shall be null and void.

Article 108.—In the district, there shall be a District Government with a District Magistrate who shall be elected by the citizens in the District General Meeting. The Magistrate shall hold office for a term of three years and may be eligible for re-election.

Only those persons found qualified in the public examinations held by the Central Government or adjudged qualified by the Ministry of Public Service Registration may be candidates for the office of District Magistrate.

Article 109.—The District Magistrate shall administer the affairs of the district in accordance with the principles of self-government and, under the direction of the Provincial Governor, execute matters assigned by the Central and Provincial Governments.

Article 110.—The organization of the District Council and District Government as well as the election and recall of the District Magistrate and the Members of the District Council shall be determined by law.

Section 3. The Municipalities

Article 111.—Unless otherwise provided by law, the provisions governing self-government and administration of the district shall apply *mutatis mutandis* to the municipality.

17

Article 112.—In the municipality, there shall be a Municipal Council, the Members of which shall be directly elected by the citizens in the Municipal General Meeting. One-third of the Members shall retire and be replaced by election annually.

Article 113.—In the municipality, there shall be a Municipal Government with a Mayor to be directly elected by the citizens in the Municipal General Meeting. He shall hold office for a term of three years, and may be eligible for re-election.

Only those persons found qualified in the public examination held by the Central Government or adjudged qualified by the Ministry of Public Service Registration may be a candidate for the office of Mayor.

Article 114.—The Mayor shall administer the affairs of the municipality in accordance with the principles of municipal self-government and, under direction of the competent supervising authority, execute matters assigned by the Central or Provincial Government.

Article 115.—The organization of the Municipal Council and Municipal Government, as well as the election and recall of the Members of the Municipal Council and the Mayor, shall be determined by law.

Chapter VI

NATIONAL ECONOMIC LIFE

Article 116.—The economic system of the Republic of China shall be based upon the Min-Seng-Chu-I (Principle of Livelihood), and shall aim at national economic sufficiency and equality.

Article 117.—The land within the territorial limits of the Republic of China belongs to the people as a whole. Any part thereof the ownership of which has been lawfully acquired by an individual or individuals shall be protected by, and subject to, the restrictions of law.

The State may, in accordance with law, tax or expropriate private land on the basis of the value declared by the owner or assessed by the Government.

Every landowner is amendable to the duty of utilizing his land to the fullest extent.

Article 118.—All subterranean minerals and natural forces which are economically utilizable for public benefit, belong to the State, and shall not be affected by private ownership of the land.

Article 119.—The unearned increment shall be taxed by means of a land-value-increment tax and devoted to public benefit.

Article 120.—In readjusting the distribution of land, the State shall be guided by the principle of aiding and protecting the land-owning farmers and the land-utilizing owners.

Article 121.—The State may, in accordance with law, regulate private wealth and enterprises when such wealth and enterprises are considered detrimental to the balanced development of national economic life.

Article 122.—The State shall encourage, guide and protect the citizens' productive enterprises and the nation's foreign trade.

Article 123.—All public utilities and enterprises of a monopolistic nature shall be operated by the State ; except in case of necessity when the State may specially permit private operation.

The private enterprises mentioned in the preceding paragraph may, in case of emergency for national defence, be temporarily managed by the State. The State may also, in accordance with law, take them over for permanent operation upon payment of due compensation.

Article 124.—In order to improve the workers' living conditions, increase their productive ability and relieve unemployment, the State shall enforce labour protective policies.

Women and children shall be afforded special protection in accordance with their age and physical condition.

Article 125.—Labour and capital shall, in accordance with the principles of mutual help and co-operation, develop together productive enterprises.

Article 126.—In order to promote agricultural development and the welfare of the farming population, the State shall improve rural economic and living conditions and increase farming efficiency by employment of scientific farming.

The State may regulate the production and distribution of agricultural products, in kind and quantity.

Article 127.—The State shall accord due relief or compensation to those who suffer disability or loss of life in the performance of military or public services.

Article 128.—The State shall give suitable relief to the aged, feeble, or disabled who are incapable of earning a living.

Article 129.—While the following powers appertain to the Legislative Yuan in the case of the Central Government, they may be exercised by the legally designated organ if, in accordance with law, such matters may be effected independently by a province, district or municipality :

1. To impose or alter the rate of taxes and levies, fines, penalties, or other imposts of a compulsory nature.
2. To raise public loans, dispose of public property or conclude contracts which increase the burden of the public treasury.
3. To establish or cancel public enterprises, monopolies, franchises or any other profit-making enterprise.
4. To grant or cancel public enterprises, monopolies, franchises or any other special privileges.

Unless specially authorized by law, the Government of a province, district or municipality shall not raise foreign loans or directly utilize foreign capital.

Article 130.—Within the territorial limits of the Republic of China all goods shall be permitted to circulate freely. They shall not be seized or detained except in accordance with law.

Customs duty is a Central Government revenue. It shall be collected only once, when the goods enter or leave the country.

The various grades of Government shall not collect any dues on goods in transit within the country, with the exception of tolls levied for the purpose of improving the waterways and roads, on vessels and vehicles making use of them.

The right to impose taxes and levies on goods belongs to the Central Government, and shall not be exercised except in accordance with law.

17*

Chapter VII

EDUCATION

Article 131.—The educational aim of the Republic of China shall be to develop a national spirit, to cultivate a national morality, to train the people for self-government, and to increase their ability to earn a livelihood, and thereby to build up a sound and healthy body of citizens.

Article 132.—Every citizen of the Republic of China shall have an equal opportunity to receive education.

Article 133.—All public and private educational institutions in the country shall be subject to State supervision and amenable to the duty of carrying out the educational policies formulated by the State.

Article 134.—Children between six and twelve years of age are of school age, and shall receive elementary education, tuition free. Detailed provisions shall be provided by law.

Article 135.—All persons over school age who have not received an elementary education shall receive supplementary education, tuition free. Detailed provisions shall be provided by law.

Article 136.—In establishing universities and technical schools, the State shall give special consideration to the needs of the respective localities so as to afford the people thereof an equal opportunity to receive higher education, thereby hastening a balanced national cultural development.

Article 137.—Education appropriations shall constitute no less than 15 per cent. of the total amount of the budget of the Central Government and no less than 30 per cent. of the total amount of the provincial, district and municipal budgets respectively. Educational endowment funds independently set aside in accordance with law shall be safeguarded.

Educational expenditures in needy provinces shall be subsidized by the central treasury.

Article 138.—The State shall encourage and subsidize the following enterprises or citizens :

1. Private educational institutions with a high record of achievement.
2. Education for Chinese citizens residing abroad.
3. Discoverers or inventors in academic or technical fields.
4. Teachers or administrative officers of educational institutions having good records and long service.
5. Students of high records and good character who are unable to pursue further studies.

Chapter VIII

THE ENFORCEMENT AND AMENDMENT OF THE CONSTITUTION

Article 139.—The term " law " as used in the Constitution means that which has been passed by the Legislative Yuan and promulgated by the President.

Article 140.—Laws in conflict with the Constitution are null and void.

The question whether a law is in conflict with the Constitution shall be settled by the Control Yuan submitting the point to the Judicial Yuan for interpretation within six months after its enforcement.

Article 141.—Administrative orders in conflict with the Constitution or laws are null and void.

Article 142.—The interpretation of the Constitution shall be undertaken by the Judicial Yuan.

Article 143.—Before half or more of the provinces and territories have completed the work of local self-government, the Members of the Legislative Yuan and of the Control Yuan shall be elected and appointed in accordance with the following provisions :

1. The Members of the Legislative Yuan : The Delegates of the various provinces, Mongolia, Tibet, and of the citizens residing abroad, to the National Assembly shall separately hold a preliminary election to nominate half of the number of the candidates as determined in Article 67 and submit their list to the National Assembly for election. The other half shall be nominated by the President of the Legislative Yuan for appointment by the President.

2. The Members of the Control Yuan : The Delegates of the various provinces, Mongolia, Tibet, and of the citizens residing abroad, to the National Assembly shall separately hold a preliminary election to nominate half of the number of candidates as determined in Article 90 and submit their list to the National Assembly for election. The other half shall be nominated by the President of the Control Yuan for appointment by the President.

Article 144.—The Magistrates of districts where the work of self-government is not yet completed shall be appointed and removed by the Central Government.

The preceding paragraph is applicable *mutatis mutandis* to those municipalities where the work of self-government is not yet completed.

Article 145.—The methods and procedure of helping the establishment of local self-government shall be determined by law.

Article 146.—No amendment to the Constitution may be made unless it shall have been proposed by over one-fourth of the Delegates to the National Assembly and passed by at least two-thirds of the Delegates present at a meeting having a quorum of over three-fourths of the entire Congress.

A proposed amendment to the Constitution shall be made public by the proposer or proposers one year before the assembling of the National Assembly.

Article 147.—In regard to those provisions of the Constitution which require further procedure for their endorsement, such necessary procedure shall be determined by law.

Appendix D

GUIDING PRINCIPLES FOR ARMED RESISTANCE AND NATIONAL RECONSTRUCTION *

THE Kuomintang is leading the entire nation in carrying on armed resistance and National reconstruction. Success in both tasks will require not only the concerted efforts of members of this Party, but also the acceptance of responsibility by the people as a whole in a united endeavour. Consequently, this Party has deemed it necessary to call on the people to abandon their prejudices and sink their differences in favour of oneness of purpose and unity in action. For this particular reason, at its Extraordinary National Congress this Party has formulated and adopted various principles governing foreign relations, military affairs, politics, economic affairs, mass movement and education, and caused their promulgation for general observance, so that the nation's strength may be concentrated and general mobilization may be attained. These principles are as follows :

I. GENERAL PROVISIONS

1. The Three People's Principles and other teachings bequeathed by Tsungli (Dr. Sun Yat-sen) are hereby declared as the highest authority regulating all war activities and the work of national reconstruction.
2. The nation's war strength shall be centralized under the leadership of this party and of Generalissimo Chiang Kai-shek in order to make possible the fullest progress.

II. FOREIGN RELATIONS

3. In accordance with the spirit of independence and sovereignty, China is prepared to ally herself with all nations and peoples who sympathize with her cause, and to wage a common struggle for peace and justice.
4. China is prepared to exert her utmost to uphold and increase the authority of any international peace structure as well as all treaties and conventions which aim at safeguarding world peace.
5. China is prepared to ally herself with all forces opposed to Japanese imperialism in order to check Japanese aggression and to establish and maintain lasting peace in East Asia.
6. China is prepared to improve still further the existing friendly relations with various nations in order to win greater sympathy for her cause.
7. All puppet political organizations which Japan has set up in Chinese territory now under her military occupation, and all their actions, both internal and external, are hereby declared null and void.

* Adopted by the Extraordinary Kuomintang National Congress, Hankow, April 1, 1938.

III. MILITARY AFFAIRS

8. Political training in the Army shall be intensified in order to familiarize all officers and men with the meaning of armed resistance and national reconstruction and to make them, one and all, ready to lay down their lives for the nation.

9. All able-bodied citizens shall be trained : the people's military ability for self-defence shall be strengthened ; military units engaged in war shall be reinforced ; and overseas Chinese who have returned to offer their services at the front shall be given special training in the light of their skills and abilities to fit them for participation in the defence of their Fatherland.

10. People in various localities who have their own arms shall receive direction and support from the Government ; under the command of the various war area commanders, they shall co-operate with the regular troops in military operations for the defence of their homeland against external foes, and also for the purpose of starting widespread guerrilla warfare in the enemy's rear in order to destroy and harass enemy forces.

11. In order to heighten military morale and raise the people's enthusiasm for national mobilization, both the wounded and dependants of the killed shall be looked after, the disabled shall be rehabilitated, the families of soldiers shall be given preferential consideration.

IV. POLITICS

12. Popular organs shall be set up for the people to participate in affairs of State, thereby unifying the national strength and collecting the best minds and views for facilitating the formulation and execution of national policies.

13. The *hsien* (county) shall be taken as the basic unit in which self-defence organizations shall be strengthened through training the people and increasing their power, and in which conditions for local self-government shall be fulfilled as soon as possible in order to provide a strong political and social foundation during war-time and to pave the way for constitutional rule.

14. There shall be a thorough reform in the machinery of all grades of government for purposes of simplification and rationalization, and administrative efficiency shall be enhanced in order to meet the needs of war.

15. The conduct of officials of all ranks shall conform to rules ; they shall be dutiful, ready to sacrifice themselves for the country, observe discipline, and obey orders so that they may serve as models for the people ; those disloyal to their duty and who obstruct the prosecution of the war shall be court-martialled.

16. Corrupt officials shall be severely punished and their property confiscated.

V. ECONOMIC AFFAIRS

17. Economic reconstruction shall concern itself mainly with matters of military importance and, in addition, with matters that contribute to the improvement of the people's livelihood. With these objects in view a planned economy shall be put into operation, investments by people both at home and abroad shall be encouraged, and large-scale war-time production shall be undertaken.

18. The greatest measure of energy shall be devoted to the development of rural economy, the encouragement of co-operative enterprises, the regulation of foodstuffs with regard to their demand and supply, the cultivation of waste land and the improvement of irrigation works.

19. Mining shall be undertaken, the foundations for heavy industries shall be laid, light industries shall be encouraged, and handicraft industries in the various provinces shall be developed.

20. War-time taxes shall be levied and the financial administration shall be thoroughly reformed.

21. The banking business shall be controlled so that industrial and commercial activities may be properly adjusted.

22. The position of fapi (legal tender) shall be fortified, foreign exchange shall be controlled, and imports and exports regulated, all for the sake of financial stability.

23. The communication systems shall be reorganized, connecting transportation by waterways, overland routes and airways shall be instituted, more railways and highways shall be built and more airlines opened.

24. No hoarding, speculation or manipulation shall be allowed, and a system of price stabilization shall be enforced.

VI. Mass Movement

25. The people throughout the country shall be aroused and organized into occupational groups such as unions of farmers, labourers, merchants and students. The rich shall be asked to contribute in money and the able-bodied shall contribute in labour service All classes of people shall be mobilized for the war.

26. The freedom of speech, the freedom of the press, and the freedom of assembly shall be fully protected by law, in the course of the war, provided they do not contravene the San-Min-Chu-I, which are the nation's highest principles, and provided they are within the scope of law and order.

27. Refugees from the war areas and unemployed people shall receive relief and shall be organized and trained so that their services may be available for the war.

28. The people's national consciousness shall be promoted so that they may assist the Government in eradicating reactionaries. Traitors shall be severely punished and their property confiscated in accordance with law.

29. Both the educational system and teaching material shall be revised. A problem of war-time education shall be instituted with emphasis on the cultivation of the people's morals, and the enchancement of scientific research and the expansion of necessary facilities.

30. Technical personnel of all kinds shall be trained and given proper assignment in order to meet the needs of war.

31. Youths shall be given training to enable them to work in the war areas or rural districts.

32. Women shall be given training so that they may be of service to social enterprises and thereby of help to the nation's war strength.

THE END

OVERLEAF
Particulars of a publication
of similar interest
issued by

GEORGE ALLEN & UNWIN LTD
LONDON: 40 MUSEUM STREET, W.C.1
CAPE TOWN: 58-60 LONG STREET
TORONTO: 91 WELLINGTON STREET WEST
BOMBAY: 15 GRAHAM ROAD, BALLARD ESTATE
WELLINGTON, N.Z.: 8 KINGS CRESCENT, LOWER HUTT
SYDNEY, N.S.W.: BRADBURY HOUSE, 55 YORK STREET

GOVERNMENT BY ASSASSINATION

by HUGH BYAS

Formerly Tokyo Correspondent of the *New York Times*

Second impression. La. Cr. 8vo. 10s. 6d. net

THIS book is to Japan what Rauschning's *Revolution of Nihilism* was to Germany. The author, who has spent twenty-three years of his life as a newspaper man in Tokyo, has written one of the most authoritative and informed volumes yet published about the island empire. He explains as explicitly and clearly as he can, how the Japanese Government works, and describes the strange men and stranger ideas that animate it. He shows how the younger army and navy officers have ruthlessly terrorized their superiors and the civilian government into conformity with their own ideals; ideals which are a weird compound of Marxism and National Socialism, transformed for Japanese uses and mixed with fanatical racial, national and semi-religious obsessions.

Japan, like Germany, believes that it is a nation with a destiny, and that war pays. The result is a sort of military socialism with the Emperor as a figurehead and the totalitarian state so geared for war that 20 per cent. of each individual's production is for himself and 80 per cent. for the sinews of conquest.

Of the future, Mr. Byas feels that, once impressed by democratic power, the Japanese might come to democracy themselves at some future date, out of their usual habit of imitating the successful aspects of foreign nations.

"It is a depressing picture that Mr. Byas spreads out before us. But he makes it very convincing."—EDWARD SHANKS in the *Sunday Times*.

"A valuable book, with much detailed information on personalities and events."—*Birmingham Post*.

"A really important book; it is fair-minded, informed and free from exaggeration."—*The Listener*.

"Well documented and absorbing."—*Manchester Guardian*.

"An extremely important book, and a considerable contribution towards understanding the nature of the side of our problem in the Far East."—*Tribune*.

LONDON: GEORGE ALLEN & UNWIN LTD